"Elaine Phillips' masterpiece on wisdom literatu[re] [...] scholarly, practical, thought-provoking, and devotional. In this book, you are invited to look at life from a multifaceted perspective, to seek wisdom above all things, and to examine the intricacies of Proverbs, Job, Ecclesiastes, and Song of Songs. With the integration of ancient Near Eastern literature and recommended readings in each chapter, the book is highly recommended as a textbook for classes on Hebrew poetry and wisdom literature."

—Hélène Dallaire
Earl S. Kalland Professor of Old Testament and Semitic Languages
and Director of Messianic Judaism Programs, Denver Seminary

"Dr. Phillips' new book is a welcome addition to the study of the biblical wisdom literature. Her approach to the material reflects a scholar's careful awareness of the original language and a master teacher's ability to communicate successfully with both beginning college students and those much more advanced. Her many insights into the complex problems of Proverbs, Job, Ecclesiastes, and the Song of Solomon help sort out how the teachings of Torah were applied to everyday issues of living. Each generation of believers faces the same problems. And every generation benefits from recognizing that there is 'nothing (really) new under the sun.'"

—G. Lloyd Carr
Emeritus Professor of Biblical Studies, Gordon College

"Phillips explores the complex questions of our day, giving students a new, approachable way to see the continuing richness and meaningfulness of biblical wisdom literature in today's world. This book will be a valuable resource for courses on biblical wisdom literature for years to come."

—Beth M. Stovell
Associate Professor of Old Testament, Ambrose University

"Phillips' writing is winsome and accessible, drawing students into the biblical text by providing just enough exposure to scholarly questions to empower—but not overwhelm—them. She proves an able tour guide, cultivating a lively conversation around the challenging subject matter of the wisdom books. I am eager to share this book with my students!"

—Carmen Joy Imes
Adjunct Professor of Biblical Studies
George Fox University and Multnomah University

"Novices to the wisdom literature will be taken aback to discover this lost treasure that has been in their Bibles all along. *An Introduction to Reading Biblical Wisdom Texts* is a personal and beautifully written book that invites us back into these essential words of revelation. It is a book about wisdom—and thus a book about work and psychology and suffering and love and sexuality and politics and . . . everything. Page after page Phillips unearths the imaginative, far-reaching, and too often neglected teachings of the ancient Hebrew sages. An invaluable resource that belongs in homes and on scholarly shelves."

—Ryan P. O'Dowd
Pastor of Bread of Life Anglican Church, Ithaca, New York
Senior Fellow, Chesterton House, Cornell University

"As I read this, I imagined my students' responses. I believe Dr. Phillips' work will be informative, readable, and formationally helpful to them. Dr. Phillips writes in a comfortable style, yet her depth of research and knowledge show through. She presents the sometimes puzzling, yet practical and profound qualities of biblical wisdom literature in a way that is interesting and accessible."

—Susan I. Bubbers
Dean, The Center for Anglican Theology, Orlando, Florida
Priest at Celebration Anglican Fellowship

An Introduction to

READING

BIBLICAL

WISDOM

TEXTS

An Introduction to

READING

BIBLICAL

WISDOM

TEXTS

Elaine A. Phillips

HENDRICKSON PUBLISHERS

An Introduction to Reading Biblical Wisdom Texts

© 2017 Hendrickson Publishers Marketing, LLC
P. O. Box 3473
Peabody, Massachusetts 01961-3473
www.hendrickson.com

ISBN 978-1-61970-710-8

Printed in the United States of America

First Printing — August 2017

Library of Congress Cataloging-in-Publication Data

Names: Phillips, Elaine A., author.
Title: An introduction to reading biblical wisdom texts / Elaine A Phillips.
Description: Peabody, MA : Hendrickson Publishers, 2017. | Includes
    bibliographical references and index.
Identifiers: LCCN 2017014130| ISBN 9781619707108 (alk. paper)
Subjects: LCSH: Wisdom literature--Criticism, interpretation, etc.
Classification: LCC BS1455 .P45 2017 | DDC 223/.061--dc23
    LC record available at https://lccn.loc.gov/2017014130

Contents

Preface and Acknowledgments

In my conversations with students, family members, and random seat partners on airline flights, there are certain questions that inevitably rise to the surface given enough time and candor. Full disclosure: I studiously avoid talking with people seated next to me when I travel, but sometimes it does happen in spite of my best efforts to immerse myself in a book or a nap. When those exchanges do begin, up front I confess that I teach Bible, and the conversation usually grinds to an immediate halt. Occasionally, however, that declaration prompts a curious question. Why on earth . . . ? And away we go.

At any rate, you can guess some of the subsequent questions in each of these contexts, I am sure. How is it that people do such horrible things to each other? In the face of overwhelming despair, what is the point of living, to say nothing of living well? For that matter, who defines what "living well" is? Why is your interpretation of right and wrong (righteousness and wickedness) any better than anyone else's? Ah, that one could get uncomfortable, and it suggests such quaint language. Righteousness? Wickedness? What do these words mean? Here is a slightly safer one: Why are some days so boring and others shot full of fearsome perils? But then come questions that are intended to poke holes in my worldview. What kind of a God holds people responsible if he exercises absolute control over their lives? Why must we endure pain? How are we supposed to come to grips with the prospect of dying? Couldn't there have been a better design?

Biblical wisdom texts wrestle with these questions and a host of others. Some of them explore good and orderly living and warn against landing in traps. Others poke a little fun at idiosyncratic human behavior. (Reading some parts of the Bible requires a good sense of humor.) While Song of Songs rhapsodizes about love, still other wisdom texts echo the heart-wrenching outbursts of agony that are only fully understood by those who suffer. No matter the focus, we find in these texts mirrors of our human longing to grasp something of these perplexing aspects of life. We would dearly love to curb unruly circumstances, subdue pain, and stave off the ominous darkness of death. We vainly think that using our good sense will advance these causes.

The Plan

Enough of the opening volley. Here's what I would like to accomplish in this book. Part One will explore an array of introductory issues, the first of which will be looking at basic definitions. We need to zero in on wisdom and folly as we see them through a biblical lens. To be sure, the pursuit of wisdom is universal; our opening questions indicate that. Nevertheless, there is also a powerful moral component of biblical wisdom that will shape the direction of our study rather significantly. It can be distilled in "the fear of the Lord," the powerful connection with Torah (God's instruction) and character traits of humility and trust. Remember those potentially nagging terms "righteousness" and "wickedness"?

A second preliminary matter has to do with the nature of Hebrew poetry. It is not an overstatement to claim that poetry is a perfect vehicle to convey rich, sometimes ambiguous, and challenging truths. Part One closes with a brief investigation of the possible historical and theological contexts for the Bible's wisdom texts. Can we legitimately place some or all of them in Solomon's tenth-century court circles, or should that suggestion be sent to the dustbin of less sophisticated interpretation?

Part Two will address the practical wisdom found in Proverbs, starting with a brief overview of the pertinent academic questions. These are fascinating, by the way. Please don't skip that chapter! Because no facet of human experience is exempt from the sages' keen observations, Proverbs is an endless treasure trove, very difficult to distill and summarize but always yielding more gems with each reading. The chapters that explore these practical nuggets focus on recurring themes: the ever-present challenge to choose between righteousness and wickedness; the power of words; character and human nature; family relationships; discipline and diligence; justice and stewardship.

Part Three focuses on Ecclesiastes. This is one of my favorites. Scholars differ as to whether the views expressed in the book are a comfortable fit with "orthodoxy." Was the author just chronically gloomy? The word that defines the book, Hebrew *hevel*, eludes easy definition. Fittingly, this word may mean "elusive," even though popular translations have opted for something like "meaningless" or "vanity." Equally compelling are "transient" or "absurd" or "enigmatic." Get the picture? This is good stuff. Ecclesiastes alternately presents the reader with disturbing and oddly reassuring realities, rocking back and forth between the perspective from "under the sun" and the reality of God's gifts. The author speaks to the frustrating and tedious nature of much of life, the anguish over the brevity of life and the finality of death, and the pain of incessant injustice. And he clings to hope in judgment—of all things. A final chapter in this section addresses several of the more challenging interpretive conundrums in Ecclesiastes 7.

Part Four is devoted to Job. What can I say? Where ought we begin? Awe, humility, trepidation, caution, hope—the character and the book drive us to our knees. As before, our first chapter is given over to the formidable array of academic issues. And then we get into it. Successive chapters address the initial confrontations between God and the adversary, Job's character and initial lament, and the friends' penchant for invoking fear as they attempted to correct Job's perception of his own situation. All of these are disturbing at their very core. Probing more deeply, we look in turn at how Job felt as he was on the cusp of life and death and at the shocking things he said about and to God. Whether Job spoke chapter 28 or it is an ethereal interlude, it merits its own chapter in this treatment. And what do we do with Job's final, powerful self-vindication? Do his words in chapters 29–31 subvert his entire case? Is he self-righteous and unlikable in the end? Elihu's speeches certainly add something to this astonishing work, but the question is *what* they add. Pressing on, God's torrential words from the whirlwind are the foundation of the whole wisdom enterprise, but they do leave us perplexed. Even God's responses, however, are not the end of the story, and we explore the implications of Job's final words, God's demand of and threat issued to the friends, and God's restoration of Job.

Finally, Part Five recognizes the potential place of Song of Songs in the wisdom tradition. Given the nature of intense human love, it is appropriate to consider it under a wisdom umbrella. After all, we need a healthy dose of wisdom when the extravagances of emotion overwhelm us! We explore the effusive descriptions of the lover and the beloved; they are often quite foreign to our ears. In addition, the love described in this text begs us as readers to probe for deeper meanings. What are all the purposes of this text?

Additional Notes

The chapters in this book are brief. That is intentional so as to sustain focus and interest. Each part closes with suggestions for further reading. Questions for reflection, details concerning Hebrew words and phrases, mentions of related literary works, and possible projects to engage readers appear in sidebars. References and very brief explanatory comments have also occasionally been included in the form of endnotes. Unless otherwise indicated, I offer my own translations, even though they are not always felicitous in English. I attempt to retain the Hebrew word order as much as possible, since subtle emphases are often conveyed through sentence structure. In addition, awkward syntax often makes us slow down as readers, and that is what I intend. Although it is a difficult choice, I have chosen to translate 'adam with "man" because all other options are either awkward ("humankind") or lose the distinctiveness of a singular individual. On occasion I simply leave it as 'adam. One further note: on the few occasions when the Hebrew text has different versification, it is noted in square brackets following the English translation reference.

While most readers will be familiar with the label "Old Testament," I have chosen to designate this portion of the Scriptures the "Hebrew Bible." The term "old" often carries connotations that are unwarranted—such as out of date or irrelevant. In fact, too many of our contemporary churches have carefully placed these extraordinary books in the equivalent of a safety deposit box, only consulting them on very rare occasions.

The divine name that represents God's covenant relationship with Israel is the unpronounced Tetragrammaton. This term refers to the four Hebrew letters that comprise the name. When it appears in the biblical texts with which we are dealing, I will render it "Lord," in keeping with major translations. This distinguishes it from the instances in which the Hebrew word 'adonay appears. This latter term means "lord" and can refer to a human master as well as the Lord of heaven and earth.

In addition to my academic objectives, my fervent hope is that our study will nurture our love for God, who is the source of our wisdom and truth. May these chapters help us wrestle with the love, fear, doubt, joy, anger, and wonder expressed by the biblical writers in the context of our own faith journeys.

Acknowledgements

It has been a privilege to engage my classes in wisdom literature at Gordon College with these developing thoughts over the years. Initially, they were in fledgling form; more recently, my students have graciously interacted with drafts of what has become this book. I'm grateful for the insights and constructive responses from each one. Sometimes, it was under duress. For example, "your midterm and final grades will be your thoughtful and honest critique of these chapters." Bless their hearts; they more than rose to the occasion and provided me, among other gifts, with cautions on what works with readers four decades younger than I!

I am also grateful beyond words for the confidence placed in me by the editorial board at Hendrickson Publishers and particularly Jonathan Kline. His wisdom and painstakingly careful direction have been invaluable at every stage of this process. Friends and family—their prayers and encouragement—have been a mainstay for me. Without the constant care of Perry, my unflappable husband, this book, along with most other projects in my life, would have remained in the "someday I would like to . . ." category. From tech support when I have panicked over recalcitrant pieces of equipment and software that definitely have minds of their own to insightful comments upon reading chapters, he has lovingly been an anchor for my soul. Finally, to God be the glory!

Abbreviations

General

BCE   Before the Common Era
ca.   circa
CE   Common Era
ch(s).   chapter(s)
lit.   literally
p(p).   page(s)
v(v).   verse(s)

Journals, Series, and Reference Works

AB   Anchor Bible
ANET   *Ancient Near Eastern Texts Relating to the Old Testament*. Edited by James B. Pritchard. 3rd edition. Princeton: Princeton University Press, 1969.
ASV   American Standard Version
BDB   Brown, F., S. R. Driver, and C. A. Briggs. *A Hebrew and English Lexicon of the Old Testament*. Oxford: Oxford University Press, 1907.
ESV   English Standard Version
HCSB   Holman Christian Standard Bible
IBC   Interpretation: A Bible Commentary for Teaching and Preaching
ICC   International Critical Commentary
KJV   King James Version
NASB   New American Standard Bible
NCB   New Century Bible
NICOT   New International Commentary on the Old Testament
NIV   New International Version
NJPS   *Tanakh: The Holy Scriptures: The New JPS Translation according to the Traditional Hebrew Text*

NKJV	New King James Version
NRSV	New Revised Standard Version
NSBT	New Studies in Biblical Theology
OTL	Old Testament Library
RSV	Revised Standard Version
SBL	Studies in Biblical Literature
SHBC	Smyth & Helwys Bible Commentary
WBC	Word Biblical Commentary

PART ONE

Where and How Do We Start?

Preliminary Observations

Before we begin our investigation of specific biblical wisdom texts, we need some background. Because I mentioned air travel in the preface, try this analogy. Prior to hopping onto a plane and heading around the globe to distant countries, it would be wise to procure maps and a guidebook. For some of us, that means apps on our cell phones. Bottom line: it helps to know where we are going and how many stops we are making. Is each destination very different? Will we be able to relate to the people? What are they like? Will language be a problem? Perhaps we should have one of those handy cards that tell us how to ask the five most important questions in any language. Are there cultural customs that we need to know in order to avoid offending our hosts? How can we avoid blundering too badly or repeating cultural gaffes? Addressing these questions adequately means acquiring and interpreting available data. Some of those data have to do with specific places to visit—palaces, temples, villages, and wayside rests. We will find rhyme and reason in this particular list of "specific places" shortly.

Let's refocus: *our* destinations are a succession of biblical texts that have characteristically been labeled "wisdom" even though not everyone agrees on the label or what is included under the umbrella. For now, however, let me set aside that argument and pose several additional basic questions. What is wisdom? Since we are talking about destinations, is wisdom a "destination" we will ever reach? Will we recognize it if and when we get there? Would our traveling companions agree with us that we had "arrived"?

Beyond the matter of destination, why go on this journey anyway? What are the human impulses and desires that compel us to pursue wisdom? Are we lacking something and know we cannot live without it? A side question: Does the specter of pride worm its ugly way in here? It might run like this: "I want to be wise so as to be better than . . ."! That is not a motive we are eager to claim, but it seems to lurk within each one of us. How do we squash it? And here is a cultural note: How much is our quest reshaped when we introduce the concept of "the fear of the LORD"? Perhaps that might be an antidote to at least part of the pride problem, but is fear constraining or freeing? Here's one more: Do wise people all manifest the same character traits? (That might be a bit tedious.) As you can see, we're all about questions here.

Even the matter of language is complicated. We're not only dealing with Hebrew but with Hebrew poetry. Although we may be quite familiar with poetry—and even like some of it—Hebrew poetry has some unique and exquisitely well-tailored characteristics for conveying God's truth. This will be the place where we think of bringing along that handy card to help us with language features that are not always familiar. Trust me, we will need it.

Finally, specific places will be important. To be sure, foundational cultural customs and values are shaped in the home no matter where we go. After all, our first and often best teachers are our parents. The family context threads its way through a good part of the material we encounter in wisdom texts. Nevertheless, there are additional shaping influences that have to do with place. The royal court, the marketplace, busy streets, and the city gate are venues where we watch wisdom in action. We will want the guidebook's descriptions of these places and their importance.

This biblical wisdom pursuit has to do with keen observations, pensive reflections, and definitive choices. Keeping a journal might help, just as we would write a travelogue about a new adventure. We initially encounter a host of wisdom gems in ancient Israel and among its neighbors, but we inevitably bring them back home and continue to relish the lessons that we absorbed during the course of our journey.

CHAPTER 1

The Universal Pursuit of Wisdom

What Is Everyone Seeking?

The search for what we are going to call wisdom crosses cultural boundaries. This is evident in texts from across the centuries and around the globe. Even more basic, it is evident in the human penchant for always asking questions. Kids ask questions without hesitation. When we adults don't know something, we ask—usually. The prior threat of revealing our embarrassing ignorance is now alleviated by the nonjudgmental internet. We simply search and receive 1,975,887 responses in one second. Then we assess which are remotely useful.

There are reasons behind this penchant for asking questions. Let me pose just a few as foundational. We will think big for starters. We live in a universe that is immeasurably vast. We humans, even with all our ingenuity and inquisitiveness, have only the faintest clues as to what is going on throughout the far reaches of the cosmos. Even in such a narrow and tiny place as our planet, we cannot wrap our minds around the complexity of ocean life, geological formations, plants, living creatures—are you getting the picture? Quantum particles and astronomical distances all defy our imagination, and they are part of what we get to explore. That's the point. Something compels us always to press beyond what we know. We have the privilege of endlessly experimenting in science labs, composing and sculpting in artistic studios, and constantly writing and rewriting our life stories. These are adventures without boundaries—just like the expanding universe.

This fledgling description has not even ventured into the intricacies of human hearts and minds as we interact with our world, with each other, and with the Presence that we seem interminably to be seeking. Even for those who do not affirm a God-centered and God-created universe, there is still that insatiable desire to seek something (Someone) beyond ourselves. In some cases, we "create" and reduce that someone to our own image. We like the likeness; it is manageable. On the other hand, a glimmer of wisdom cautions us. If we can "manage" that likeness, its value might be questionable.

All of this is to say that our identities (no matter who and where we are) compel us to search for answers as to how to live and live well in our world(s). Okay, so how do we do that? Using reason is an important component of this quest. We have minds that are remarkably equipped to deal with our complex living quarters! What we observe about our wider world helps us determine how best to adapt. Let me pose an example from my own geographical context. Is it snowing today? Boots and gloves will be in order as I venture outside. Living well means mastering information so as to exercise some control over our circumstances. Is it snowing today—again? Okay, that has tipped the accumulated snow total over one hundred inches this year; next year we are hiring someone to clear our driveway. Another way of putting this is that we seek to create security in a world that is always filled with potentially fearsome prospects. No point in being caught entirely off guard when a bit of proactive wisdom might have served well. (Truth is, though—I like shoveling snow.)

Fine, reason fuels the search. What else is essential? We might add to critical reason the capacity to love people, to love beauty, and to hate whatever robs us of joy and hope. That is a slim sample of endless emotional responses to our day-to-day living. These responses are interwoven, tempered, and enriched by passing time and changing circumstances— ever-changing circumstances. We are perpetually evaluating and reevaluating; how we *feel* about those circumstances matters. In the midst of all this, we strive to discover what is good and, in our best moments, we choose accordingly. We learn about consequences, especially when they are sobering. Our reason, sensitivity to goodness, and dogged determination form the fabric within which we develop moral resolve. The "we" in these paragraphs encompasses pretty much every breathing soul. These are things "we" do because we are human. But there is more.

Our finite minds run up against boundaries in all realms, and at the same time we know there are things beyond those boundaries, just out of reach—so tantalizing. The author of Ecclesiastes put it well: God "made everything beautiful in its time; he set eternity in the hearts of humans, but they are not able to find out what God has done from the beginning to the end" (Eccl 3:11). This is, frankly, a recipe for endless frustration. In this sphere arise questions about the meaning of life in the face of intense suffering, in the face of apparent absurdities, and in the face of emptiness. As if these are not enough, we agonize over how to pick our way through the minefields of human relationships, the pain of love, and the horrifying love of hatred that destroys so much in its path. In sum, there is a sense of what *ought* to be, but life is fraught with inexplicable tragedies. These are the questions that drive some to despair, some to deep hope, and all to question and seek greater wisdom. These questions are universal. Biblical wisdom literature is but one slice of the global pie, but it is an important slice.

Wisdom "Attitudes" and Behaviors

In the survey above, the disciplines of psychology, anthropology, and sociology made cameo appearances along with the realms of the natural sciences and aesthetic pursuits. Here we circle back to explore what wise people are *like*. How do we know a wise person when we meet her? The following character traits are not in any hierarchy; each is simply an integral part of a whole person. Even though we are still exploring wisdom through a cross-cultural lens, we cannot help but make connections with biblical descriptions.

No matter what wisdom tradition we visit, a defining characteristic of wisdom is humility. To be sure, this sounds counterintuitive at first. In fact, we worry that gaining wisdom will result in pride, and we warn against such a treacherous path. We probably know a few people who think they embody wisdom—and they let us know. Nevertheless, true seekers of wisdom soon realize how little they know. They are humbled at how few questions can really be answered but are still deeply curious. They realize the limits of human understanding and come to rest in an odd way in the fact that they don't have to try to control the universe.

This results in the ability to trust, a positive by-product of experiencing our limitations. Coming head-to-head with limits, a proud and self-dependent individual succumbs to anxiety and eventually despair. One who is wise learns to rest. "It is what it is, and I now leave it in hands that are much stronger and more capable than mine." We do the best we can and then learn to practice confidence and hope in our sovereign God. Part of this means giving up the expectation that we can always explain and fix everything! No one said this path to wisdom was easy or short.

It seems that kindness is also a constant companion to humility and therefore to wisdom. Perhaps this is because humble folk are more sensitive to pain and hurt, and they seek ways to lessen the impact of suffering. Experience has been for them a sober teacher. Another way of expressing this trait might be to call it compassion and love—unfailing love for our neighbors and, from our biblical perspective, love for the Creator of all good gifts that we enjoy.

Wise persons, no matter where they come from, are observant. "Attentive" might be an even more precise adjective. It suggests a developed and systematic focus on each aspect of the surrounding environment without mentally straying away to distractions as they come along. Developing the ability to attend to something is part of education. It is clear when we read Proverbs 30 that the author had been attentive to aspects of nature in order to discover moral lessons embedded in what he observed. Not everyone singles out ants, locusts, and lizards as models for exemplary character traits (Prov 30:25–28).

Speaking of the ant, diligent work and discipline are also part of the fabric of wisdom. They are in harmony with our affirmation that the universe is the work of a Master Creator. Our existence in it requires that we engage in the tasks of preservation; these labors are gifts from God (Eccl 2:24; 3:13; 5:18–20; 9:9–10). Wisdom literature addresses responsible study, just government, family maintenance, and the value of all sorts of manual labor. The self-disciplined person is recognized as wise. Idleness is an affront to God. It is not happenstance that laziness is characterized so negatively in Proverbs.

Humility coupled with the need to learn trust, diligence, and attentiveness send us in search of mentors. We need master instructors, teachers who can model the character traits we wish to embody. We also need those with whom we can exchange ideas, cross intellectual swords, debate, and agree to disagree. "Iron on iron together . . ." (Prov 27:17a). Biblical wisdom is often expressed in riddles, puzzles, fables, parables, and allegories. These are, by their very nature, tests of the intellect and the product of keen thinking and acquired skill and knowledge. In our study of the book of Proverbs we will examine these spheres of reason, discernment, and understanding in much greater depth.

Finally, there is a good deal of value in silence. Excessive words bode ill for wisdom. We cannot help but think of politicians of all stripes. Casting the net more widely, folks who are noisy are generally thought to be fools. There are a number of biblical proverbs that affirm this observation (e.g., Prov 10:19; 12:23; 17:28).

Our Invitation

We are invited to explore everything within sight and "walking distance" as well as the faint images resting at the very edges of our horizons. We are compelled to embrace this pursuit, savor every part of our experience, cling to wisdom, and rejoice in the precious honor that wisdom grants us. This is not a sterile or confined structure that we enter under duress. This is our very life.

Admittedly, we have moved in the course of this chapter from a global understanding of wisdom toward the biblical understanding. In preparation for the next chapters, let me suggest you read each segment below out loud, slowly.

> Acquire wisdom; acquire understanding.
> Do not forget and do not turn from the words of my mouth.
> Do not forsake her and she will guard you.
> Love her and she will protect you. (Prov 4:5–6)

There is no place for neglect, to say nothing of willful rejection, of wisdom. That would be perilous. On the contrary, we are to invest our emotional energy as we *love* wisdom and enjoy the assurance of protection she affords.

> Wisdom is first; acquire wisdom,
> and above all your acquisitions, acquire understanding.
> Esteem her and she will lift you up.
> She will honor you when you embrace her.
> She will set on your head a garland of grace;
> a crown of splendor she will give to you. (Prov 4:7–9)

In case we did not hear it the first time, here it is again: "Get wisdom and understanding." It seems wisdom is vital. In addition to love and protection, honor and esteem are part of this deeply personal engagement. We wrap our figurative arms around wisdom, taking her as ours, and in turn we wear grace like a crown, evident to all not in ostentatious finery but in radiance. What better way to walk through life?

CHAPTER 2

What Makes *Biblical* Wisdom Unique?

Introduction

The previous chapter gave us tantalizing hints as to how we might begin to think about biblical wisdom against a much broader backdrop. To review: wisdom, plain and simple, is highly valued no matter what community or culture we visit. When practical wisdom is really lodged in our guts, it often serves as a caution—"don't go there!" In company with wisdom, we find good advice on how to conduct ourselves so as to avoid major catastrophes and minor embarrassments. When we are robing ourselves in this necessary garb to deal with life, we add a "garland of grace." That means others are also attracted to what they see and experience.

Now we probe further to see what distinguishes the wisdom texts we encounter in the Bible. Our question now has a new dimension. Have you noticed? Previously, we were talking about wisdom; now we are talking about wisdom texts. That means that vibrant and living gems of wisdom have been crystallized in order to pass them along. My mother's favorite sayings, expected and spoken at key points, are now only remembered because I have written some of them down. "Boredom is the sign of a small mind" is one of my favorites, and it was best in living context!

We first need to describe the range of biblical texts that have traditionally come to be called "wisdom literature." The texts are varied, to say the least.

Which Biblical Texts—and Why?

The centerpieces of biblical wisdom are Proverbs, Job, and Ecclesiastes, which for a good long time have been presumed to represent a distinct genre. The fact of the matter is, however, that they are quite different from one another, in terms of both form and content. Add to this a relatively recent newcomer, Song of Songs, and we have a conundrum. How is it that these four books fit within any kind of single genre boundary? What defines the genre—form or content or both? Even where we start to engage this question affects where we end up!

I have chosen Proverbs as our starting point. It is in many ways the least perplexing of these books. A father teaches and admonishes his son so that the son will be wise in very practical ways. The instructions are intended to cultivate discernment and shape character. They are by and large succinct and to the point, and they are often quite funny. Yes, this fits within a "wisdom" category. The fool is warned of deadly consequences for rejecting the ways of righteousness; the wise person is praised. While life and death are in view, Proverbs' particular set of lenses focuses most closely on here, now, work, words, and living with both feet on the ground. That takes a good measure of practical wisdom.

We can next see Job and Ecclesiastes going together; they deal with the unanswerable questions of suffering and death. Pain and frustration enter the picture, and uncertainties abound. There is not much that is funny about Job and Ecclesiastes. Can these possibly merge with the Proverbs perspective, or are we simply predisposed to make this work? We may tentatively affirm that they can do so, although "merge" may not be the best concept. Let's just say that these books bring to the table more mature, sober, and necessary perspectives on life; to avoid them would indeed be utter folly.

But what about Song of Songs? How is it that some two decades ago scholars began to suggest that this unique, lyrical book could be lassoed and brought into the wisdom corral? Here is one response: the Song has to do with love—and if there were ever a place where wisdom is needed, it is in regard to the matter of love! To be sure, if we were simply assigning books to the wisdom category based on the appearance of the themes of life, death, and love, we could end up with every biblical book being a candidate. Nevertheless, as we will see, Song of Songs lodges its presentation of human love in a multilayered context that beckons us to revisit, among other places, Genesis and the garden of Eden. That should be enough of a hint for now.

In sum, the Bible's wisdom texts front-load instruction, debate, warning, description, and reflective questions. They capture our attention with poetic imagery. Narrative, particularly narrative within the covenant framework, plays a lesser role. In spite of the differences among these texts that we have noted above, their overall poetic forms and their thematic emphases do serve as tethers between them. They are free to roam a bit but are still bound together.

Just for the record, there are also wisdom psalms, although there is not a lot of agreement as to which psalms should be classified in this way. Psalms that are widely acknowledged to fit in this category share vocabulary and themes with our texts. A classic example is Psalm 1, with its contrast between the way of the wicked and that of the righteous. Psalm 8 compels us to be attentive to creation, another wisdom theme. In Psalm 39, we come face-to-face with the fleeting nature of our lives; our days are said to be but a "handbreadth." Psalm 49 starts off with characteristic wisdom vocabulary, including "understanding," "proverb," and "riddle." Others that you can explore are Psalms 14, 32, 73, 88, and 94. As you do, reflect on why these have also been deemed wisdom psalms.

A Biblical Definition of Wisdom

Given the exercise in which we have just engaged, "defining" biblical wisdom seems an audacious enterprise. If the diverse characteristics of the literature tax our ability to spread one net over the whole, the substance poses an even greater challenge. To wit, the attempt to put into words something that is intrinsic to the character of God seems presumptuous. How can finite and fallen creatures undertake such a task? Even as we make observations about human nature and the fabric of the created order, we press up against the unanswerable. And we want to offer a definition?

Yes—with appropriate fear and trembling. For starters, how about "the fear of the LORD is the beginning of wisdom" (Prov 9:10; Job 28:28)? "Fear of the LORD" is also an end point: "The end of the matter; everything has been heard; fear God . . ." (Eccl 12:13–14). The requisite obedience that results from proper fear of the Lord is unique to the wisdom literature of Israel. Fearing God links those unanswerable questions with practical guidance and instruction. God has given instructions (the Torah) that are entirely suited for his image-bearers. God designed us; he knows what is necessary for us to fulfill our remarkable potential. Think of the Bible and particularly the Torah and wisdom literature as the owner's manual, straight from the design center. In those areas that we simply do not understand, we take *our* Owner's directions seriously.

Notice that we are still wrestling with the tension between the charge to pursue wisdom with all of our being because it does guide and protect, and the realization that it cannot be fully attained; our minds are finite but wisdom stretches far beyond (Eccl 3:11; Job 28). Parts of it are off-limits because we live "under the sun," a favorite phrase in Ecclesiastes. Thus, any definitions we suggest will run the risk of omitting significant components of biblical wisdom. Nevertheless, I do keep coming back to this one: "Wisdom is the discipline of applying truth to one's life in the light of experience."[1] I like it, even though it may land more in the practical, proverbial wisdom camp than in the realm of the speculative material.

Under this rubric, wisdom involves our absorbing several bodies of knowledge. We learn the traditions that are handed down over generations. In this case, we are talking about Torah (God's instruction) as it is embedded in covenant (God's declaration of his relationship with his people). We also activate our capabilities of observation and exercise our intellect to evaluate what we learn and perceive. There is a proper order of truth and goodness, and we are able to attend to it. Finally, we discipline our wills; unless we apply truth, there is no point to the previous intellectual exercises.

Let it be noted that observation, evaluation, and application can unfold in the most daunting circumstances prompted by suffering and death. We wonder and question at those times. Moral discourse is part of each step; we seek further wisdom and understanding in the face of life's challenges because we are convinced that wisdom knows how things should be. Wisdom compels us to expect things to be better and to choose to make them better. It is in this context that we heed admonitions in Torah and the wisdom literature to pursue righteousness and justice, to eschew idolatry, and to fear the Lord. This tall order necessitates the work of the Holy Spirit and a hefty dose of humility. In sum (for now), the intent to pursue wisdom *is* wisdom, and it flourishes best in covenant community.

Additional Implications: Creation, Evil, and Biblical Wisdom

It would be a mistake to leave our overview of biblical wisdom without an introductory consideration of Genesis 1–3. God *spoke* the entirety of the created order into existence. That sequence of creative words was powerful beyond our most extreme imagined possibilities. "The LORD by wisdom founded the earth; he established the heavens by understanding" (Prov 3:19). God's wisdom ordered all of creation; we will revisit this in conjunction with our investigation of Proverbs 8.

God's prohibition and pronouncement in Gen 2:16–17 focus on the tree of the knowledge of good and evil. There is a stunning ambiguity at this point both in the nature of this "tree" and its relationship to the tree of life (Gen 2:9). Further, temporality and finitude threaten ominously in the last clause of Gen 2:17: "... *in the day* you eat from it, you will *surely die.*" These are *the* issues with which we humans wrestle in our pursuit of wisdom. Back in Eden, existence is already represented in the harsh polarities of life and death, good and evil; and so it continues into the temptation scene itself: "You shall be as gods, knowing good and evil ..." (Gen 3:5).

The serpent, called more wise (*'arum*) than all of the creatures (Gen 3:1), sowed doubt, blurred the boundaries between good and evil, caused pride to blossom, and ruptured all relationships with its deception and blatant lie. We will engage in an extended study of words related to wisdom in conjunction with the book of Proverbs. For now, it is sufficient to note that *'arum* has both positive and negative connotations. Here we read it as "crafty" in the most negative sense. After all, look at the results of the serpent's terrible scheming. Nevertheless, the word appears in a series of proverbs with primarily positive emphases. One of the reasons the serpent may have been so beguiling and appealing to Eve was that this aspect of its intellectual prowess, "wisdom" after a fashion, looked pretty good. That continues to be the problem, doesn't it? How do we sort through deception and skewed perceptions, especially when the options "look pretty good"?

Falsehood, deception, exaggeration—they are all related in Genesis 3. For her part, Eve intensified the original prohibition, distorting the word of God in order to "protect" it. Then, with the serpent's false assurance in her ears, Eve saw that the tree lived up to its prior description. It was "good for eating, pleasing to the eye (cf. 2:9) and pleasant for enlightenment" (3:6). The initial two conclusions Eve reached were based on the correspondence between her observations and reality. She exercised good practical "wisdom." Regarding the tree of the knowledge of good and evil, however, she had to connect what she *saw* with something beyond empirical evidence. She had to take "on faith" what the serpent said in regard to gaining "enlightenment" from eating the fruit of the tree. This is not the standard Hebrew word for wisdom (*ḥokhmah*). Often translated "for gaining wisdom" in Gen 3:6, the basic meaning of the word *lehaskil* is debated. The verbal root seems to be related to seeing, giving attention to, and pondering; derivative meanings range from having insight to being wise or prudent and acting circumspectly. While it is God who gives this kind of insight (1 Chr 22:12; 28:19; Dan 9:22), the issue in Genesis 3 is that humans would acquire it through willful disobedience.

Contrary to the word of the serpent, God's word was correct on the death issue. He made it certain by banning them from the tree of life. (Proverbs 3:18 equates the tree of life with wisdom.) What had been deliciously close to the tree of knowledge in the center of the garden was now unattainable. Instead, fear and alienation shaped interactions between God and his creatures and among humans.

That brings us full circle to the fear of the Lord. It became a necessity once Adam and Eve landed themselves in the rebellious camp. Not surprisingly, Torah has more admonitions to fear the Lord than to love him, not because God wants to terrorize us but because God knows us well and knows that we operate always under the dark shadow of evil inclinations and temptations. The fear of the Lord is a gift.

One final question for now: Given the pervasive nature of evil and the need for fear of the Lord to curb our inclinations, is it possible for unregenerate folks to be wise? Truly wise? Think about that as we move through these texts.

CHAPTER 3

Biblical Poetry: The Perfect Form(s) for Wisdom Expressions

Introduction

Drop a sentence about poetry into the conversation among a gathering of your friends and watch their reactions. It is an interesting exercise—and of course it depends on the contents of your sentence! Nevertheless, some will practically gush over how much they love poetry and others will vaguely nod, indicating they have likely not read any poetry since tenth grade. Our task is to introduce Hebrew poetry to a wide range of readers, from the one extreme to the other, as well as everyone in between.

We have two objectives. The first is to explore why poetry is such a powerful medium of communication, especially in terms of its prominence in the Hebrew Bible. The second is to tread into the characteristics of Hebrew poetry, both those that are quite distinct from our familiar Western poetry forms and those that we already know from our studies in classic English literature.

Why Poetry "Works"

The line between poetry and prose is not nearly as stark as this initial presentation might suggest. We can all think of prose that is so lyrical in cadence and vocabulary that it bears the same powerful emotive quality that we often accord poetry. On the other hand, I have run aground in pieces that purport to be poetry but seem only to be chopped-up lines of bad prose. No doubt I have missed something profound in them. My point is that there are gray areas in this discussion.

Approximately one-third of the Hebrew Bible is poetry. This is remarkable. Of course, the songbook for the Israelites (Psalms) is poetry, but that is only the beginning. A substantial portion of the prophets' words are poetic, and most of our wisdom texts are as well. There are even examples of poetry incorporated into the Torah and the historical books. The question practically pleads to be addressed: Why so much? After all, the New Testament has precious little poetry. Instead, it is shaped by narratives, theological formulations, and exhortations about practical living.

I will address the contrast with the New Testament first and just briefly. The unparalleled story of God becoming flesh, suffering in that flesh, dying, and rising again is the culmination of the metanarrative that shapes all of human history. The main point of the grand story lies in God's victory over sin and death, foreshadowed repeatedly throughout the Hebrew Bible and now coming to fulfillment. The apostles' responses to that event are couched in the language and forms of their Greco-Roman culture. Among other factors, this was a context in which texts and writing were accessible and in which written documents moved easily.

By contrast, the social world of the Hebrew Bible was much more dependent on hearing and listening in order to remember and obey. Poetry served an extraordinarily important purpose, providing cadences, patterns, and language that would make the messages memorable. As we will see, that is especially true as the key patterns emphasize repetition and attention.

In addition, no matter the cultural context, poetry evokes a depth of emotion beyond what even excellent prose conveys. Contributing to this are vivid imagery, unusual word choices, and much more compressed expression. We will be looking at examples of each of these below. In the meantime, one further comment is in order. Because of the spare nature of poetry, each word counts. Sometimes words have to "count" in multiple ways. Poetry is often ambiguous, both because it is terse and because the words chosen can carry multiple valences.

Unique Characteristics of Hebrew Poetry

Consider the following noble hymn text penned by Isaac Watts:

When I survey the wondrous cross
On which the Prince of Glory died,
My richest gain I count but loss
And pour contempt on all my pride.

And the verses continue, compelling us to contemplate *our* response to the gospel narrative. Each word choice strikes deeply in our hearts.

"Wondrous" sets the cross into a sphere that is beyond remarkable. "Prince of Glory" draws together a host of echoes from the Hebrew Bible and the New Testament. "Pouring contempt" on the chief sin that plagues each of us forces us to come to grips with whether we nurse our pride or really hate it.

In addition to these word choices, however, both rhyme and rhythm are at work, making the verse easy to sing and thus more easy to memorize. (That is one of the precious treasures embedded in musical settings.)

In contrast, there is only a faint and occasional sense of rhyme in Hebrew poetry. Something else is powerfully at work. Instead of rhythm of sound, there is what we might call a rhythm of thought. Ideas are juxtaposed in successive lines of text, creating symmetry of thought. This is called "parallelism," and most scholars identify it as the primary characteristic of Hebrew poetry. Think of it as the structural backbone that binds the lines together. Parallelism establishes conceptual relationships.

Synonymous Parallelism

Put in the simplest terms, when two lines of poetry convey the same basic message using different words, we have "synonymous parallelism." With apologies to Isaac Watts, here is what that first verse might look like reworked into a structure that manifests synonymous parallelism:

> When I survey the wondrous cross
> and gaze upon the tree of glory,
> that tree on which the Prince of Glory died,
> the place he was crucified—
> my richest gain I count but loss,
> everything I have ever worked for means nothing to me,
> and pour contempt on all my pride,
> I despise everything that I have always boasted about.

You get the point. The repetition of each idea makes us pause and revisit the initial concept. If this rendition were more felicitous, we might pause with less dismay! "Synonymous" parallelism is a slight misnomer because the "repeating" lines are rarely exact repetitions, nor do they always contain synonyms. Mere repetition would be numbing. Instead, the second line intensifies the initial thought, introduces a slightly altered perspective, and compels the reader to slow down and circle back to the point to see what has been emphasized.

Full disclosure—there are ongoing discussions in regard to the best way to map out types of parallelism. Nevertheless, I will follow the traditional rubric with just a few additional notes. As we have already seen, in synonymous parallelism the second line responds with, broadly speaking, the same general implications as the first. Here are several biblical examples:

> The fear of the Lord is the beginning of wisdom
> and knowledge of the Holy is understanding. (Prov 9:10)

> Even a fool, when he keeps silent, is considered wise;
> the one who closes his lips, discerning. (Prov 17:28)

We can see how this works. What is interesting, even in these two examples, are the gaps in Hebrew that we fill in based on the overarching parallel structure. For example, the Lord is the defining Person in the first line. Thus, even though the second line simply has "holy" in the plural, we read it in conjunction with the declaration about the Lord and presume it is referring to knowledge of the Holy One. That knowledge, in turn, is intimately related to understanding, which is intrinsic to wisdom.

The second example, too, does not present a simplistically matched set of synonyms. Instead, we are first introduced to a fool, but he is one who does something that is actually quite wise and that earns him this judgment in public: he manages to keep his mouth shut. The point is emphasized in the second line. Fools can pull off a change in public persona.

We do not want to limit our examples to the book of Proverbs; here is just one from Job:

> Oh that my anger were surely weighed,
> and my calamity also lifted in the scales. (Job 6:2)

For now, just note that Job's calamity was the cause of his anger. Both are weighed, and we can imagine the near breaking of the scales.

Antithetical Parallelism

Antithetical parallelism does not appear as frequently, but it serves a very important purpose. As the second line expresses an opposite or contrasting idea, it again makes readers linger and possibly inquire, "Should I be going down that path or not?" It is like saying, "Yes, but . . ." It introduces a perspective that needs to be considered, even if only as a foil to the primary point. These antitheses are most prominent in Proverbs 10–15, where, as we will see, they are an excellent tool for modeling discernment for youthful seekers after wisdom. Two examples to consider:

A wise son (heeds) the discipline of his father,
but a mocker does not hear a rebuke. (Prov 13:1)

A gentle answer turns away wrath,
but a harsh word stirs up anger. (Prov 15:1)

Each of these is a commentary on life! They do not require an explanation so much as a decision. In the latter case, what words and tone will I choose in the next possibly inflammatory situation?

Synthetic Parallelism

While this is one of the traditional categories that have been proposed to help us identify different types of parallelism, a word of caution is in order. In some ways, this category has become a vast catchall for the lines of poetry that are unquestionably bound together but do not easily fall into synonymous or antithetical patterns. When we think of "synthesis," we think of putting two or more components together into a whole that speaks its own message. Synthetic parallelism, then, builds from the first clause by adding further information in each successive line. Consider the following text:

A word was secretly brought to me,
my ears caught a whisper of it.
Amid disquieting dreams in the night,
when deep sleep falls on men,
fear and trembling seized me
and made all my bones shake.
A spirit glided past my face,
and the hair on my body stood on end. (Job 4:12–15 NIV)

To be sure, this can be viewed as successive lines of poetry (some of which might require the synthetic scaffold), or it could simply be Eliphaz's melodramatic description of his harrowing experience. Because our current translations have typeset these lines to read as poetry, I am inclined toward the former option. We can track Eliphaz's growing terror from line to line as the "word" is whispered into the dark night, as dreams capture him, and as something from another sphere shakes him to the core.

However we settle this issue, we cannot simply label successive pairs of poetic lines with one of the handy designations "synonymous," "antithetical," or "synthetic" and be done with it. In most biblical poetry apart from Proverbs, the parallelisms are interwoven into complex combinations, and they often involve more subtle relationships than the three we have already surveyed. Here is one final gem:

> The path of the righteous is a shining light,
> growing brighter until the full light of the day.
> The way of the wicked is like deep darkness;
> they do not know in what they have stumbled. (Prov 4:18–19)

At first glance, these are two contrasting lines about the paths that righteous and wicked people choose to take and the accompanying brilliance and gloom. The subtle differences, however, in terms of conditions and results grab our attention. The righteous walk into increasing light; it is a dynamic journey. Tragic ignorance accompanies the wicked in their bondage to constant darkness.

Two additional categories or labels might help us, even as we recognize that none of these can be applied in a rigid manner.

Emblematic Parallelism

As we read through the witty and trenchant observations in Job, Ecclesiastes, and Proverbs, we often come across lessons drawn from careful observation of nature. We do the same thing. Consider "In a battle between elephants, ants get squashed." The "lesson" is implicit; little people are hurt in large-scale conflicts. Most often in biblical emblematic parallelism, that moral deduction is explicit. The first line of the pair presents an "emblem" drawn from nature, and the second connects that illustration directly to a lesson in the moral sphere. For example:

> Dead flies cause the oil of a perfumer to stink;
> so a little folly is more prominent than wisdom and honor.
>   (Eccl 10:1)

We see an abundance of this kind of statement in Proverbs 25 and 26, such as "Like snow in the summer or rain at harvest time, so honor is not fitting for a fool" (26:1). Each of the weather "emblems" is ill suited to its immediate context, and "rain in harvest" has damaging consequences. So also we can imagine a fool abusing a position of honor: "Like a dog that returns to its vomit, a fool repeats his folly" (26:11). This is not the last we see of this bitter (pun intended) observation. Peter adds a tragic twist to the picture as he describes the fate of false teachers who, after a time of enjoying the benefits of walking in righteousness, are entangled again in their corruption (2 Pet 2:19–22).

Character and Consequences

Many of the parallel lines in Proverbs focus particularly on consequences. Again, the point is to acknowledge relationships and interactions that matter. Who we are, what we do, how we think, and what we demand of others all have consequences. We see this over and over in life—and in Proverbs:

> The one who is kind to the poor lends to the LORD,
> and he will pay him his reward. (Prov 19:17)

There are variations on this theme. Commands are issued in contexts that require responses, and what a given response might be determines the next developments. Here is an example from Ecclesiastes:

> Sow your seed in the morning and don't rest your hand in the
>   evening,
> for you do not know which will succeed. (Eccl 11:6)

In other words, in the face of uncertainty, diligence is the key to any possible success. It is not a matter of knowing the outcome so much as taking care to cover all the bases. Try this last one:

> Discipline your child for there is hope;
> do not lift your soul to his death. (Prov 19:18)

We might think strict discipline curbs a young person's joy in life, but the opposite is the case. Hope lies within those strict boundaries, while the ugly specter of untimely death accompanies an undisciplined rebel.

Large-Scale Parallelisms

In addition to these relatively small units, overarching parallel structures and repetitions are foundational to some of the wisdom literature that we read. Here are simply two examples to which we will return. In Proverbs 9, the message is clearly cast in terms of a radical contrast between Lady Wisdom and everything that she embodies and Woman Folly and her dangerous characteristics. A more subtle structure may be discerned in Ecclesiastes as the preacher/teacher alternates between a steady drumbeat of anguish and occasional glimpses of gifts from the hand of God. The frustrated and gloomy drumbeat dominates, because we live day by day in a twisted world. Nonetheless, at intervals, the preacher/teacher draws our attention upward to the presence of God through breaks in the clouds.

Circling Back: Parallelism Enriches the Message

All right; so what? Our examples have demonstrated that repetition with expansion is forceful. It does not allow the hearer or reader to nod off. Why? Because we are not entirely certain how the second line might be enhancing and expanding the message, we must be attentive to figure it out. The same is true with what we have called antithetical parallelism. As it sets up the contrast, we see and hear discernment between right and wrong modeled, but we also grow in our understanding of the limits and contours of those moral categories. Of course, the consequences that appear repeatedly in Proverbs are pointed warnings and are generally not very subtle.

One more "so what?" is worthy of mention. It always delights me that parallelism is the prominent characteristic of Hebrew poetry. As parallelism creates symmetries of ideas and rhythms of thought, it not only serves as a vehicle for much-needed repetition, but also transcends language barriers much more easily. Consider the challenges of translating the kind of poetry that is structured around rhyme and rhythm. The translator has to labor to find words that fit the pretty rigid rhyme and rhythm patterns and that at the same time maintain the depth of meaning of the poem. All we need to do to explore this challenge is look at older hymn texts that originated in German. You might want to consider "O Sacred Head, Now Wounded" as an example. It has taken masterful translators to capture the meaning of the original and transfer it to the receptor language. If you read German, you will especially appreciate this point.

Additional Poetic Features

In addition to its parallel structures, poetry grabs our emotions through figures of speech, unusual choices of words, and patterns that indicate the superlative or comprehensive nature of a statement. In this section, we will focus primarily on figurative language. This broad category involves a range of comparison strategies, sound patterns, and powerful images and symbols. As with all language, there is a never-ending array of possibilities. Established boundaries between one figurative type and the next are regularly defied by new explorations with language. What, after all, are the boundaries of metonymy? (You might want to look this word up in several dictionaries. Whose definitions do we accept?)

Figurative language compels us to establish relationships in our minds. This remarkable quality of language increases exponentially the rich associations that we can make among all the aspects of our experiences, memories, and imaginations.

Types of Comparisons

Of the numerous figures that we might pursue, I will focus solely on five of them, always mindful that they interweave through and push boundaries in biblical poetry. The ones that are probably most familiar to us from our previous study of literature come first.

Personification is giving human qualities to abstract ideas or inanimate objects. This is the "nutshell" definition and, as we will see further on, there may be potential overlap between this kind of representation and what happens when emotions and abstractions are represented by parts of the human body. But for now, let me mention what is likely the most familiar example from the texts we will study: wisdom and folly (two abstractions) make their appearance as two unforgettable women in Proverbs 9. We will visit these women at length when we get to our exploration of Proverbs.

Metaphors establish unusually striking or memorable comparisons between two entities that are unlike. In doing so, the juxtaposition speaks of one thing or concept *as if* it were another. The emotional impact of metaphor resides in the tension created by the seemingly absurd pairing of two dissimilar things. This forced conjunction enables us to see and experience things differently.

Similes accomplish the same juxtaposition but make the comparison explicit by saying one thing is "like" another. Along with metaphors, similes appear frequently in the emblematic parallelisms in Proverbs. One of the difficulties in separating these two comparison types is that English translations frequently insert a "like" when it is absent in Hebrew. Here are several examples. The first two reflect the absence of the explicit comparison (metaphor). Literal translation comes in handy:

> The crucible is for silver, and the furnace is for gold,
> and the One testing hearts is the Lord. (Prov 17:3)

It does not take much to get this picture. Crucibles and furnaces are hot, and the fire is fierce in order to refine the metals. So also the refining process that our hearts need.

> Apples of gold in webbings of silver;
> a word spoken on its "turnings." (Prov 25:11)

"On its turnings" may best be understood as "in the right conditions." This is the only place this Hebrew form is used. The basic Hebrew root word has to do with wheels. Perhaps implicit here is that, as a wheel always comes round properly, so also words.

This second juxtaposition has several layers to visualize, starting with "apples" of gold set into silver. Once we have that picture of exquisite beauty in our minds, then we have to deal with the second image, that of the wheel turning around and around. In what sense can that describe words and then be related to something precious and beautiful? Your call!

Our next example includes the explicit comparison established by the presence of "like":

> Like a stone bound in a sling,
> so is giving honor to a fool. (Prov 26:8)

What a picture! Tying up a stone in the sling that is supposed to send it rocketing toward its target is ignorant. It might also be dangerous if that stone drops back on the slinger's head!

Metonymy presses further the matter of representative comparison. And just for the sake of complexity, let's add in *synecdoche* while we are at it. They are closely related—like everything else we are combing through right now—and often confused. Metonymy refers to an attribute or related item that comes to represent the real deal. The descriptive word is linked to the particular entity but is not part of it. Synecdoche takes a part of something and compels it to represent the whole. Got it?

Here are several examples from Proverbs. Metonymy first. "Grandchildren are the crown of the aged" (Prov 17:6a); here "crown" represents honor. The most common synecdoche in biblical literature might be the word "heart" as it represents the whole of a person—will, mind, and intentions. Likewise, "eye," particularly in conjunction with "good" or "evil," represents the whole person. In the same general vein, "burning nose" is the idiomatic Hebrew way of representing anger. Here are two more examples of synecdoche:

> The lips of the righteous feed many . . . (Prov 10:21a)

> The lips of a fool enter into strife,
> and his mouth summons blows. (18:6)

These are only beginning explorations of the endless wealth of word pictures, images, symbols, and allusions in the texts we are studying. I have drawn most of the examples from Proverbs simply because they are shorter, but Job, for example, is a veritable gold mine (note the metaphor) for layers of rich meaning.

Sounds

Because most of the examples of sound effects depend on hearing the Hebrew, we will not spend time on them here. Just be apprised of the fact that puns, onomatopoeia, assonance, and alliteration all walk through the chapters of our texts and give them added zest.

Comprehensive Declarations

We have one final category to highlight. Hebrew poetry has several ways of saying "Pay attention to the following statement!" In some cases, such a statement is intended as a comprehensive declaration about the given topic. In others, it implies that this is about as over-the-top as we can get—a superlative.

Acrostic patterns in Hebrew poetry are those in which each successive line begins with the next letter of the Hebrew alphabet. The order and sequencing of each line suggest that the carefully ordered observations together convey a sense of completeness. The most familiar acrostic in our wisdom books is the description of the remarkable woman in Prov 31:10–31. She is utterly capable in every way, a true ideal.

Numbered patterns are best illustrated by Prov 6:16–19. This sober passage commences with "these are six things the LORD hates; seven are an abomination to him." The list is not a happy description. More lighthearted numbered patterns appear in Proverbs 30—"three things . . . yea, four . . ." The reader gathers that Agur, the author of this section, has been watching his world pretty carefully and has taken to heart some lessons from nature.

Ready for Work

We are now in a place to tackle the meaty substance of each piece of wisdom poetry in the Hebrew Bible. There is simply one more bit of necessary background that we will survey in the next chapter.

CHAPTER 4

Contexts: Solomon's Court as a Wisdom "Hub"?

Introduction

We have proposed that the quest for wisdom characterizes every sentient person. We have further noted the unique characteristics of biblical wisdom, particularly its intimate relationship with the Lord of the covenant. To understand as clearly as possible *what* the texts are saying, we have explored the nature of Hebrew poetry. Now it falls to us to determine how these biblical wisdom expressions fit within the wider ancient Near Eastern contexts, what social and cultural concepts will help us understand "education" in these contexts, and why Solomon's name is associated with three of the four books.

The Ancient Near East

How did the universal quest for wisdom play out thousands of years ago in cultures significantly different from those of the twenty-first-century Western world? Texts from Egypt, dating from approximately 2500 to 1000 BCE, are our best sources to explore this question. The climate of Egypt is hot and dry, conditions that tend to preserve texts better than those that were found in the more humid, river-based cultures of Mesopotamia. Composed particularly within court contexts, many texts sound like instruction manuals, emphasizing behaviors that would serve a court functionary well. Speaking well was right up there at the top. Because there are a number of examples of Egyptian wisdom instruction that are rather like biblical proverbs, I am saving specific illustrations for the next unit, which is devoted to Proverbs. There are also extant texts from Mesopotamia that both offer practical advice and explore the nature of suffering.

The classic volume *Ancient Near Eastern Texts Relating to the Old Testament*, edited by James Pritchard (3rd ed.; Princeton: Princeton University Press, 1969), is the easiest place to access the widest range of texts. The only drawback is the dated and sometimes stilted translation style. For renditions in more contemporary English, see *The Context of Scripture*, vol. 1 (Leiden: Brill, 1997), edited by William W. Hallo and K. Lawson Younger.

Not surprisingly, we find references in biblical narratives to wise counselors whose jobs were in foreign courts. Joseph's unexpected rise to prominence in Pharaoh's court came about because the wise men of Egypt failed at their interpretive task (Gen 41:8). Some of this wisdom was later intertwined with a form of the occult—divination and the like. We see this especially in conjunction with the Exodus narrative. Wise men in Pharaoh's court were able to conjure up the same effects as Moses and Aaron for the first two plagues against Egypt (Exod 7:22; 8:7 [3]), and this was instrumental in keeping Pharaoh's heart hardened against the Israelites' pleas. Even they, however, recognized when the divine Opponent was too much for them (Exod 8:18–19 [14–15]). With Egypt still in focus, we read in Isa 19:11–15 a scathing condemnation of Egypt's "wise" counselors who gave senseless advice. Our point, however, is that they were there and had the ear of Pharaoh. No surprise, really. All leaders make a point of surrounding themselves with presumably helpful voices.

It is instructive to note that the description of Solomon's superior wisdom is lodged next to the names of the most eminent scholars of his day. They came from all over "the east" and from Egypt, and were sent by "all the kings of the world" (1 Kgs 4:30–34 [5:10–14]). While this is referring to the kings of the numerous small city-states in the ancient Near East, the implication is that the Jerusalem court was not a second-rate meeting place. It may have even been like going to the Cavendish Laboratory in Cambridge for a conference on experimental physics. To repeat, Solomon's wisdom was reputed to be greater than all the others of his day. We will revisit this aspect of Solomon's biography shortly.

Social Contexts

Just for the record, there is an ongoing discussion as to whether official wise men (we might think of academics, Supreme Court justices, members of the National Security Council, or presidential advisers as equivalents) were the primary source of wisdom material in the ancient Near East, or whether it really originated at the grassroots level. After all, there are a number of biblical passages that suggest that wisdom was fruitfully brewing in the family and clan. Note, for example, that Samson displayed his penchant for posing riddles at his wedding party. We wonder if he had any idea of the swath of destruction his small riddle would leave (Judg 14). Or consider the "wise woman" who was just down home in Tekoa when she was used as Joab's mouthpiece to get King David's attention (2 Sam 14).

At the same time, the Bible mentions Israelite professionals. During David's reign, both Ahithophel and Hushai served as counselors, and they were both good at it, though for different reasons and toward different ends. It's a gripping story; you can read it in 2 Samuel 15–17. Isn't it interesting that both the wise woman of Tekoa and these two advisers weighed in regarding David's problems with his son Absalom? It seems Absalom was a wily sort himself, and a good deal of wisdom was needed to subvert his ill designs on David's kingdom.

Many of the trenchant observations in the Bible's four wisdom books are the stuff of the market, the gate, the vineyard, and the sheepfold, as well as the home. In point of fact, these venues might not have been as foreign to advisers and rulers then as they would be to urban, inside-the-beltway types today. In the culture of "shepherds who were kings," we might ask what "courts" actually looked like. Even the imposing Egyptian temples and palaces were much closer to the dwellings of the ordinary folk who served in and around them. And no doubt everyone, whether court-bred or frequenting the local dispensary of barley brew, would know of bribes and the "king's wrath"!

Perhaps, as with all things that have to do with living, we ought to skip trying to pinpoint a singular "source" for wisdom. Every context generated its own rich collections, and it seems that precious little wisdom was under the tight control of "elitist" classes. We might contrast this with other significant culturally defined roles. For example, priests were in the temple orbit. Some prophets were in the court circles; they might have challenged the ruling figures but, nonetheless, that was their venue. Wisdom, however, belonged to everyone.

What Are the Connections with Solomon?

You have noticed, I am sure, that so far we have been presuming that Solomon was indeed closely associated with these books. His name or distinct likeness appears in three of the four (Proverbs, Ecclesiastes, and Song of Songs). Very few contemporary scholars, however, think these texts actually date to the tenth century BCE, that is, the period of Israel's history in which Solomon lived. There are a number of reasons for this. Some have to do with the presence in these books of what seem to be later forms of Hebrew. Some are based on the assumption that the biblical picture of the united monarchy under David and Solomon is hopelessly idealized and not a reflection of reality. Instead, it is thought, tenth-century Jerusalem was small and not a place for gatherings of international dignitaries. These judgments reflect a larger tendency to drive a wedge between religious texts and history.

I offer just a few responses for the moment. We will deal with Solomon's association with the book of Proverbs in particular in much greater detail as we study that book. First, it is always a bit dicey to use language as an indicator of a book's composition. Our sample of biblical Hebrew is a very small slice of what was a much larger living language. When we move into poetry, the number of times we encounter words used only once or twice is notable, but this does not mean these words were rare and later additions to the language. They were just not part of the traditional covenantal rhetoric. The Bible's historical texts, for example, use standardized syntax and grammar as ways of moving the narratives forward. In the instructions (Torah), we find a relatively prescribed set of commonly used terms. We might think of this as reflecting more conservative use of language for civil and ritual stipulations. No surprise there. In contrast, we would expect the brief zingers in Proverbs and the speculative wisdom of Job and Ecclesiastes to use quite different vocabulary. This does not necessarily mean the texts are later.

Second, the assumption that the narratives associated with David and Solomon are embellished and do not represent historical reality reflects a much larger discussion that is beyond the purview of this study. Thus, I make only a few observations here. There is a growing body of evidence from the field of archaeology that substantiates the existence of a sizable kingdom centered in Jerusalem in the tenth century BCE. The reason we do not read of this dynasty in ancient Near Eastern sources (as we do for the Israelite reigns of the Omri dynasty in the ninth century) is that during the tenth century the Assyrian empire was in a downsizing mode. Politics had gone temporarily south, and the Assyrians had to be concerned with events in their own territories. The Assyrians were the ones who later had lots to say about their exploits to the west, but they simply were not going in that direction in the tenth century. That, in God's providence, was likely one reason why David and Solomon after him were able to flourish as they did.

If the biblical narratives about David and Solomon are representative of historical reality, then at this time traffic through Israel from all points of the compass would have brought wisdom and wealth in abundance into the royal courts in Jerusalem. From the standpoint of historical geography, this land was a crossroads for commercial and military traffic from every major empire and minor kingdom. In like manner, it was the podium for political and religious messages. But that moves into another book for another time.

Kenneth Kitchen's *On the Reliability of the Old Testament* (Grand Rapids: Eerdmans, 2003) is a good place to engage the main issues here. Kitchen has also written very helpful materials on the likelihood that the collections found in the book of Proverbs do indeed reflect the tenth century. See chapter five and notes.

What can we say about Solomon that might support the contention that Proverbs, Ecclesiastes, and Song of Songs are products of his thought? For one thing, the description of his wisdom in 1 Kgs 4:29–34 [5:9–14] corresponds with the contents of Proverbs. Verse 32 [5:12] indicates that he spoke three thousand proverbs; our canonical book has only 915 of them. The others may have been a significant part of the court rhetoric if we accept the contention that many formal proceedings were conducted in poetic form. Taking it in a different direction, verse 33 addresses the wide-ranging nature of Solomon's curiosity. He was the interdisciplinary Renaissance scholar of that time, and many of the objects of his study appear in the emblematic parallelisms in Proverbs. Finally, as we will see in our focus on Proverbs, a good case can be made for formal parallels between Proverbs and Egyptian wisdom from the tenth century, not texts from five centuries later.

Solomon is also the figure that we have in mind as we read Ecclesiastes. The preacher/teacher of Ecclesiastes seemed to view life through lenses that were jaded. He had seen it all and experienced most of it. There is little youthful idealism running through the text. By the time Solomon was at the end of his reign and life, we can easily imagine that his inner reflections might have sounded a lot like Ecclesiastes. The disillusionment that comes after a life of poor choices is powerful.

There are significant question marks regarding how the name of Solomon is woven into the Song of Songs, but we can table most of that discussion for now. Suffice it to say that Solomon may not be the devoted lover so exquisitely described by the beloved but rather an external threat to the rustic young couple. Whatever Solomon's literary role in this text, the name association was no doubt the product of his notorious relations with far too many women.

There are reasons for this prominence of Solomon outside the historical books. Think about it. He was the king responsible for formalizing worship in the temple. We have only a fleeting sense of how the temple-centered worldview would have shaped popular perceptions. Places of religious worship have a relatively minor and separate role in most modern Western countries. Not so in the ancient Near East, and not so for the place in Jerusalem where the Lord had chosen to place his name. That Solomon had completed this structure elevated him to a position we can hardly imagine. From a pragmatic standpoint, the temple would also have served as the national "bank"; it was the safest place because the people, in their good days, would have defended its sanctity and treasures to their last breath. Solomon's international stature, prodigious wealth (likely accumulated in conjunction with his wide-ranging trade arrangements), and reputation for wisdom all interfaced to ensure that he was indeed a larger-than-life figure.

Wisdom and Worship

Solomon offered his prayer for wisdom as he was worshipping at the high place at Gibeon (1 Kgs 3:3–15). Specifically, he asked for a "heart that hears in order to discern between good and evil" (3:9), so that he could judge the people equitably. God granted that prayer, and immediately Solomon went to Jerusalem, stood before the ark of the covenant, and offered sacrifices. The very next episode in the text illustrates that God answered Solomon's prayer for discernment (3:16–28). And so he launched into his reign, which was dominated, as we have already seen, by his international political acumen on a number of fronts and by the temple construction project. Thus, even in the literary presentation of Solomon's entrance onto the scene, worship and wisdom are interwoven.

The temple would be the central place of worship, taking the stationary place of the movable tabernacle. It represented sacred space, the place where God would dwell in the midst of his people, and thus it represented "access to heaven." The cloud of glory (2 Chr 5:13–14) appeared, as did fire from heaven (7:1–3). These manifestations of the presence of God were palpable reminders of the transcendent "stuff" of the wisdom quest. So were the very structure and furnishings of the temple. The altar, the laver stationed on wheels, the cherubim, and the separating curtain all provided an avenue by which to move toward the ineffable. Not surprisingly, the description of Ezekiel's visions into the heavenly realms captures the same objects—wheels, cherubim, and the wide expanse between the cherubim and the radiance of the throne (Ezek 1; 8). Because Ezekiel had been a priest before the exile, he would have known the significance of what he saw in those celestial visions. The temple was a "connection" between earth and heaven. Likewise, God planted "eternity" in the hearts of humankind (Eccl 3:11), compelling us to reach beyond the things that are solely of this world.

One more observation fits under this umbrella: central to worship is obedience. Choosing righteousness over wickedness is high profile in the practical instructions in Proverbs. Without an obedient ("hearing") heart, it is dangerous business to venture into God's presence. When our rebellious hearts trample all over the holiness of God, God is not pleased. Proverbs 15:8 is simply one articulation of this principle: "The sacrifice of the wicked is an abomination to the LORD, but the prayer of the upright is his delight." Ritual Torah has everything to do with approach to God. While the components of worship do not appear frequently in the wisdom literature, fear of God and care with vows in God's house figure into the preacher's/teacher's admonitions in Ecclesiastes (5:1–7), the practice of intercessory prayer characterized Job (1:5), and Job's quest for God was laced with pleas and prayers of lament.

This suggests another connection. The Psalter, Israel's worship book, provided an avenue for God's people to sing their observations about God's creation, God's Torah, and the ways of the righteous and the wicked. Through the psalms, God's people came into his presence confessing their fear of mortality, their despair at unjust suffering, and their utter frustration at rampant evil. These too are of one piece with wisdom.

In sum, we do not want to presume a chasm between biblical sages as represented in the wisdom texts and those who were responsible for worship in Israel. To take just one example, Psalm 88 is attributed to one of the sons of Korah, a Levite. That psalm is a microcosm of the book of Job.

Reprise: Theological Themes

As we conclude our introduction, let us recapitulate the overarching theological themes in the Bible's wisdom texts. This literature is all about human nature, often in its less pleasant manifestations. A classic term for this might be theological anthropology; the doctrine of sin, sometimes viewed as a bit quaint, practically shouts from these texts. We encounter deceit, anger, pride, doubt, and the cruelty of words. We are people in need of help, and this help comes as trust, faithfulness, love, wisdom, and humility beckon us. A steady drumbeat echoes around the matter of honesty, possibly because it is so elusive in every sphere of our day-to-day interactions.

This brings us to the theology of relationships with God and with our fellow humans. Both rest under the umbrella of covenant and Torah.

The covenant articulates the love-based relationship and obedience to God's instructions (Torah) that are essential to well-being, both for individuals and within social structures. The covenant is the backbone of the character and consequences repeatedly stressed in Proverbs. God's covenant name, the Lord, is especially prominent in the central chapters of Proverbs (15–16). The covenant is also the backdrop for Job and Job's friends as they all presume God's justice in the cosmic spheres as well as in earthly contexts. Relationships of the most enchanting kind weave together the poetry of Song of Songs, with its multiple layers of intended meanings.

In the end, we return to the place from which we started our definition. The fear of the Lord is not only the beginning of wisdom; it was the completely proper response of the people to Moses as the words of the Sinai covenant were overwhelming them (Exod 20:18–21). In that relationship, fear was good and healthy. Thus, fear of the Lord is also the "conclusion of the matter" (Eccl 12:13–14).

For Further Reading

Alter, Robert. *The Wisdom Books: Job, Proverbs, and Ecclesiastes*. New York: Norton, 2010.

Brown, William P. *Character in Crisis: A Fresh Approach to the Wisdom Literature of the Old Testament*. Grand Rapids: Eerdmans, 1996.

———. *Wisdom's Wonder: Character, Creation, and Crisis in the Bible's Wisdom Literature*. Grand Rapids: Eerdmans, 2014.

Clifford, Richard. *The Wisdom Literature*. Nashville: Abingdon, 1998.

Crenshaw, James L. *Old Testament Wisdom: An Introduction*. 3rd ed. Atlanta: Westminster John Knox, 2010.

Dell, Katharine. *"Get Wisdom, Get Insight": An Introduction to Israel's Wisdom Literature*. Macon, GA: Smyth & Helwys, 2000.

Estes, Daniel J. *Handbook on the Wisdom Books and Psalms*. Grand Rapids: Baker Academic, 2005.

Hess, Richard. "Wisdom Sources." Pages 894–901 in *Dictionary of the Old Testament: Wisdom, Poetry and Writings*. Edited by Tremper Longman III and Peter Enns. Downers Grove, IL: InterVarsity Press, 2008.

Kidner, Derek. *The Wisdom of Proverbs, Job and Ecclesiastes: An Introduction to Wisdom Literature*. Downers Grove, IL: InterVarsity Press, 1985.

Klingbeil, Gerald. "Wisdom and History." Pages 863–76 in *Dictionary of the Old Testament: Wisdom, Poetry and Writings*. Edited by Tremper Longman III and Peter Enns. Downers Grove, IL: InterVarsity Press, 2008.

Murphy, Roland E. *The Tree of Life: An Exploration of Biblical Wisdom Literature.* 3rd ed. Grand Rapids: Eerdmans, 2000.

Penchansky, David. *Understanding Wisdom Literature: Conflict and Dissonance in the Hebrew Bible.* Grand Rapids: Eerdmans, 2012.

Perdue, Leo G. *The Sword and the Stylus: An Introduction to Wisdom in the Age of Empires.* Grand Rapids: Eerdmans, 2008.

———. *Wisdom and Creation: The Theology of Wisdom Literature.* Nashville: Abingdon, 1994.

———.*Wisdom Literature: A Theological History.* Louisville: Westminster John Knox, 2007.

Rad, Gerhard von. *Wisdom in Israel.* Nashville: Abingdon, 1972.

Weeks, Stuart. *An Introduction to the Study of Wisdom Literature.* T&T Clark Approaches to Biblical Studies. London: T&T Clark, 2010.

PART TWO

Practical Wisdom: Proverbs

A sampling of life's mundane questions might look like this: How can I possibly deal with that person who just plain annoys me? What about those insufferable types who talk endlessly? Oops, am I one of them? Did I really hear what I think I heard? Is anyone anywhere speaking the truth? How do I figure it out? We've got a child who is just like I used to be when I was three; what do I do when I feel like swatting her? That comment really hurt; how do I respond? While we are covering the gamut of life in the trenches, what about abuses of power and corruption in high places?

We could go on and on with these kinds of questions. No doubt you have your own; they surface each day and address the feet-on-the-ground parts of living. Sometimes, the questions defy answers entirely. Other times, our valiant attempts at answers run aground. Enter the book of Proverbs! Its gems are, by and large, one-liners, and many of them are zingers! Reading them is an exercise in slowing down, for reasons we will explore further. Years ago I heard a chapel speaker suggest that we resolve to read one proverb a day for the rest of our lives—just one, because that is all we can absorb if we are to take seriously the challenge to apply the truths embedded in these nuggets.

I commence this unit with some hesitation. How can we wrap our minds around 915 proverbs, especially since, after the first nine chapters of the book, so many of them seem to stand alone? Here's the plan. The introductory chapter will explore further who might have written Proverbs and why, situate the book's teaching method in its contemporary cultural context, chart a course through the book as a whole, focus on interpretive principles that might work for slivers of wisdom, and then ruminate on possible lessons to be drawn from the book. Sounds daunting! In the chapters that follow, we will take a thematic approach, starting with the profound theological foundation laid in chapters 1–9. Yes, we're going to miss a lot; that is why you are going to read a proverb a day for the rest of your lives. In the meantime, it does not hurt to return to the admonition in Prov 9:10: "The fear of the LORD is the beginning of wisdom, and knowledge of the Holy One is understanding." That declaration distills the theology of this unique book.

CHAPTER 5

How on Earth Should I Make Sense of Proverbs? An Overview

Authorship and Compilation

Because Solomon's name appears three times in the book of Proverbs (1:1; 10:1; 25:1), it is reasonable to suggest that the collection might have originated in the court of Solomon in the tenth century (approximately 950) BCE. Perhaps the expression "proverbs of Solomon" indicates that he was the person who authorized the collection for court use. Just a reminder, by the way, that this connection is not a foregone conclusion. As we noted in chapter four, a significant number of scholars tend to place the book much later. Nevertheless, if the biblical accounts reflect even a modicum of historical reality, the tenth-century reign of Solomon was marked by interaction with a wide range of international wisdom circles (1 Kgs 4:29–34 [5:9–14]) in addition to international commerce and trade (1 Kgs 10). Think of New York City, London, or Tokyo, with their array of academic institutions, judicial systems, and economic nerve centers.

All of this would have been fertile ground for Israel's own library of vibrant and developing wisdom traditions. According to the account in 1 Kings, Solomon himself wrote over three thousand proverbs (4:32 [5:12]), and likely there were many others in the "library." His awareness of plant and animal life (4:33 [5:13]) surfaces in memorable lines about fig trees (Prov 27:18), ants (30:25), and lizards in kings' palaces (30:28).

Kenneth Kitchen has demonstrated that the structure, length, and nature of the proverbs in chapters 1–24 (what he calls "Solomon I") fit into the tenth-century international wisdom context. This was the time of Solomon. See Kenneth Kitchen, "Proverbs 2: Ancient Near Eastern Background," in *Dictionary of the Old Testament: Wisdom, Poetry and Writings*, ed. Tremper Longman III and Peter Enns (Downers Grove, IL: InterVarsity Press, 2008),

552–66. See also Bruce Waltke, "The Book of Proverbs and Ancient Wisdom Literature," *Bibliotheca Sacra* 136 (1979): 211–38.

Even though a core of Solomonic material is a possibility, it is also apparent that the entire book is a compilation and that some parts were added considerably later. How do we know that? Proverbs 25:1 indicates that the "men of Hezekiah, king of Judah" copied proverbs of Solomon. We need just a bit of historical context to make sense of this. After Solomon's death, the united monarchy suffered an irreparable schism, and the northern tribes formed their own kingdom, Israel. This occurred in 931 BCE. Both the north and the south (Judah) endured increasing pressure from the international superpower of the day, Assyria. The north succumbed first (722 BCE); Hezekiah became king in Judah during that tumultuous time (2 Kgs 18:9–13).

The Composition of Proverbs: From Solomon to Well after Hezekiah

1010–931 BCE: United Monarchy
1010–970: David's reign
970–931: Solomon's reign—temple built
931: split in the kingdom (north and south)

931–722: Divided Monarchy
728: Hezekiah (south) begins coregency with Ahaz
722: fall of north to Assyria

722–587/6: Judah Alone
715–686: Hezekiah's reign
701: invasion of Sennacherib (Assyria)
587/6: destruction of temple (Babylonians)—into exile
539: edict of Cyrus—return of Jews to land
516: completion of second temple

It is not difficult to imagine fear laced throughout court interactions in Judah in those difficult days. Reading further in 2 Kings 18–20 and the parallels in 2 Chronicles 29–32, we learn that Hezekiah was a God-fearing king who also scored high marks for careful preparation against the Assyrian onslaught. While he appealed earnestly to God and enlisted the help of the prophet Isaiah, he also boldly resisted the Assyrian king, Sennacherib, and had his engineers construct walls and water reservoirs. It may be that in addition to monumental efforts to strengthen Jerusalem's defenses, Heze-kiah undertook the preservation of its precious archives. Among the works included in these archives would have been the proverbs of Solomon.

> Throughout history, we see evidence of deep concern to preserve cultural treasures when enemies threaten the existence of a people. Examples from across the centuries leap to mind. Whoever the inhabitants of Qumran (on the northwest corner of the Dead Sea) were, they took pains to deposit their precious texts in jars that they hid in caves. The Liberty Bell was re-moved from Philadelphia and taken farther to the north and west when the city was threatened by the British in the War of 1812. We read of the heroic efforts of members of the Warsaw ghetto to archive everything they could that reflected a life they knew was coming to an end. In regard to this last, see Samuel D. Kassow, *Who Will Write Our History? Emanuel Ringelblum, the Warsaw Ghetto, and the Oyneg Shabes Archive* (Bloomington: Indiana University Press, 2007). The examples multiply.

Back to the biblical book of Proverbs: the final work was compiled at some unknown point after the unsettling times of Hezekiah. It incorporated the words of two foreign kings, Agur and Lemuel. Just who they were and when they were active participants in the wisdom enterprise is unknown.

Ancient Near Eastern Connections

One of the most engaging aspects of the book of Proverbs is its universal appeal. We have already gained some familiarity with global perspectives on wisdom. Now in Proverbs, pithy sayings and hilarious caricatures are the main fare. We have to laugh at many of them—and at ourselves. Why not? Even as they are products of particular, often peculiar, circumstances, these circumstances are the kind that human beings encounter no matter the time or the place. We find collections of proverbial wisdom in just about every corner of human culture. They are, simply put, about life—then and now, and everywhere.

We think of "getting your ducks in a row" or "putting your feet to the fire," and we have a pretty good idea what is being said, even though we may not be lining up ducks every day or burning the soles of our slip-pers. An example of a recurring and timely biblical proverb surfaces in Isa 24:17–18 and is echoed in Jer 48:43–44. The opening words of these texts, "terror, and pit, and trap," sound similar to each other (*pahad vaphahat vaphaḥ*), and there is an ominous quality about the repeated vowel and the guttural growl. The warning continues: "(these) are against you, O inhabitant of the earth. The one who flees from the sound of terror will fall into the pit, and the one who climbs up from the pit will be caught in the trap" (thus Isa 24; Jer 48 is slightly different). Following these statements, Isaiah and Jeremiah contextualize the dire threat for their own situations, but we do not need to be living back in the seventh or sixth centuries BCE to get the point: there is no way out. An even more familiar proverb fell from Ezekiel's lips: "The fathers have eaten sour grapes, and the children's teeth are set on edge" (Ezek 18:2). He even labeled it a proverb (*mashal*).

For our purposes, the geographically immediate contexts of Mesopotamia and Egypt are the most important. Instructional literature from Egypt spanned from the mid-third millennium (approximately 2500 BCE, the middle of the Old Kingdom) to well beyond the New Kingdom (1550–1000 BCE). Likewise, Sumerian texts from Mesopotamia were composed in the same time frame, even though they are not as numerous. Altogether there are over forty such texts, indicating that the book of Proverbs joined a long and venerable tradition. Among the most notable Egyptian texts are the following: the Instruction of Ptah-Hotep (ca. 2450 BCE); the Instruction of Meri-ka-Re (ca. 2100); the Instruction of Amenemhet I (ca. 1950); the Instruction of Any (early New Kingdom: 1550–1400); and the Sayings of Amenemope (ca. 1200). Note that all of these precede the time of David and Solomon. It is thus not unreasonable to claim that Solomon's court officials participated in a robust wisdom environment.

Egyptian instructional materials often addressed the sons of court officials; some of the texts tended to be autobiographical, providing a context for the practical wisdom that the fathers were about to hand along. Ptah-Hotep's introduction to his instructions provides a poignant example of anguish in the face of aging:

> O king, my lord! Age is here, old age arrived,
> Feebleness came, weakness grows,
> [Childlike] one sleeps all day.
> Eyes are dim, ears deaf,
> Strength is waning through weariness,
> The mouth, silenced, speaks not,
> The heart, void, recalls not the past,
> The bones ache throughout.
> Good has become evil, all taste is gone,
> What age does to people is evil in everything.
> The nose, clogged, breathes not,
> Painful are standing and sitting.[1]

Generally, these texts did not consist of erudite or metaphysical speculations. They focused on garden-variety reminders of living with integrity, exercising piety and generosity, and treating family, friends, and enemies appropriately. The excellent use of words has a high profile, as do sobriety and discipline. These are not earthshaking reminders, but they are necessary, especially from experienced and perhaps chastened fathers to exuberant sons. This would be especially true for the court context, in which religion and politics had to be addressed with the highest level of socially appropriate behavior. We see an interface between court and family concerns in these proverbs. The following is just a small sampling:

If you are a man who leads,
Listen calmly to the speech of the one who pleads;
Don't stop him from purging his body
Of that which he planned to tell.
A man in distress wants to pour out his heart
More than that his case be won. (Instruction of Ptah-Hotep)[2]

The tongue is [a king's] sword;
Speaking is stronger than all fighting,
The skillful is not overcome . . .
Those who know that he knows will not attack him,
No [crime] occurs when he is near;
Justice comes to him distilled,
Shaped in the sayings of the ancestors. (Instruction for King
    Meri-ka-Re)[3]

Beware of a woman who is a stranger,
One not known in her town;
Don't stare at her when she goes by,
Do not know her carnally.
A deep water whose course is unknown,
Such is a woman away from her husband.
"I am pretty," she tells you daily,
When she has no witnesses;
She is ready to ensnare you,
A great deadly crime when it is heard. (Instruction of Any)[4]

If you find a large debt against a poor man,
Make it into three parts;
Forgive two, let one stand,
You will find it a path of life. (Sayings of Amenemope)[5]

As we will see, these have conceptual parallels with biblical proverbs.

One additional cultural connection merits our attention. In the Egyptian worldview, there was a basic sense of divine order and balance. Called *ma'at,* it was the essence of existence and a necessary counter to chaos. Pharaoh, a human representative of the gods, was responsible for maintaining *ma'at* and ordering what we might call a just society. *Ma'at* was equally important in the lives of individuals; order went hand in hand with truthfulness. In some ways, *ma'at* sounds a good deal like biblical wisdom (*ḥokhmah*), a term to which we will return.

This section would not be complete without noting that since the 1920s scholars have recognized that Prov 22:17–24:22 shares parallel themes and possibly even structural similarities with the Sayings of Amenemope (abbreviated SA). There is, however, disagreement as to just what this implies. Central to the discussion is the meaning of a word in Prov 22:20 (*shilshom*), translated by some as "thirty sayings," by others as "excellent things," and by yet others as "previously." If indeed it ought to read "thirty sayings," then the parallel with SA appears quite strong because that text also refers to "thirty sayings." Some would go so far as to say that this section of Proverbs was actually a translation of that Egyptian work. On the other end of the interpretive spectrum, Kenneth Kitchen claims that the thematic parallels are so general that we should not presume a specific relationship between the two documents. For example, the concept of "wealth taking flight like birds" (Prov 23:4–5 and SA 10:4–5) is evident already in a Sumerian text that pre-dates SA by eight hundred years. Many of the connections are shared with other texts because they express what is simply good common and ethical sense. The sequence of the Egyptian sayings and the sayings in Proverbs is not remotely the same. From another angle, *shilshom* could simply be an abbreviated form of a known Hebrew idiom, *'etmol shilshom* ("previously"), and thus we need not posit a direct verbal link with SA (Kitchen, "Ancient Near Eastern Background," 562–64).

The words of Ahiqar represent a period in wisdom instruction that is several centuries after our tenth-century date for Solomon's court, notably that of the Assyrian courts of Sennacherib and Esarhaddon (seventh century BCE). The same concerns of life are evident. In fact, as our next example demonstrates, perhaps Ahiqar shared the strong sentiments about discipline that we find in Prov 23:13–14. Ahiqar reads: "Withhold not thy son from the rod, else thou wilt not be able to save [him from *wickedness*]. If I smite thee, my son, thou wilt not die, but if I leave thee to thine own heart [thou wilt not live]."[6] We discover additional parallel images in Ahiqar and Proverbs. For example, Ahiqar states, "I have lifted sand, and I have carried salt; but there is naught which is heavier than [grief],"[7] and Prov 27:3 declares, "Stone is heavy and sand a burden, but provocation by a fool is heavier than both" (NIV).

If we had time for further sampling of ancient Near Eastern wisdom texts, however, we would see with increasing clarity a unique feature of Proverbs. The covenant name of Israel's God is a reassuring presence. Even as we encounter life in the fields, the home, the marketplace, and the court, we cannot forget that the Lord watches, hears, tests, weighs, and hates. All of our activities are under God's all-seeing eye, and sometimes they are displeasing to him. At the same time, God establishes plans, takes up the cause of the needy, and loves those who pursue righteousness. It does not hurt to repeat again the lesson that Scripture repeats: the fear of the Lord is the beginning of wisdom. This fear is not mindless terror; it is accompanied by *knowledge* of the Holy One (Prov 9:10). This is spirituality at its best—recognizing that the whole of God's creation is infused with his wisdom. Proper fear of the Lord requires our humble submission to his sovereign majesty and covenant love.

Structure of the Book

While our initial impression might be that there is precious little evidence of structure in the book of Proverbs, we are going to map out as much as we can. The task might not be as impossible as it first seems.

Introduction to the Book (1:1–7)

Given the prominence of instructional literature in the ancient Near Eastern courts, the introduction reads like a set of course objectives in the royal tutoring institution. Verses 2 through 6 declare:

> for knowing wisdom (*ḥokhmah*) and discipline (or
> instruction—*musar*);
> to understand words of understanding (more on this later);
> to take instruction (*musar* again) for enlightening;
> righteousness, justice, and uprightness;
> to give to the simple prudence;
> to the young man knowledge and discretion.
> Let the wise hear and add wisdom (*lekaḥ*);
> and let the one who (already) understands acquire guidance (or
> direction) to understand a parable (*mashal*) and interpretation;
> words of the wise and their riddles.

I need to pause at this point and acknowledge how excruciatingly difficult it has been to choose one best English word to represent each Hebrew counterpart in this list. In the next chapter, we will explore this whole array of interrelated words that together give us some sense of the richness of the pursuit. In the meantime, one final word from the text, in verse 7—"the fear of the LORD is the beginning of knowledge; wisdom and discipline fools despise." This declaration sets up the counterpoint that shapes the rest of the book.

The Father Speaks (1:8–9:18)

The father's admonitions to heed wisdom are severe warnings, visiting and revisiting the contrast between wisdom and folly. This is no time for gentle appeals and veiled allusions to generic problems. The father knows that radical evil is on the prowl to capture and destroy young, naive sons (and daughters), and he describes it over and over. The figure of the adulteress, a strange woman who seduces, is especially prominent and troubling as this section develops. There is little doubt that the allure of idolatry lurks behind this figure.

One feature of Proverbs that distinguishes it from its cultural counterparts is the role that mothers also play in this instruction and warning process. We see the home as well as the royal school here, as the child is admonished to obey his mother as well as his father (1:8; 4:3; 6:20; see also 31:1, 26).

Individual Sayings (10:1–22:16)

"Individual sayings" is often the default label for the content of chapters 10–22, and our fledgling attempts to divide and conquer this book seem to fade at this point. Here we find twelve chapters of apparently unconnected adages. So much for structure! Nevertheless, let us be cautious about treating these as an undefinable mass and then forging beyond them in search of an organizing rubric. There are several striking features to be noted.

For one thing, chapters 10–15 are made up almost entirely of antithetically parallel statements. Following the overarching themes of chapters 1–9, we now confront a steady parade of contrasts. What is more, these contrasts start with a distinct emphasis on righteousness, the righteous, and the upright *in contrast to* the wicked (chs. 10–12). We must not miss the implications. The father's admonitions to make critical life-shaping choices are not left in the abstract. The antitheses present stark, mundane, day-by-day choices. Will the words uttered be life-giving or death-dealing? Can a person know that s/he will be delivered, or will hope perish? Basic choices between right and wrong have consequences in every facet of life, and chapters 13–15 make that clear. Three direct references to the "fear of the Lord" in chapter 14 (vv. 2, 26, 27) serve as pointers to the center of the book, chapters 15 and 16, where the figure of the Lord dominates the discourse.

Just when we were getting used to the oppositions, the drumbeat of antitheses ceases after chapter 15. In conjunction with the focus of chapters 15–16 on the Lord, chapter 16 brings the king into the picture. Human rulers, mostly not in evidence up to this point, will be making more frequent appearances from here on. And we note that the Lord is the King who is trustworthy (16:20). Moving on, there are few structural features that guide our engagement with chapters 17–21. We are simply left to revel in the richness of each poke and jab.

"Words of the Wise" (22:17–24:34)

As noted above, we see in this section some affinity with the thirteenth-century BCE Egyptian text the Sayings of Amenemope. Even if this part of Proverbs is not drawn directly from SA, it is certainly distinct from what has preceded it. Prior to this point, the proverbs are primarily one-two punches. Here we are treated to the development of each thought, sometimes with powerfully emotional overtones. For example:

Don't move an ancient boundary,
and don't enter the fields of orphans.
Because their Redeemer is strong,
he will take up their cause (lit., strive their strife) with you. (23:10–11)

The extended description of the perils and consequences of excessive drinking merits our attention. This hits home no matter what culture we live in. Wine may go down smoothly, but it bites like a serpent, stings like an adder, and leaves the drunkard seeing strange things, speaking improprieties, feeling numb, and demanding another drink when he wakes up (23:29–35).

And one more just to challenge us:

If you turn weak in the day of trouble (*tsarah*), your strength is *tsar*.
Rescue those being taken to death and tottering toward
 extermination.
If you hold back because you say: "Look, we did not know this,"
does not the One who established hearts understand?

> And the One who watches over your life,
> he knows, and will return to a person according to his deeds.
>   (24:10–12)

Needless to say, this is a sobering word to those of us who prefer to shrink to the sidelines when crises are flaring.

Proverbs Edited in Hezekiah's Time (25:1–29:27)

Chapters 25–29 capture our attention again, just in case we have been dozing a bit. Many of these proverbs fall into the category of "emblematic" parallelisms. The reading audience is challenged to think analogically; a verbal picture, an "emblem," is what helps us connect the dots. Whereas the two-liners in chapters 10–15 taught discernment—this, but not that— now we are to see "this points to that and the connection teaches us something further." These proverbs practically plead for us to sketch them!

> A club and sword and sharp arrow—
> a man who gives false testimony against his neighbor. (25:18)

> As a dog returns to its vomit,
> so a fool repeats his folly. (26:11)

> A roaring lion and a charging bear
> is a wicked man ruling over a helpless people. (28:15)

In addition, we encounter moral declarations:

> The one who turns his ear from hearing the law,
> even his prayer is detestable. (28:9)

> Do you see a man who speaks in haste?
> There is more hope for a fool than for him. (29:20)

Furthermore, there are occasional "clusters" of proverbs. Those that have to do with the sluggard are classic examples (26:13–16). So are the "fool" collections (26:4–12). We will say more about these in future chapters.

The Wisdom of Agur and Lemuel (30:1–31:9)

Though the words of these kings constitute a relatively small portion of Proverbs, they carry some heft. Perhaps they both came into Solomon's court with their own proverbial observations, and Solomon authorized them. Since this is the last we shall see of them, we will spend just a bit of time here.

Agur's opening words in chapter 30 are both a delight and an enigma. Did he commence by naming an unknown audience (Ithiel and Ucal as proper names), or should we interpret these words as an acknowledgement of his own weariness? The latter requires a small alteration in the text but actually fits better with what comes next. It seems that Agur despaired of addressing the stuff of weighty theological speculation, claiming ignorance and lack of wisdom. I prefer to translate verses 2–3 somewhat differently than most: "Though I am more ignorant than anyone and do not have the understanding granted to humans, and have not learned wisdom, *yet* knowledge of the Holy One I do know." Even so, Agur bowed before the mystery of power in the heavenly realms. His questions in 30:4 sound a bit like Job 38.

That posture is the perfect segue to the next declaration, warning, and prayer: "Every word of God is purified. He is a shield to those who find refuge in him. Do not add to his words, lest he rebuke you, and you become a liar" (vv. 5–6). "Two things I ask of you" comes next, and the following verses plead that Agur be spared from falling into the web of deceit, as well as from poverty that would turn him into a thief and abundance that would harden his sensitivity to God's provision (vv. 7–9). The rest of his words are equally engaging; Agur delighted in learning lessons from nature and couching many of them in numbered sequences: "... three things ... no, four ..." Each is masterful. Just one example will suffice: "There are things that are never satisfied — *sheol*, the barren womb, land that never has enough water, and fire" (30:15b–16).

From Agur we transition to the words of Lemuel, notably attributed to his mother (31:1). They are wise advice for a king, warnings against craving women and drink and ignoring the obligation to care for the oppressed (31:2–9).

Closure: The Woman of Strength (31:10–31)

Lemuel's words may also include the final encomium to this remarkable woman of strength, or it could be a separate entity. Whichever is the case, this acrostic poem also functions as a comprehensive closure to the entire book. Several observations are in order at this point. First, the personification of wisdom in the first nine chapters is now embodied in this picture. To be sure, she is an ideal, but nevertheless she is an ideal with substance! We observe her daily activities, including careful investment and energetic engagement with traders and merchants. She nurtures family relationships, extends her strong hand to the needy, and offers faithful instruction. Needless to say, she is not confined to the field or the hearth. Second, the closing description of her is that she "fears the LORD" (31:30) and thus merits praise in the public arena of the city gate. This echoes the "fear of the LORD" admonition in 1:7, and it also reminds us of the public persona of Lady Wisdom as she makes her case in streets and the public square (1:20–21).

Tiptoeing around Interpretive Pitfalls

We have established the fact that proverbs, which are evident throughout the ancient Near East, were intended to be instructional. On the face of it, this should make the prospect of interpretation easy. Nevertheless, an array of questions confronts us. How do we apply bumper-sticker-sized truths? How can poetry that is replete with figures of speech be authoritative? What about proverbs that are caricatures, happily poking fun at other people? Are they too funny to be taken seriously? What about those proverbs that seem to be so obvious we wonder why they are even mentioned? Here is an example: "Whoever speaks the truth gives honest evidence, but a false witness utters deceit" (12:17 ESV). It does not take a rocket scientist to get the point; was it necessary to write this one down? On the other hand, some proverbs leave us scratching our heads. For example, "The sluggard is wiser in his own eyes than seven men who answer discreetly" (26:16 NIV). Wrap your mind around that at the first go-round.

Bumper-Sticker-Sized Truths

Let's start with the relative brevity of each proverb. Their brevity indicates that there is clearly more to be said, and, as a matter of fact, it is actually a subtle invitation to further thought, to response, to "yes, but . . ." And this is good. It also means that we expect to gain additional perspectives as we keep reading. In many ways, proverbs are a perfect postmodern teaching mechanism because they intrinsically recognize the complexity and perspectival nature of truth. Each individual proverb is a generalization born from experience in a particular context. It must be read in balance with the rest of the proverbs in the collection, each of which also rises from specific circumstances of place and time. When we read or hear proverbs from any cultural context, we encounter distillations of accumulated traditional wisdom founded on lived experiences.

In themselves, proverbs are not absolute declarations, nor are they intended as guarantees. "Train a child in the way he should go, and when he is old he will not turn from it" (22:6 NIV) is a classic "abused promise," and it has prompted anguished soul-searching on the part of earnest parents who have watched helplessly as their errant children have made choices that are clearly departures from "the way he should go." Perhaps an observation can serve as a corrective here. It might be best to understand this in terms of guiding a young person, exercising deep sensitivity to his or her gifts and abilities (the "way" that is best for that child), and not forcing the child onto a path prescribed by someone else. The latter happens all too often, and that prescribed path does end up being rejected.

The Locus of Authority

The next obvious question is this: How can these sometimes impertinent observations about human nature bear authority in the lives of believers? There is more to say about this, and we will get to it momentarily, but one caution might be helpful from the outset. We might pose the same query regarding snippets of other biblical genres as well. For example, to what extent is a genealogy authoritative for my life? Or what about descriptions of boundaries and city lists (Josh 15)? To be sure, we can suggest that good theological implications are embedded in each of these examples, but it takes a bit of work to get to that point. Thus, perhaps we ought not hold Proverbs to a higher standard of directly applicable authority than we do other parts of God's word. Our interpretive task always involves figuring out how to interface each of these genres with our own circumstances so that the word is active, living, and transformative *for us*.

Let's start with figures of speech. How do they work as inspired Scripture? For one thing, metaphors, personifications, unexpected turns of the language, and imagery captivate us; they grab our attention when it is sometimes dulled. In making the message more memorable, they serve actively to point us toward significant truths that we could easily miss.

Here is a related direction we might explore. The very fact that so many proverbs do poke fun at human foibles leads us to ponder the importance of character in this book. Who we are (our character) has everything to do with how we act. That connection is central to Proverbs. Some proverbs focus on the consequences of our combined character and actions; others are evaluative. These observations are most powerful when they surprise us just a bit.

The book emphasizes the basic virtues of truth, humility, justice, and prudence, often by juxtaposing them with their negative counterparts. In many of these cases, the proverbs are clear warnings and prohibitions. It is difficult to avoid the matter of authority in those cases. The proverbs intentionally warn against all manner of evil and folly. Those sound very much like concerns of the covenant, even though the tone is quite different from the prophetic literature. Here is the bottom line—again. The fear of the Lord in the context of life well lived is the substance of these pursuits. We cannot get more orthodox.

Obvious and Obscure

Some of the problems that arise in this context have to do with the challenges of translating Hebrew poetry into English that sounds at least somewhat felicitous. That is not an easy task, as witnessed by my attempt above to render 24:10–12. Hebrew poetry is spare, the word order is often not what we expect, and occasionally the words chosen are unusual companions of more familiar synonyms used in prose. Once we slow down and work through a literal rendition, we might not think a proverb is so "obvious." If it is, perhaps we are to see that "obvious" does not automatically lead to our truly apprehending the essence of the declaration. Maybe we do need to be hit upside the head with elementary truth—over and over again.

At this point, let us revisit the "obvious" declaration about truth and falsehood found in 12:17. A literal rendition of the verse runs like this: "He breathes out faithfulness; he tells righteousness; but a witness of false things—deceit." That has some heft to it. The first part is getting at fundamental character traits that actively issue forth in corresponding faithfulness and righteousness. On the other hand, the one who speaks of false things will be the source of deceit. Note one small detail. In contrast to the essence of breathing and telling the truth, there is no verb in the second half. Perhaps *that* character is presented as more evasive. We might even say "slippery." The same focus on the danger of deceit reappears in 14:5: "A truthful witness does not deceive, but a false witness pours out lies" (NIV). Again, a literal translation, while more awkward, is telling: "A witness of truthful things will not lie; but one who breathes out lies is a false witness." In fact, the number of proverbs about the menace of false witnesses is striking. There is, after all, something here for us to absorb.

What about those obscure tidbits? Some of the obscurity might be eliminated once we do our cultural homework. For example, many proverbs primarily grow in simple agrarian and home-based environments. Ponder 14:4: "When there are no cattle, the manger is clean, but abundant produce comes from the strength of an ox." What is the point of this one?

How does it hang together? We may not get the whole message, but the first step is to reconstruct the scene and enjoy the language. Some folks might like a clean feeding trough in the barn. It sure beats having to shovel out waste every day. On the other hand, "clean" could imply "empty." Even more, the word translated "clean" can also mean "grain," which adds yet another layer. If we transport ourselves to an agricultural society, not having the animals in the barn is like not having your tractor ready. Woe betide us when we try to head out to the fields to harvest by hand! That ox, fueled by lots of food in the feeding trough, is pretty messy, but that's okay. It's more than worth it. And, from a slightly different angle, perhaps there *is* grain, but if there are not cattle consuming it, then it rots, and what is the use?

Is there an "authoritative" spiritual takeaway here? Think a moment on your own before you read one simple suggestion. Now try this. The richest and most productive parts of life involve messiness. We need to expect that.

I am not neglecting the other cryptic proverb noted above, 26:16. Here again is the NIV translation: "The sluggard is wiser in his own eyes than seven men who answer discreetly." The first part is a setup that we might expect. In other words, it does not surprise us that sluggards would have unrealistic notions about themselves. But what does the point of comparison imply? Let me offer a literal translation of the second part. "The sluggard is wiser in his own eyes than *seven who respond tastefully* (i.e., with good judgment)." The word "seven" usually carries the symbolism of perfection. Sluggards have so reconstructed reality that they have set themselves at the top of the heap. Unfortunately for this slothful fool, this exists only in his or her completely compromised vision.

Gleaning in the Fields: Practical Theology

Before we launch into our next chapters, let us chart a course through lessons that will repeatedly surface. Here they are, without much fanfare. At the end of the day, we are to embrace wisdom and eschew folly. Practical ways of doing this include our intentional choices to *practice* righteousness at each decision point; to speak in ways that are edifying, truthful, and encouraging; to do justice and uphold truth; to cherish family and friends; to accept the tasks of discipline and self-discipline; and to conduct ourselves as good stewards, using our material and emotional well-being to bring comfort and hope to the poor and poor in spirit. These activities will keep us occupied for the rest of our lives—and we will be reminded of them as we read one proverb each day!

CHAPTER 6

Wisdom and Folly and Their "Children" (Proverbs 1–9)

Introduction

It is worth pausing for a bit of review. As we have tackled the challenge of defining wisdom, we have been both incessantly drawn forward into that challenge and also stopped in our tracks at the edges of the unfathomable. We have explored poetry as a perfect vehicle for our journey into the simultaneous order and surprise of living. We have visited the palaces and courts of sages from the ancient Near East. Lastly, our investigation has begun to zero in on those worthy traditional instructions handed from generation to generation—proverbs.

Proverbs 1–9 serves as the theological "handle" for the entire book. These chapters contrast wisdom and folly, both richly personified as women who actively seek devotees. Each segment of instruction in these introductory chapters is followed by illustration; wisdom and folly are not left as passive and abstract qualities. If we simply trap them on paper, we effectively dismiss any real engagement with either. In the garb, however, of beckoning women, they tread into our lives—over and over again. They are key actors on our stage, bringing along a cast of supporting actors and costume changes designed to bolster their appeals. We meet them in these initial scenes and get acquainted. By the end of the book, both wisdom and folly have developed quite extraordinary personalities.

Wisdom climbs to the podium at the head of a busy street and challenges, mocks, and cajoles—anything to get the attention of the numbed passersby (1:20–33). Her message starts with stark judgment but promises hope. She is compelled to repeat this public address because it is so utterly crucial (8:1–21); everyone from fools to kings and rulers needs her. Both wisdom and folly extend invitations to sumptuous feasts (ch. 9). Wisdom has one decided advantage; she is an intimate friend and associate of God (8:22–31). Having been present at creation, she offers a perspective on all of life that is absent from folly's persona. The appeals of wisdom bookend these first discourse chapters.

> The Hebrew word for wisdom is plural in this introductory salvo (1:20). The same form occurs in Prov 9:1, as wisdom issues her invitation. Her voice gains authority with this plural form, and this authority is necessary given her seductive opponent. While the singular form, also translated "wisdom," occurs well over one hundred times in the Hebrew Bible, the plural is rare: we see it again only in Prov 24:7 and Ps 49:4.

With this chapter and those that follow, we draw extensive quotations of the biblical text into *our* text. There is no other way to engage the proverbs; we need to see them before us as we ponder their implications. For the most part, I will offer my own translations—unless I find the proverb too gnarly and need some help!

Responses to Two Vignettes

The best way to get to know the two women, wisdom and folly, is to watch and listen to them in action. Therefore, think of the following as "clips" or "trailers."

Lady Wisdom on Her Podium

Wisdom's public platform is really an outdoor pulpit. She preaches, and it is a very public scene.

> Wisdom cries aloud outside;
> in the streets she raises her voice.
> Above all the noise she calls;
> at the opening of the city gates she speaks. (1:20–21)

As you read this excerpt, redescribe for yourself in contemporary terms what is happening. Does your city or town have a public park where lots of folks congregate? How would you respond if someone got up on a makeshift podium with a megaphone and began saying the following words? We need to read this slowly—perhaps out loud.

> How long, O immature fools, will you love being simple?
> And mockers take pleasure in their mockery,
> and fools hate knowledge?

If you turn back at my rebuke, behold I will pour out for you my
   spirit;
I will make my words known to you.
Because I called, but you rejected me—
I extended my hand, but there was no one listening—
(because) you have ignored all my advice,
and my rebuke you have not desired;
I will laugh at *your* calamity.
I will mock when your dread comes;
when, as a crashing ruin, your dread comes,
and your calamity arrives like a whirlwind;
when misery and distress come against you.
Then they will summon me but I will not answer;
they will seek me but they will not find me.
Because they hated knowledge and did not choose to fear the LORD,
and did not desire my counsel, and rejected all my rebukes,
they will eat from the fruit of their way,
and they will be filled with their own counsel.
For the turning away of those who are immature kills them,
and the false sense of security of fools destroys them.
But the one who listens to me will dwell in safety,
and will be at rest from the dread of evil. (1:22–33)

In this extensive quotation of Prov 1:22–33, note the switch in person from
"you" to "they" immediately after the dire warning that "misery and distress will come against you." At this point, wisdom distances herself even
beyond mocking laughter at their ruin. "They" will seek but not find her.
She disappears entirely from their perceptual field, and even the grammar
shows it!

What did you think as you read that? Note this preacher's tone! She
intentionally accuses and threatens. There is nothing particularly "correct" about her approach, but before we dismiss her as an antiquated
crackpot, let us consider two things. First, Lady Wisdom knows disaster
is indeed around the corner for those who deliberately ignore virtue
and plunge headlong into self-gratification. Her declaration of judgment
is based on the reality of approaching horrors that simpletons refuse
to see because their eyes have been blinded by the false advertising of
every component of the fool's world. This is a desperate moment, and
strong words are essential. Second, wisdom's words here, intimidating
as they are, end with an invitation to listen and return to safety and rest.

She continues to beckon her audience toward more noble things—truth, righteousness, honor, and riches far beyond mere gold and silver (8:1–21). We will return to her invitation to the sumptuous feast of wisdom and fear of the Lord (9:1–12) shortly.

Gullible and Foolish

The gullible young fool might make us readers even more nervous than the loud preaching of Lady Wisdom. Along with the "father" who is narrating (7:1–5), we watch the young fool wander into the sticky net of a calculating and truly wicked woman. We want to shout "Stop! You fool. You don't know what you are doing! Stop! Stop!" As you read the following, ask yourself how you would respond to this person if he were one of your peers—or your own child. I have abbreviated and paraphrased the biblical description to get the point across to a contemporary audience.

> I saw a naive young man—he obviously lacked good sense—crossing the street near the house of a woman who was known for cheating on her husband. It seemed to him to be a good time to follow his impulse; it was dusk, no one would see as he slipped in. But he did not need to linger and lurk. She boldly came out to meet him; that was her pattern with others as well. She took hold of him, reduced any shreds of his resistance with her overpowering presence, and enticed him into bed. Her assurances that her husband would not find out sealed the deal; they spent the night in sexual ecstasy. Except that he was now utterly trapped and ruined. His life, moving toward sexual addiction of the worst kind, would never be the same. (a summary of 7:6–23)

This is even more insidious today because our young fool does not need to be out in the street. His (or her) gullible heart can just as easily be trapped and slaughtered in front of a screen filled with pornography. How do we intervene? How does this young fool find the courage to resist?

Benefits of Wisdom and Her "Helpers"

We can imagine our personified wisdom viewing that scene with deep sorrow. It was the outcome about which she had warned her audience. Oh, how she longed instead for open hearts to hear her appeal. What she could offer if only, if only, they would listen *and* work to lay hold of wisdom, knowledge, discipline, understanding, and discretion (1:1–6)! Accompanying wisdom are the "helpers" just mentioned. Each contributes to the armor necessary to resist the evil that invariably dons the mask of thrill and excitement. These assistants do not just flutter into place; this is a quest that involves attention and memory of wisdom's instruction, seeking, calling out, hearing, and understanding (2:1–5). Yes, it is a task, but one laced with hope and joy. Love and faithfulness are part of this picture as well (3:3).

Let us take a brief tangent in order to explore the implications of the words that are most often used in conjunction with wisdom (*hokhmah*). It is not an accident that these show up in the book of Proverbs' "course objectives" (1:2–6); they are important parts of our character structure from the get-go. In several cases, this will necessitate just a bit of Hebrew, so bear with me!

In Proverbs, a common parallel to "wisdom" is "knowledge" (*da'at* in Hebrew). It is not a specialized brand acquired only through graduate study. Instead, this very basic term applies to all of God's truth. In other words, everywhere that we cast our inquisitive eye—and mind—we find something new to explore, to analyze, to synthesize. There is no end to knowledge, and that is a good thing. It means we never need to sink into boredom. In fact, doing so is a bad sign because it implies our minds have turned numb to the richness of God's creation and our ability to experience it. There are always new angles for inquiring minds to investigate.

"Understanding" is one way of translating the Hebrew word *binah* and its relative *tevunah*. Another possibility is "discernment." As we sort through the implications of this, it will help to know that another related Hebrew word is a preposition meaning "between." Get it? When we develop discernment or understanding, we are cultivating the ability to choose *between* one good option and another that might be less appropriate or downright evil.

The Hebrew word translated "discipline" (*musar*) has a very wide range of meanings depending on the context. Sometimes it denotes instruction and reproof. These are the milder forms of discipline that come in verbal doses. Training and correction sound a bit more emphatic. Chastisement that involves some physical aspect also comes under this "discipline" umbrella. All take time and most involve pain of some sort!

This is by no means intended to be an exhaustive list, but two more concepts do require our brief attention. First, "discretion" (*mezimah*) implies consideration and purposeful assessment. In other words, we take some time and turn an issue around in our mind, looking at it from a variety of perspectives. How, for example, might this course of action play out once several additional parties weigh in? Or what effect will these words, quickly dropped into that social media outlet, have as they go viral? The one who lacks discretion has neglected the obligation to think about possible unintended consequences.

Finally, we are also called to be "shrewd," to exercise "prudence," and to be "clever." There is a sense in which this might be a double-edged sword. The Hebrew adjective that is translated by all these words is 'arum, and there are related noun and verb forms as well. In Proverbs, this word has a generally positive connotation and is used in contrast to people who are undeniably foolish (12:23 and a handful of additional references). At the same time, the calculating and destructive side of the concept conveyed by this word comes out in Gen 3:1; the serpent was described as more 'arum than all the other creatures that the Lord God had made.

With these expanded definitions in mind, we have a keener appreciation for the strong admonitions to pay attention! More than anything else, our young and immature fool (who, in case we have not wrapped our minds around this yet, represents each of us) needs the protection and guidance that wisdom so freely offers.

> Discretion will guard you;
> understanding will watch over you
> to rescue you from the evil way,
> from a person who speaks things that are upside-down (perverse).
>   (2:11–12)

The text goes on to describe these evil ones. They walk in darkness and enjoy every aspect of evil, from its completely twisted nature to the chaos that it causes. Nevertheless, wisdom will "deliver you from the strange woman, from the foreign woman with her slippery words" (2:16). This is the promise of rescue from the horrible end of the wayward and naive fool described in chapter 7.

We also discover assuring descriptions of spiritual and moral illumination that wisdom, discretion, and discipline provide. All of these are a tremendous benefit in a world where sin and lies abound. We remind ourselves that wisdom enters with the indwelling Christ, the Holy Spirit, and God's word.

> My child . . . keep sound thinking and discretion,
> and they will be life for your soul and a graceful garland for
>   your neck.
> Then you will walk securely on your way, and your foot will not
>   stumble.

> When you lie down, you will not be in terror.
> When you lie down, your sleep will be sweet.
> Do not be afraid of sudden terror
> or of the crashing ruin of evil when it comes;
> for the LORD will be your confidence
> and will keep your foot from being caught. (3:21–26)

> Keep, my child, the commandment of your father,
> and do not forsake the instruction of your mother.
> Bind them on your heart always;
> wind them around your neck.
> When you walk, she[1] will lead you;
> when you lie down, she will keep you;
> and when you get up, she will converse with you.
> For the commandment is a lamp, and instruction is a light,
> and in rebuke and discipline is the way of life. (6:20–23)

As we can see from this brief sketch, we have the privilege of active participation in this task. We "keep"—and wisdom "keeps." Further, in a passage we have already visited, we are called to *embrace* her, a powerful image in the personification:

> Acquire wisdom; acquire understanding . . .
> Do not forsake her, and she will protect you.
> Love her, and she will guard you.
> Wisdom is at the forefront;
> get wisdom, and among all of your acquisitions, acquire
>   understanding.
> Esteem her, and she will exalt you.
> She will honor you when you embrace her.
> She will set on your head a garland of grace,
> and a splendid crown she will give to you. (4:5–9)

This is not a sterile and wooden obedience as we trudge along a narrow path of restrictions and laws. Wisdom attracts us, we embrace her, and the lasting nature of that embrace weathers the assaults of the wicked woman's temptations. Not only that; wisdom adorns us with honor instead of shame, with crowns instead of dunce caps.

In case we are not convinced this is a good path to take, here are just a few more accolades for wisdom. It was linked with life in the land, an important assurance to those who understood that covenant promise (2:20–21). It has everything to do with favor with God and our fellow human beings (3:3–4); it is intertwined with health and peaceful prosperity (3:7–10, 16). Above all, Proverbs deems it precious beyond words, a source of life and blessing (3:13–18). The "tree of life" reverberates with echoes of Genesis 3; that tree is not permanently out of reach after all. Those who seek God's wisdom diligently will find her (8:17).

Perils of Folly

Folly is another word from an earlier era. Who, after all, thinks in terms of anything being folly—or sin, for that matter? We are immersed in a culture that preens and excuses itself at every turn. We are quick to assert our rights instead of asking God to search us in order to see if there be any grievous way in us (Ps 139:23–24). Because this is so, it might help to describe folly and the wide range of fools whom we will encounter should we veer onto this dangerous path. Once we have reviewed the gallery of fools, we will watch Woman Folly take center stage multiple times; she just does not stop. A related matter: just as there are a number of Hebrew words for fool, there are also multiple words that are translated "sin," "iniquity," and "transgression." Apparently, these were important concepts! I would maintain they still are.

"Foolishness" is the easiest synonym with which to replace folly, but both of them could be tainted by our contemporary lighthearted dismissal of activities that are silly, perhaps even idiotic and irrational, but not necessarily damaging. Folly in the biblical sense, however, carries a much more serious burden. A biblical fool deliberately rejects God's instructions, and the result is deadly. We have already heard Lady Wisdom's assessment of this track—it leads to disaster (1:24–27) and inner wreckage (1:32). Those who engage in folly taste and sample evil of all descriptions and find themselves trapped in the end by an insatiable appetite for wrong (1:11–19).

> For they do not sleep if they have not done some evil,
> and their sleep is robbed unless they have caused someone to
>   stumble,
> for they eat the bread of wickedness
> and drink the wine of violence. (4:16–17)

While bloodshed and adultery are very high profile—and we will return to them—it is also instructive to take a good, hard look at what the Lord hates (6:16–19). This will give us further benchmarks for folly:

Six things the Lord hates; seven are an abomination to him:
haughty eyes, a tongue that lies,
hands that shed innocent blood,
a heart that sows evil plans,
feet that hasten to run to evil,
a false witness who pours out lies,
and one who creates strife among brothers.

This six/seven pattern may have a skeleton chiastic structure to it. What does that mean? Directly in the center is the *heart* that devises evil schemes. On each side of this are limbs (hands and feet) that carry out those evil plans, wreaking havoc against innocent victims. These are all encompassed in a nest of deception. In fact, "a false witness who pours out lies" describes a habitual liar—whose every breath is a pack of lies. The haughty eyes at the outset are marginally matched at the end by the intentional sowing of discord among brothers. We might surmise that a major factor in this enterprise could be one form of injured pride or another.

This list follows a description of a thoroughly abominable person in whose heart is perversity and who sows evil all the time wherever he goes (6:12–14). It should not escape us that two of the seven detestable characteristics have to do with lying. Central to folly and sin is deceit; it is also one of the deadliest sins for all the irreparable damage it does.

What kind of fools *do* we encounter on the way? It turns out that not all fools are equal; some are more vacuous than others, and some are more fearfully lethal. We will do well to acquaint ourselves with the whole rogues' gallery.

The immature and naive young man who was drawn into the adulteress' bed (ch. 7) was not beyond all hope. The Hebrew word for this man, *peti*, implies a gullible, inexperienced, and relatively "harmless" type. This word is related to the Hebrew verb that means to "deceive" or "seduce." Our *peti* is mentally naive; "a simple person believes anything" (14:15a). That person needs to get up the backbone to resist the loud messages from the surrounding cultural megaphones. The strong temptation to continue in foolish ways leads to much more serious conditions. The simple person can end up being morally irresponsible; "the waywardness of the simple will kill them" (1:32a).

The second and third words in Hebrew, *kesil* and *'evil*, are pretty much interchangeable. Both imply that the people they describe are stubborn and obstinate. Such people are dull, not in terms of intellectual apparatus but because they have hardened their hearts. Their consistent choices for evil instead of good have hard-wired them. Their inclination to reject God's ways has developed into a pattern. These types often demonstrate that they are also stupid in practical affairs that require wise and good choices. We can tell they are going to fare badly because discipline will not soften them; even a hundred blows will not make a difference (17:10).

The brutal, utterly godless fool, the *naval*, appears only three times in Proverbs. Implicit in this is a faint silver lining in the dark cloud of fools hovering over this book. There is still hope for the rest of the fools who are repeatedly described and caricatured. That is good, because many of them sound painfully like us. By the way, the Hebrew word for this last fool is the basis for the name Nabal, husband to Abigail (1 Sam 25), who clearly lived up to his name as he ranted, threatened, and failed to meet his obligations to David and his men.

One final word merits some comment. A mocker (*lets*) is not viewed positively. This person scoffs at what is right and good. We might want to pause—again—to think about contemporary culture. What passes for humor in the public square, stand-up comedy, late-night shows, and political lampooning? How often is our humor at the expense of people of integrity? Just a thought.

We have saved the worst for the last. The threatening and at the same time alluring figure of the wayward woman, the adulteress, the seductress, is on center stage in these first nine chapters. Segments of chapters 2, 5, 6, and 7 are given over to vivid descriptions. In succession these pictures are enlarged with ever more details of the snares and the horrific results. The message is writ large—"stay away!" She captivates and captures, and the end result is shame and death.

> For her house leads to death,
> and her footpaths to the *rephaim* (spirits of the dead).
> All who go to her do not return,
> and they do not come to the ways to life. (2:18–19)

> And her end is as bitter as gall;
> sharp as a sword is her mouth.
> Her feet go down to death;
> her steps lay hold of *sheol*. (5:4–5)

> Keep your way far from her;
> don't approach the door of her house,
> lest you give to others your strength,
> and your years to the cruel . . .

At your end, you will groan
as your flesh and remnants are finished,
and you will say, "How I hated discipline!
And my heart despised rebuke.
I did not listen to the voice of my instructors,
and did not incline my ear to those who would teach me.
I am almost completely ruined in the midst of the assembly and
  congregation." (5:8–14)

Not only does the wayward fool face public shame; there is also the prospect of the adulteress' jealous husband, whose rage is white-hot and lethal (see 6:24–35). Each description is extended from the previous one. The stakes are higher; self-gratification is the intent, but it leads to a terrible, *real* end—the utter darkness represented by *sheol*, the grave. This is indeed a dark path: "The way of the wicked is like deep darkness; they do not even know into what they have stumbled" (4:19). The figures of adulteress and idolater are comingled with folly. In sum, lurching mindlessly into the arms of another man's unfaithful wife is deadly. "The one who commits adultery with a woman lacks will; he destroys himself when he does this" (6:32).

While Lady Wisdom is intimately related to the fear of the Lord, Woman Folly, the adulteress, sends her prey running after other gods, the idols of immediate self-gratification. Her victims will find themselves trapped by and in their own sins. The inescapable matter of moral responsibility hovers over each one of us.

The Message Matters: Two Invitations (Proverbs 9)

This stark choice between wisdom and folly, between God and idols, reaches its highest tension point with two invitations to dine. In ancient cultures, eating together presumed relationship—perhaps even covenant relationship. It would be easy to say that the contrast between the two women could not be more obvious. Just note, however, that their invitations sound unnervingly alike at the outset. "Whoever is simple, let him turn in here!" they both beckon. The unscrupulous Woman Folly parrots the opening words of her better counterpart. Unsuspecting simpletons would be left scratching their heads and wondering which way to go— whose dinner to attend—if they did not pay attention to the demeanor of each woman and the contents of the feast.

Lady Wisdom has actively built her house, a metaphor for character construction. She has worked diligently to make this meal a stunning success, and she sends out messengers with the carefully crafted invitation and challenge. Come on in, enjoy the exquisite food and drink, and then work at reconstructing your lives. To drive the point home, she includes a brief sermonette on the contrast between those who are wise and fear the Lord, and those who do not.

By way of contrast, Woman Folly lounges at her doorway, with a voice and suggestive laugh that cast a spell—though it is not a good one. She too is in an obvious place; it is hard to miss her even if one tries. Whereas Lady Wisdom's bread and wine are the product of labor and sacrifice, Woman Folly unabashedly admits that hers are stolen. In fact, she is proud of it; she knows there is something irresistible about the excitement of treading into forbidden territory and trying to get away with it. She exploits that thrill for all it is worth. Folly's delicacies must be consumed in secret, and that is the most enticing part of it. Note there is no wine or meat—just stolen water and bread. The simpleton who goes to her has no taste whatsoever. She has duped her young fools to follow their impulses instead of thinking of consequences. When they get inside the house, however, they find a company of dead guests. We will leave them there for the time being.

Through Another Lens: Wisdom's Unique Relationship with the Creator

Laced through these first nine chapters is another thread that winds wisdom right into the very fabric of creation. In other words, wisdom has to do with the theology of everything. Every intellectual and personal quality that interfaces with wisdom, such as knowledge, discretion, understanding, and prudence, is a unique capacity borne only by God's image-bearers and evidenced in the context of God's created order. This is heady stuff.

We hear echoes of Genesis 1, first and somewhat faintly in Prov 3:19–20, then thundering in Prov 8:22–31, and reverberating all the way into the New Testament. We will commence with Prov 3:19–20.

> The LORD with wisdom founded the earth;
> he established the heavens with understanding.
> By his knowledge, the deeps were split apart
> and the clouds dripped dew.

We already know that "in the beginning God created the heavens and the earth" (Gen 1:1). Now we see that wisdom is the principle that ordered all creation and continues to manifest God's sustaining power in that creation.

As we zero in on Prov 8:22–31, let me make a practical suggestion. Have several Bible translations open in front of you. That will help immensely as we sort through each of the verses and see that the translators have had to make some tough choices. In a moment, we will turn to some of the translation issues, but even prior to that, note that verse 22 is talking about the "beginning" of the Lord's "way" and his "work" from of old. In other words, the text is going to address the creation *process*. The quandary is how to do this in words that both are truthful and make sense to creatures lodged in time and space.

Let me put this another way as we try to wrap our minds around the problem we confront. Once we attempt to put these "events" into language that makes sense to us, we inevitably reduce processes (the only word I can think of, even though it is not entirely sufficient) that have been unfolding in the infinite context of eternity. How do we talk about the existence of wisdom prior to having the conditions that define existence as we know it? It seems that Prov 8:22–31 articulates the farthest reaches of reality as we know them and places wisdom before and beyond them. Because it gives these limits in our reality, however, we may be tempted to force wisdom *into* those confines as well. That would be a mistake.

One more component of this discussion is essential. This passage addresses relationship and particularly the relationship between wisdom and the Lord. Initially, the role of wisdom sounds passive. The passage starts as follows, amplified here to convey even a minimal sense of the complexity.

> The LORD acquired/possessed (*qanah*) me —
> the first/beginning/top (*re'shit*) of his way,
> before his works from then/from time (*me'az*).
> From eternity I was woven/poured out/appointed (*nasakh*);
> from the head/first, from before the earth. (vv. 22–23)

In this context, the verb *qanah* implies relational existence; wisdom is intrinsic to the Lord's nature. With this same word humans are exhorted to "acquire" wisdom (Prov 4:5); it ought to be intrinsic to *our* natures as well. The verb for "acquire/possess" also occurs in Ps 139:13, regarding the creation of humankind. In God's image, we are to be and do the same as he.

Articulating the *nature* of the initial relationship between the Lord and wisdom pretty much eludes us. Nevertheless, the words pique our interest and compel us further into the mystery. What we can say is that the word for "first" or "beginning" is a clear connection to Gen 1:1—"in the beginning, God . . ." Wisdom is also inherent in the visible creation and intimately related to it, just as it is to the Creator.

> When there were no deeps, I writhed/ twisted/danced
> (passive form—often used in conjunction with giving birth and
>   suffering);
> before the mountains were rooted,
> before the hills, I writhed. (vv. 24–25)

This unavoidably involves "limiting" language, juxtaposing phenomena that humans know experientially as permanent—the great unfathomable deeps and the hills—with the movement and agony of birthing. Wisdom was active prior to the existence of the immovable.

From here the passive tone transitions seamlessly into presence. "When he established the heavens, I *(was) there!*" (v. 27). Wisdom was in attendance as boundaries were inscribed for the waters and the foundations of the earth (vv. 28–29). Finally, presence is transformed into participation in these remarkable processes of creation. By the end of the passage, wisdom is fully engaged with delight.

> I was with him, the master Artisan,
> and I was daily a delight (masculine plural noun),
> playing (feminine singular participle) in all time,
> playing (feminine singular participle) in/on/with the world of the
>   earth (the whole earth);
> and my delight is (masculine plural) with humankind. (vv. 30–31)

See Michael V. Fox, *Proverbs 1–9: A New Translation with Introduction and Commentary*, AB 18a (New York: Doubleday, 2000), 285–86, for a succinct discussion of the possible meanings of *'amon* in verse 30. They include (1) artisan, (2) ward/nursling, and (3) the adverbial meaning "constantly." The last is unlikely; Fox favors the second because the image of wisdom growing up in God's care and giving God delight fits the immediate context. Nevertheless, "artisan" or "craftsman" indicates that wisdom was involved in the creative process with God, a concept that fits with 3:19.

This description of wisdom is a sparkling jewel. Whether the persona is a skilled artisan or a young child, the presence of wisdom brings joy and delight in this vast arena of creation. Wisdom is depicted as delighting and playing, perhaps even boisterously and robustly so. Two additional grammatical details speak volumes, even though they are easily overlooked. There is balance and surprise built into this small chiastic structure. After the declaration of identity, wisdom's joyful activity is represented in two masculine plural nouns (delight) that embrace the two feminine singular participles (play). In other words, even the gender and number of the engaged wisdom are complex and compelling.

A consummate rabbinic scholar, the apostle Paul knew these multiple layers of meaning. They no doubt underlie his affirmation of the incomparability of Jesus:

> He is the image of the invisible God, the firstborn of all creation. For by him all things were created, in heaven and on earth, visible and invisible, whether thrones or dominions or rulers or authorities—all things were created through him and for him. And he is before all things, and in him all things hold together. (Col 1:15–17 ESV)

Reprise and Prospectus

Here we have it—the choices we make matter, and they matter a lot. Yes, wisdom is hard to come by. It means fearing the Lord, cultivating humility, and doing what is right. It means obeying, listening, curbing our insatiable appetites, and caring for others. As we mine the precious gems in Proverbs 10–31, we will peer at wisdom's characteristics through one lens after another. And yes, we are only beginning.

Likewise, the unsavory, unpleasant, unlikable, and yet persistent fool continues to surface after this initial appearance. In some costumes, the fool appears comical, but most often he or she is leaving a path of destruction and shattered relationships. These descriptions make us pause because they sound far too familiar. Let us determine to read sufficiently slowly in order to learn from the small drama in each verse.

CHAPTER 7

Character Matters

Introduction

Teachers periodically remind their students that education is about character formation. That is all well and good, but how do we rescue that concept from such glib expressions as "she's such a character" or "you are going to play the character of the villain in the school production"? To be sure, both of those examples do draw on the substance of this term; each implies something distinct and noticeable, a mark, as it were. To mark or engrave is the meaning of the basic Latin word. There are all sorts of directions we could go with that, but for now we will simply note that each choice, each word, each action etches particular qualities more deeply in our being—whether for good or bad.

In our introductory overview of the book of Proverbs, we noted that chapters 10–15 are packed with antithetical parallelisms whose point is to teach discernment between wise and foolish choices. Front-loaded in chapters 10–12 are righteousness and wickedness and a host of related terms. To this skeletal character structure we will eventually add the flesh of humility, integrity, and truthfulness.

"Above All Guarding, Watch Your Heart" (4:23a)

This entire verse reads, "Above all guarding, watch your heart, for from it are the goings-forth of life" (Prov 4:23). This is assuredly not a translation I would publish for posterity, but it represents pretty closely what the Hebrew says. On more than one occasion, I have heard explanations of this verse that run something like this: "Be careful about giving your heart to someone too soon in a romantic relationship. Take your time because the rest of your life will be shaped by this one choice."

While that is good advice, this particular verse is saying quite a bit more. To be sure, in our cultural context, hearts are central to the whole mysterious process of falling in love. In fact, we easily get the impression that our romantic endeavors are the most important part of our existence. "My heart beat faster"; "my heart broke." Hearts swell, burst, ache, and are tender—or hard. Most of these ideas are bound up with emotion, and I don't for a moment intend to undervalue emotions; they are a gift to be treasured and indeed guarded. Aching hearts may lurk underneath laughter. Jealousy may harden tender hearts. We must be mindful of its deep and damaging consequences (Prov 27:4).

The Hebrew word for heart, however, carries significantly more weight. The heart (*lev*) is the source of all thought, action, and will. The psalmist implored God to "create for me a clean heart and renew in me a right spirit" (Ps 51:10). In other words, my heart is central to my character. It is a living part of me, shaped and molded by every instruction (good or ill), every sight, word, and experience. It is impaired and dulled by absorbing endless streams of garbage. It is strengthened by truth, hope, and joy. How appropriate, therefore, to think carefully about what goes into my heart! Guarding means establishing well-reasoned safeguards and filtering the inflow. Two different words are used in Prov 4:23a to emphasize the need for vigilance in this process. It might help to think of the categories into which our e-mail is sorted. My e-mail program separates out "clutter" and "junk mail." This enables me to focus more carefully on what needs to be addressed as I think, evaluate, and determine the best possible course of action. Back to character formation, our hearts are at the center of the process, and their health is vital. "A heart that heals is life to flesh, but envy rots the bones" (Prov 14:30). As you continue to read Proverbs, whenever you see "heart," think back to these initial observations.

What we determine to do in response to any and every situation comes from our hearts. Our choices are, in other words, the "goings-forth of life," as Prov 4:23b so aptly puts it. Use your biblical imagination for a moment. Springs of water gush forth from the ground; in the biblical world, that is a powerful figure for nurturing and restoring life. If our hearts are right, they nourish others.

The phrase "goings-forth" is admittedly awkward. While the related Hebrew verb form (meaning to "bring out") is common, the derived noun that appears here is used much less frequently, just slightly over twenty times in the Hebrew Bible. There is a related, provocative echo in Mic 5:2 [1]. Using an even less common form, Micah spoke of one who would come forth from Bethlehem as ruler of Israel, whose "goings-forth" were from before, from the days of eternity. This reminds us of our exploration of wisdom's position in the preceding chapter. Let us weave this web of possible connections even further. In John 7:37–38, Jesus spoke on the last day of the Feast of Tabernacles as follows: "If anyone thirsts, let him come to me and drink. Whoever believes in me, as the Scripture has said, 'Out of his heart will flow rivers of living water.'" The person who has received the water of life from Jesus will be a source of that same life-giving water. Could it be that Jesus had Prov 4:23 in mind? On the flip side, Jesus admonished the rule-observing Pharisees in his audience to pay much less attention to the "clean" state of the physical food they were ingesting and to be much more concerned with the "goings-forth" from their hearts—"evil thoughts, sexual immorality, theft, murder, adultery, coveting, wickedness, deceit, sensuality, envy, slander, pride, foolishness" (Mark 7:21–22). This could be an expansion of the things the Lord hates as described in Proverbs 6. Smack in the middle of that list of seven things is a "heart planning wicked schemes" (6:18).

The Dominant Word Pair:
Righteousness and Wickedness

Righteousness and wickedness—what is wrong with these words? Yes, you read that question correctly. It suggests that something might be amiss with these fundamental biblical words. If so, what might that be?

While those who have been nurtured in the church's embrace will resonate with the life implications of these words, they carry a significantly different weight in the public square. Let me sketch a small scene.

There is a Midwestern city that has in one of its public parks a series of small inscribed pillars that are intended to convey socially meaningful messages to runners, dog walkers, and anyone else who happens by for the first time. (After multiple sightings, they simply merge into the visual landscape.) The laconic snippets include such admonitions as the following: fight fear; fight prejudice; live softness; live compassion—all sounding a bit hackneyed, but basically bland and "nice." They run in this general rut until we encounter the following one: oppose righteousness; oppose violence. And an add-on for good measure: overcome righteousness. When I first saw these warnings against righteousness, I was so vexed I composed a letter to the municipal parks authority. My better judgment prevented me from actually sending it! But what is going on here?

I'm sure you have figured it out. Our language is biblical language, and this is not a bad thing until it runs up against perceptions of the

world outside the church. What we view as a worthy goal to pursue, the general public perceives and has retooled as *self*-righteousness. Sometimes, sadly, their perceptions are painfully on target. Our work is cut out for us as we labor to "overcome" those perceptions. A major accompanying component will be humility.

The opposite matter has to do with wickedness. The simple lens on this is that we live in a cultural environment that is loath to use words like "sin," "evil," and "wickedness." They are too, well, condemning, and that is the last thing we want to be. Who wants to be perceived as a judgmental bigot, after all? So we soften our view of the moral terrain and allow the boundaries and horizons to be dim and fuzzy.

Chapters 10–12 of Proverbs stop us in our "please like me" tracks. They do not allow us to get away with that approach. We are confronted with one antithetical parallelism after another, many of which compel us to *choose* between righteousness and wickedness, between good and evil and their inevitable consequences. We cannot escape the call to evaluate and discern; the pairing continues through the rest of the book, albeit at a lower decibel level. No postmodern perspectivalism here.

Constellations of Words

Of the ninety-one verses in chapters 10–12 of Proverbs, forty-two mention some form of the Hebrew words related to "righteous" and "wicked." Of those, twenty-five explicitly pair "righteous" with "wicked" or "righteousness" with "wickedness."

The Hebrew word *tsedek* means "rightness" or "righteousness," and its near relative *tsedakah* refers to righteousness and righteous acts. *Tsaddik* is an adjective that describes a person who is righteous, just, correct, and lawful. Forms from this cluster are used sixty-six times in Proverbs. There seems to be a focus on *being* and *doing* what is right. The (masculine) plural of *tsaddik* is *tsaddikim*, "those who are righteous." Proverbs does not waste time getting to the point; one of the "course objectives" right from the get-go is to receive instruction in righteousness (1:3). The results of fearing the Lord and seeking knowledge of the Holy One include understanding righteousness and justice (2:9).

The characters at the opposite end of the spectrum are deemed *rasha'* (an adjective that also stands in as a noun meaning "wicked" and "wicked person") and *resha'im* (the plural form). *Resha'* means "wickedness." We also find a related verb that means "to cause to do wickedness or evil." While it is entirely acceptable to translate *rasha'* as "evil," there are a number of additional Hebrew words that also mean evil—no surprise there. I intend to hammer away at our cultural refusal to recognize "wickedness" as a fully contemporary concept.

Righteousness and Wickedness Have Consequences

Just as wisdom is bound together with knowledge, discretion, discipline, prudence, and understanding, so the righteous person embodies these qualities—and they *matter*. Our choices—all of them—have life-altering consequences. Put another way, righteousness is living out day by day the wisdom we so earnestly seek and the truth we claim to believe. Those who are righteous hate what is false (13:5), and they act in accordance with that mindset.

There are benefits. The one who chooses to be righteous is assured of life and delivered from death (10:2). A *tsaddik* may fall seven times, but he rises again; the wicked stumble in their evil (24:16). Even in the face of inevitable death, the righteous have a refuge (14:32). By way of contrast, no amount of hoarded treasure will help the wicked in that dreaded day (10:2; see also 11:4). Variations on the theme are no less sobering.

When the whirlwind passes, the wicked are no more,
but the righteous have a foundation forever. (10:25)

The righteous live forever; they are not moved,
but the wicked will not dwell in the land. (10:30)

Surely righteousness leads to life,
    but the one who pursues evil—death. (11:19)

Righteousness guards (same word as in 4:23) the one whose way
        is whole,
    but sin overturns the wicked. (13:6)

We recall the invitation from Woman Folly (9:13–18); she entices gullible youngsters to spiral downward into wicked ways that are abominations to the Lord. Flashback to chapter 5: "The wrongdoing of the wicked
person will trap him; the cords of his sin will hold him fast" (5:22).

By way of contrast, the righteous person enjoys a solid measure of
stability, peace of mind, and meaningful existence. There are not only assurances for whatever the future may hold; those who are righteous also
have a sense of wholeness in the present. In increasingly anxiety-ridden
societies, that is not inconsequential. "Blessings are on the head of the
righteous, but the mouth of the wicked covers violence" (10:6).

Stop for a moment to allow this contrast to settle in. It juxtaposes
two rather incongruous images. Blessings on the head could not be more
visible. Yes, this is a figure of speech, but the point is that the righteous
experience obvious benefits. On the other hand, wicked persons have to
muffle the reality of their violent natures. Their words are a thin disguise
for the horror underneath; it would be unseemly to have it prominently
displayed.

This worrisome observation recurs. "The mouth of the righteous is
a fountain of life (benefiting others), but the mouth of the wicked covers violence" (10:11). Just one more for good measure: "The work of the
righteous leads to life, (but) produce of the wicked to sin" (10:16).

Additional images make us pause. The righteous are remembered for
a blessing, contrasted with the repulsive image of the rotting name of the
wicked (10:7). The longing hope of the righteous is joy; the fleeting hope
of the wicked perishes (10:28; see also 11:7). The tongue of the righteous
is likened to fine silver, while the heart of the wicked is little (10:20). In
other words, the righteous person speaks that which is truly valuable,
but the very essence (heart) of the wicked has no value.

Living long in a state of terror does not have much appeal; that prospect is reserved for the wicked, while the desires of the righteous are
granted (10:24). Righteousness makes the way of the righteous straight
and delivers them, but the wicked end up in the unenviable position
of being trapped by their own twistedness and falling (11:5–6; see also
12:12). The house of the righteous stands, but the wicked are overturned
and are no more (12:7). Bottom line: evil persons are self-destructive in

their deliberate choices; they could have opted for a better way. The righteous, for their part, enjoy security and freedom from hunger and distress (10:3; 11:8), two ever-present threats for ancient Near Eastern peoples. Once we pause with these images, etching them in our hearts and minds, they make us long to be righteous—above all else.

That is not all. Righteousness has communal consequences. The righteous are a fountain of life (10:11); their lips nourish many (10:21); and they care about justice for the poor (29:7). They are careful in counsel, weighing answers (15:28). They bring joy to their parents (23:24). In the face of so much overwhelming family heartache, this declaration is compelling.

By contrast, what passes for "kindness" in the wicked person's system is more akin to cruelty (12:10). As we might expect, the comprehensive effects of evil, particularly of wicked words, are destructive. Godless persons destroy their neighbors with their evil speaking (11:9); even a village can be ruined by the mouth of the wicked (11:11). Really? Really! The counsel of the wicked is deceitful (12:5). And words of the wicked lie in wait to ambush (12:6).

We do not want to neglect national implications; they are timely. "Righteousness exalts a nation, but sin is a disgrace to a people" (14:34). It could not be much clearer than that. Seems we have major work before us. Here is one more, just to challenge us in our successive waves of election seasons. "When the righteous increase, the people rejoice; when the wicked rule, the people groan" (29:2).

> The Hebrew word translated "disgrace" in Prov 14:34 is actually *ḥesed*, which only here and in Lev 20:17 has a very different meaning from its common one of "unfailingly loyal covenant love." These two contexts require that *ḥesed* carry a tragically negative burden.

Let's circle back and confront those little pillars of popular wisdom that I described earlier. The biblical proverbs we have been considering are decidedly *not* about self-righteousness. Instead, they put love for the Lord and for our neighbors above all self-seeking inclinations. This has nothing to do with publicly wagging our rebuking finger under the noses of those with whom we disagree.

In sum, the Lord loves those who pursue what is right (15:9b). Active seekers after righteousness and loving-kindness (*ḥesed* in its typical meaning) will find life, righteousness, and honor (21:21). Pause with the words "pursue" and "seek." This adventure is likened to a chase and a quest. We will not have time for gaping yawns and naps. Instead, excitement abounds as we seek what is right; life and honor are bonuses. According to these proverbs, it is a no-brainer that righteousness is the only choice that makes any sense, especially since the fear of the Lord adds days to one's life, while the years of the wicked are cut off (10:27).

Additional Contrasting Threads in the Fabric

We have focused on the deepest marks etched into our ideal righteous character. In three subsequent chapters, we will watch that ideal character actively pursue righteousness in speaking, in discipline, and in engaged stewardship. In the meantime, however, Proverbs reminds us that there are additional traits that we will do well to cultivate while performing major slash-and-burn eradications of their negative counterparts.

Humility and Pride

"Haughty eyes" are listed first in the six/seven things the Lord hates (6:17). The same image accosts us near the end of the book. In the course of describing a whole raft of unsavory types, Agur observes with dismay those whose eyes are high and their eyelids lifted up (30:13). It seems he hardly knows how to process the utter arrogance. And we can construct a caricature in our mind's eye—individuals looking down their very long noses at someone they perceive to be so small as to be almost entirely inconsequential.

That may be an amusing picture, but the reality behind it is anything but funny. Setting ourselves up in judgment over another person is really attempting to join God on his throne. This is not a good place to be; whenever we presume to climb to those lofty heights, it is not long before we face a reality check—and it can be a rough experience. There are a number of variations on this proverbial theme: "Pride goes before destruction; a haughty spirit before a fall" (16:18 and parallel expressions in 11:2; 18:12; 29:23). Needless to say, there are also social consequences: "Pride only leads to strife; wisdom is with those who are advised" (13:10).

Because we image-bearers of God are so prone to usurp his place, we need constant reminders of the virtue of humility, especially since it does not fit well with our culture's version of success. Which of us, after all, wants to be humble, even humiliated on occasion, unrecognized for the major contributions we make, passed over for awards that we are certain we deserve? You know the circumstances; we have all been there. We bristle when that half-rate, obviously lazy, schmoozing glad-hander gets the bonus—and it is a public recognition! Into that arena come two timely admonitions: "Don't put yourself forward before a king, and don't stand in the place of great ones; it's better to be told to come up than to be lowered" (25:6–7), and "Let another praise you, not your own mouth" (27:2). That is difficult, especially when no one else *does* praise us or ask us forward.

This matter of humility is yet another indication of the rich wisdom tradition that was laced through the life and teachings of Jesus. We are reminded of the gentle rebuke Jesus offered when he noted guests rushing for places of honor at the Sabbath dinner of a prominent Pharisee (Luke 14:7–11).

Nevertheless, let's not forget the ultimate humiliation that Jesus endured on our behalf. The apostle Paul put it this way: "Though (Jesus) was in the form of God, (he) did not esteem equality with God something to be grasped, but made himself nothing, taking the form of a servant" (Phil 2:6–7). Just prior to that, Paul urged his audience to have the same mindset. So do a significant number of proverbs—here is a sampling:

Pride comes and so does disgrace; with the humble is wisdom. (11:2)

Fear of the LORD, discipline, wisdom—humility is before honor. (15:33)

Better to be lowly with the poor than divide the spoil with the rich. (16:19)

The reward for humility and fear of the LORD includes riches, honor, and life. (22:4)

Haughty eyes and proud hearts are not only distasteful; they are *sin* (21:4). Everyone who is arrogant is an abomination to the Lord, and that person will be punished (16:5). Do we really get this? It's not a matter of whether or not I like that high-handed and self-absorbed person. The sober reality is that *God* does not, and he will not countenance this ugly trait in anyone, including each one of us.

One far too common verbal expression of arrogance is scoffing, mockery, and the quick one-liner put-down (21:24). These are feeble attempts to exalt our own presumably superior intellect at the expense of others. We will address the damage that is caused by scoffers in the next chapter. These are the worst kind of fools, and their characters are fundamentally flawed because they do not listen to rebuke (13:1). In addition, there are consequences. "(The LORD) mocks those who mock, but to the humble, he gives grace" (3:34). Here is one final shot, directed at those who seek self-affirming laughs by demeaning their parents: "The eye that mocks a father and scorns to obey his mother will be plucked out by ravens" (30:17). That's a graphic way of saying that this individual will not be properly buried, the epitome of shame. This punishment is measure for measure: the end of the one who shames his or her parents will be endless shame.

Truthfulness and Mendacity

While pride gets the top spot in the list of "six, no seven" things that the Lord finds abominable, lying and false testimony also secure places in the list. No wonder; we find a trail of destruction in the wake of a practiced liar. At this point, I will introduce temporarily an artificial (I hate to say "false" in this context) dichotomy. We will investigate at length the matter of false *speaking* in the next chapter because it deals with the consequences specifically of words. Nevertheless, because lying is evidence of a much deeper character flaw, we need to address it here. Deceit lodges in our hearts and shapes words and actions.

Truth is central to God's being; lying is the prime characteristic of Satan. None other than Jesus said, "You belong to your father, the devil, and you want to carry out your father's desire. He was a murderer from the beginning, not holding to the truth, for there is no truth in him. When he lies, he speaks his native language, for he is a liar and the father of lies" (John 8:44 NIV). Our summons to be righteous includes a clarion call to stop deception in its tracks wherever it rears its head, and instead determine to know truth and to be truthful. We might ask ourselves the following question: In what major areas of life, according to the book of Proverbs, do deceit and falsehood wreak the most havoc? Dishonest weights in commerce reflect the underlying greed of the merchant. Character assassination rages through all walks of life and into circumstances as presumably innocent as gossip and as destructive as slander. False testimony in court is devastating. These last few will occupy us in the next chapter.

Particularly alarming are the layers of deception that compound so many of our daily interactions. The hypocrisy of charmers who mean nothing of what they say is particularly vexing.

> Silver dross covering earthenware are fervent lips and an evil heart.
> With his lips one who hates disguises himself,
> but in his innermost being he places deceit.
> Though his voice is comforting, do not believe him,

because seven abominations are in his heart.
Hatred is covered by deception,
but his wickedness will be revealed in the assembly. (26:23–26)

Don't miss the high profile for wickedness, evil and deceitful hearts, malicious nature, and abominations that fill the heart, all concealed under a slick surface. The pattern entrenches itself as liars feed on each others' webs of falsehood: "The wicked one listens to evil lips; a liar pays attention to a malicious tongue" (17:4).

These twisted ways of the heart are the basis for cheating, basically falsifying the relevant data to make my take a lot better than I deserve. No matter what the context, it is a way to get ahead without the real effort needed for honest gain. In the ancient Near East, this often took the form of the use of unbalanced weights and measures to increase profit in an economy that was based on measuring produce. If you were buying two pounds of fresh tomatoes from me, but my "pound" measures were actually only three-quarters of a pound, your tomatoes in the other side of the scale would be far less in amount. It would have been relatively easy to shave a bit off the weights and get away with it, but it seems that God took that deliberate modification rather seriously. "Scales of deceit are an abomination to the Lord, but a whole stone is his delight" (11:1). Using the whole stone meant the buyer got what he paid for, a case of economic justice. "Honest scales and balances are from the Lord; all the weights in the bag are of his making" (16:11). Just to make sure we really get it, the lesson is repeated.

Differing weights and differing measures—
the Lord detests them both.
Food gained by fraud tastes sweet to a person,
but he ends up with a mouth full of gravel.
The Lord detests differing weights,
and dishonest scales are not good. (20:10, 17, 23)

In our twenty-first-century Western and global sprawl, there are innumerable and complicated ways of hiding unjust profit in the economic sphere. Equally detestable, cheating extends its long tentacles into the academic world all too often. Future positions and tempting profits are presumed to rest on an impeccable transcript, and there are far too many shady ways to get there.

The antidote to the cheating mindset—get as much as you can for as little effort as possible—is the following: "Buy the truth and do not sell it—wisdom and discipline and understanding" (23:23).

Integrity and the Crooked Path

First off, what is "integrity"? It is a word I use regularly, especially when writing letters of recommendation, and I suppose I could come up with a bland, garden-variety definition. But let's pull this apart just a bit and see where that gets us. The Hebrew word *tam* implies the following: blameless, innocent, sincere, quiet, pious, pure, and healthy. Maybe I should not use this term so loosely in my strings of accolades for applicants. *Tamim* (the plural) suggests complete, whole, and blameless. Related to these Hebrew words is *tom*, meaning perfection and completion. Now *that* is integrity, and it is a tall order! A common word for those who embody this quality is *yesharim*, often translated "the upright" (lit., those who are "straight" [*yashar*]). Add to this the recognition that the issue is how we *walk*, how we conduct ourselves in every sphere.

A sampling here will serve us best. Remember you are reading slowly. Look for unexpected consequences in the first and second halves of each proverb. Some of them are surprises.

> The one who walks in integrity walks securely;
> crooked ways are found out. (10:9)

Think about that picture. In spite of circuitous routes taken to avoid detection, the devious character is outed. In the meantime, the person of integrity has no worries.

> Integrity of the upright guides;
> crookedness of the treacherous destroys. (11:3)

Again, ponder the implications of this. Integrity does not overpower or squelch. Instead, guidance suggests freedom with a clear direction in mind. The contrasting figure, however, indicates one unavoidable end, and it is not pretty.

> An abomination to the Lord are those twisted in heart,
> but his delight—those whose way is blameless. (11:20)

> The one who walks in upright ways fears the Lord;
> the one whose way is devious despises him. (14:2)

Both the Lord and humans have deeply vested emotional interests in these relationships. The Lord despises crooked hearts, and they appear to despise him in turn. What a twisted tragedy! The hopeful prospect is again the fear of the Lord as a rock-solid and secure map for the journey.

At the same time, however, the choice to walk the right way is not free from trouble. "Bloodthirsty men will hate the one who is blameless, and they will seek the life of the upright" (29:10). Even so, "a poor man walking in integrity is better than rich men whose ways are crooked" (28:6), because persons of integrity are not shortsighted; they keep their sight focused on the end.

What Kind of Person Will I Be?

We encounter additional pairs of character traits in the book of Proverbs, but we have to stop at some point and assess where we are and how this ought to change us. Yes, that is a bold statement. Nevertheless, all our quotes and observations are useless exercises unless the word transforms us. Thus, we must pose some questions to ourselves. How do I want to end up? How will I be perceived, both by the people closest to me and by God in heaven above? Momentary stop: God in heaven is actually closer than any of the others in my personal space. This might be one reason for giving more than lip service to the "fear of the LORD." It is a recurring theme in the book of Proverbs and bears planting deeply in our hearts. (Remember what "heart" in Hebrew means.) One last parallelism for now: "Hatred stirs up strife; love covers all offenses" (10:12). It's not difficult to decide where we want to land on that one.

CHAPTER 8

The Power in Words

Introductory Questions and Observations

Here is a question to get us rolling. How do words and language work to help us process our worlds, engage our friends, and leave some kind of a memory behind us? We not only talk with others; we also talk to ourselves—a lot. Why might that be? Even these two questions sound so small in light of the inexpressible potential in this gift of verbal communication. While we could multiply our questions endlessly, the bottom line runs something like this: words and language systems are formidable components of our humanity.

In the biblical worldview, God created simply by speaking—"let there be . . . ," and when God spoke, "it was so." While *God's* words were sufficient to bring everything into being, I am stymied by the prospect of even beginning to describe the wonders of creation in *my* words. What a vast difference! Nevertheless, this much we can say (it will sound a bit academic, but it is a necessary starting point): because the whole of the created order is inextricably linked with words that had their origin in God's being, we image-bearers have the capacity to perceive, interpret, and talk about that creation—with words. Even as we recall the past, some part of us hopes to speak into the future. Beyond remarkable!

Let's pursue this just a bit further. While basic needs can be "communicated" with somewhat primitive language and nonverbal signs, our thoughts and feelings, those wonderful products of our emotional, intellectual, and spiritual spheres, need a sufficiently complex language system. How, after all, would I communicate that I expect my students to be honest if I had only facial expressions and hand signals? To be sure, sometimes all the necessary words still do not get our messages across; but God did make communication at those deeper personal levels possible, even revealing himself through the written word and the Word Incarnate. As with all of God's good gifts to humankind, however, the gift of language suffered severe disruption after Adam and Eve chose to disobey God's words. Instead of perfect communication, words too often create and perpetuate misunderstanding, deception, and pain. Do you get the impression that we are engaging in a significantly complicated task?

Words in Proverbs: Initial Observations

A good number of the most striking proverbs about words make their case with reference to the actual apparatus for speech ("mouth," "lips," and "tongue"), creating striking verbal pictures. There may also be a subtle further message. These parts of the body *can* be controlled. One of my favorite children's sermon illustrations has delightful five-year-olds gripping their tongues with their little hands and then trying to say something. Whatever they are attempting to articulate comes out utterly garbled.

"A fool's lips enter into a fight, and his mouth invites a beating. A fool's mouth is his ruin, and his lips are a snare to his soul" (18:6–7). There are a number of references in Proverbs to "guarding" lips, mouth, and tongue. Doing so has significant consequences. "He who guards his lips guards his soul, but he who opens wide his lips will come to ruin" (13:3). "The one who guards his mouth and tongue keeps himself from calamity" (21:23). Perhaps we ought to practice covering our mouths with both hands and sealing our lips with duct tape.

What are the occasions when you and I repeatedly get trapped by our mouths (lips, tongues)? Very likely they reflect recurring themes articulated throughout Proverbs. Here is a quick overview of these themes; we will explore many of them in much greater depth.

- Lying surfaces in Proverbs repeatedly, and that ought not surprise us (10:18; 12:17, 19, 20, 22; 14:5; 26:23–28; 30:7–8)

- Its cousins, slander and gossip, are equally repulsive (11:13; 18:8; 26:20, 22)

- We're at our best when we keep words to a minimum (10:19; 12:23; 13:3)

- There is something especially annoying about chattering fools (10:8, 10; 14:3; 15:2; 18:2, 6, 7)

- Words have the potential to do extensive damage, but carefully chosen words can be healing (15:4)

The list of verses in this overview is useless unless we do something with it. Here is one suggestion. Read through the clusters in chapters 12 and 26, and see how each works its way from the deception in the heart through the lying and gossiping lips to the ruinous damage that results. Be on the lookout for these seamless connections between character and consequences.

Truthfulness and Lying

In the previous chapter, we focused on truth as a quality essential to righteous, godly character. Its dark counterpart, deceit in all its forms, drew us back to the garden of Eden, where the serpent's temptation had everything to do with lying and compelling Adam and Eve to lie as well. Jesus rightly nailed the devil as "the father of lies" (John 8:44) responsible for the tangle of self-deceit, cheating, trickery, false testimony, and fraud that we encounter daily. Abraham Heschel's compelling indictment is unmatched:

> What is one of the major roots of evil in our insane world? . . . mendacity, falsehood, wantonness of words, perversion of the heart. Falsehood is a refuge, an asylum for the cruel, the violent, for consummate criminals. What begins as a lie ends in blasphemy. Rarely does an individual's falsehood remain a private affair. It is so dynamic, so infectious and expansive that it bursts all secrecy, all privacy, affecting ever more people.[1]

Righteous character is inseparably linked to righteous words and actions; those who shape their lives around the core of truth will unfailingly tell the truth. We never need to question the trustworthiness of their words. They know that all forms of verbal deceit are abhorrent to God. "Lying lips are an abomination to the LORD, but those who act faithfully are his delight" (12:22; review again 6:16–19). They know that their social fabric is torn apart by lies because lies foster hatred. "A lying tongue hates those it crushes, and a slippery mouth works ruin" (26:28). We would do well to pray for an ongoing awareness of the disastrous consequences of each untrue word that escapes our lips. Perhaps we should practice "biting our tongues" just a bit more frequently, or holding them, as our children's sermon illustration instructed.

Justice and Truth-Telling

Speaking the truth in the public arena, particularly the court context, is high profile in the book of Proverbs. Testimony in court has life-and-death consequences. Ironically, truthfulness is too frequently a stranger to the public square. We dismiss it as "bias," whether in the context of a court case or politics in general, and we take for granted that figuring out what really happened or what was really said is beyond our limited perspectival gaze. Shame on us! We need to revisit this business of telling the truth when lives and reputations are at stake.

I will render the following maxims with somewhat wooden translations because, again, we need to slow down. As I have already noted, more readable renditions occasionally preclude our actually absorbing what is being said.

"One who breathes out truth will declare righteousness (*tsedek*), but a false witness . . . deceit" (12:17). What is this saying besides the obvious? Perhaps a brief commentary is in order. The verb "breathing out" implies exhaling with gusto. Intrinsic to this person's character is truth-telling, and it is unmistakably evident. His or her reputation has been built on a long-standing foundation. When *this* person takes the stand, we trust the testimony. The ESV and the NIV translate *tsedek* here as "honest evidence" and "honest testimony," respectively. We have the negative side in 6:19—a "false witness breathing out lies" (see also 14:5, 25). Breathing out presumes also breathing in; together these actions reflect the essence of someone's ongoing life. In far too many cases, deceit, fraud, and lies are inhaled, processed, and exhaled to do more damage.

There seems to be an important judicial principle wrapped in here: find witnesses who are reputable. Proverbs is insistent on this. This should not surprise us. God's cosmic justice is to be mirrored in the court scenes that unfold among his covenant people. If righteousness and justice are the foundations of his throne (Ps 89:14 [15]), then we are under obligation to preserve them when human well-being and livelihood are at stake. "A truthful witness saves lives, but he (the false witness) breathes out lies and treachery" (14:25). The picture is painted with an even finer brush. "A witness of *belial* (a worthless witness) mocks justice, and the mouth of evil ones swallows down iniquity" (19:28). What kind of people, we ask ourselves, would make a mockery of justice? One answer, among countless possibilities, would be those who pay bribes to court and government officials in order to keep lucrative sex-trafficking operations in business. And what kind of people gulp down evil every chance they get? Those who have given in to their addictions, are shackled by them, and cannot bring themselves to confess the truth.

Even though the current landscape is often utterly disheartening, justice will prevail, and consequences will be visited upon the perpetrators of lies: "A false witness will not go unpunished, and the one who breathes out lies will perish" (19:9; see also 21:28a).

Our sages take several steps back at this point to include in the court scene not only the witnesses, both reputable and otherwise, but the process itself: "To show partiality in judging is not good: The one who says to the evil person, 'You are righteous'—peoples will curse him, and they will denounce him before nations. But it will be pleasant for those who convict (the guilty), and good blessing will come upon them" (24:23b–25).

The national danger of listening to advice based on lies is not a recent phenomenon: "If a ruler listens to a false word, all his officials will become wicked" (29:12).

Listening to Liars

Speaking and listening are all of one piece; the one who listens to (and believes) an endless string of falsehoods is in as much jeopardy as those who breathe them out so freely: "One who is wicked listens to evil lips; a liar pays attention to a malicious tongue" (17:4). Unfortunately, lies give malicious people more ammunition in the war against righteousness.

So far this reads a bit like a series of sound-bite sermons. For a change of pace, Proverbs offers a vignette that equally illustrates the damage level of what we sometimes style as "small and inconsequential" lies— little jokes that need to be covered and re-covered. "Like a madman shooting firebrands, arrows and death, thus is a man who deceives his neighbor and then says, 'I was only joking!' " (26:18–19). Firebrands and arrows—and death—are pretty serious.

"Death and Life Are in the *Hand* of the Tongue" (18:21a)

"Hand" in Hebrew is often a figure of speech denoting power, because hands were the limbs that wielded instruments of force. In addition, the right hand could be lifted up in oath, which was itself a powerful declaration.

The quotation of Prov 18:21a above is a literal rendition. "Power" is usually substituted for "hand" (*yad*) here, but the point is clear whichever way we translate it. The verse continues, by the way, with "and those who love it (the power?) will eat its fruit." Our focus, however, is on the first part. This is not an exaggeration; every century is drenched with the blood of people who have been caught up by powerful rhetoric designed to ignite passionate and catastrophic violence. This destructive pattern continues unabated even in our presumably enlightened twenty-first century. It is instructive that "death" is the first word; "life" follows. Sadly, examples of powerful human eloquence in the service of good causes are not nearly as evident. In like manner, it is much easier to find proverbs on the damage that we do with our mouths than on the good. That could be a commentary on basic human nature as well as ancillary factors like selected media coverage—which plays to the less-exalted side of human nature.

Once words are uttered, they can never be recalled. They have their own life, it seems, and they are going places! We ought never think of words as static and dead. As words burrow into the hearts of listeners, whether one individual or a captive audience of thousands, misinterpretation enters the picture as well. What a recipe for potential suspicion and division! Far too often, we find ourselves apologizing, explaining, groveling, or constructing an ever-growing web of deceit. By way of contrast, the description in Hebrews 4 of *God's* word as "living and active" is a heartening example of the power of words.

Wherein Lies This Power?

I am indebted to Derek Kidner's commentary on Proverbs in the Tyndale Old Testament Commentaries series (pp. 46–49) for the basic rubric underlying this next section. The directional components of penetrating, on the one hand, and spreading, on the other, keep us focused on the active power of words. In fact, these two movements cover just about every locus.

Words Penetrate

Words do not simply float in some neutral space until they disintegrate. On many occasions, we might wish they did, or at least that the hearers would have a major episode of amnesia. Instead, however, words penetrate our hearts, where there is already a thick fabric of beliefs and convictions, and there they get down to business. Every day, our attitudes toward others are deeply affected by what we hear about them. What we *hear* is what someone else has *said*, and it nestles in to stay, usually more effectively than all the lectures on being good, kind, and obedient. Likewise, we are in the process of shaping the minds of people around us by what we say and how we say it. Our expectations are conveyed by words. Our joy or displeasure at the responses of friends, spouses, and children are fundamentally conveyed by words.

Let's start with Prov 12:18a: "There is one who speaks rashly, like sword thrusts." These words wound and damage, perhaps even kill, and it seems that the speaker is intent on inflicting as much damage as possible. There are multiple "thrusts" of the sword. Absorb another verbal picture: "Crookedness [of the tongue] crushes the spirit" (15:4b). Crooked words reach deep inside, where they do their greatest damage.

Proverbs 18:8 captures yet another image of penetrating words: "The words of a gossip (a malicious whisperer, or one who murmurs to stir up discontent) are like choice morsels; they go down to the chambers of the belly." What an image! We cannot get more internalized than that. And these words stay there; people savor them as much as they love choice morsels. They rarely forget the words of a gossip, and their perceptions have been changed—permanently. Equally sobering is how the words of a gossip spread. We crave those choice morsels, perhaps because they give us an edge ("*I* know something *you* don't know"), but we also tend to embellish and season them with each repetition. It seems that this problem is a verbal plague. "He who repeats a matter separates close friends" (17:9b; see also 16:28b—"a whisperer separates close friends").

> The word translated "choice morsels" in 18:8 is used only in that verse and in 26:22 (which contains the exact same statement). It seems these tidbits are swallowed and gulped down greedily.

Lest we despair, however, Proverbs also affirms the good that penetrating words can accomplish: "A rebuke goes deeper into a person of understanding than a hundred blows into a fool" (17:10). When we recall instances when friends and associates have had the courage to question our bad judgment, it is usually with a combination of embarrassment for having been so stupid, gratitude for having been stopped short in that reckless path, and resolve not to get called out again. At least we are on our way to being people of understanding.

Words Spread

Sometimes the nature of words is ratcheted up from gossip, as bad as that is. "A worthless man (a man of *belial*) digs for evil, and on his lips it is as a scorching fire" (16:27). Not only does the fire burn painfully, but the speed with which it spreads is breathtaking. Witness the images of wildfires in tinder-dry countryside. Only with monumental effort are they controlled, and that is usually after untold damage has occurred. There are ways to curb these fires, though: "Without wood, a fire goes out; without gossip a quarrel dies down" (26:20).

In literary sources that postdate the Hebrew Bible, Belial (also Beliar) comes to refer to a major evil power. We see that implication in 2 Cor 6:15; the contrast between Christ and Beliar could not be more stark. In the Hebrew Bible itself, the word is used just under thirty times; in almost half of these cases, the word is preceded by "sons of." These texts are primarily narratives that describe truly unsavory characters. The Hebrew word in question, *beliyya'al*, is likely a compound word meaning "without value."

Here is the positive counterpart: "The mouth of the righteous is a fountain of life" (10:11a). So also, "Instruction of the wise is a fountain of life, turning from the snares of death" (13:14). Fountains spread water in abundance; so also a righteous person's instruction spreads goodness, grace, and restoration. "From the fruit of his lips a person is filled with good things, and the work of his hands rewards him" (12:14).

Sharpening the Vision

When was the last time you sat in the optometrist's chair and the assistant switched in and out a series of lens changes to determine which gave the most clarity? Proverbs does the same thing, adding to and tweaking our perception of the penetrating and spreading power of words. How, for example, do things look after an onslaught of ill-tempered and evil words? Our verdict declares the scene a swath of destruction. Proverbs nails the wicked character that prompts those cruel words, while it extols the opposite. "With his mouth the godless destroys his neighbor, but with knowledge the righteous are delivered" (11:9). "Words of the wicked lie in wait for blood, but the mouth of the upright delivers them" (12:6).

Mockery and contempt are particularly reprehensible. "One who lacks heart shames his neighbor, but a person of understanding remains silent" (11:12). "The one who mocks the poor shows contempt for their Maker" (17:5a). The second statement is particularly chilling. We may be tempted to view mockers with a bit of sympathy, presuming that their cruelty comes from their own insecurity. This lens, however, sharpens our focus on the real problem.

Next we slip in flattery—what many think of as harmless and perhaps even heartening. "Slip in" is a deliberate choice; the Hebrew word translated "to flatter" means "to be smooth or slippery," and that is not a good thing. This is not simply a matter of making someone feel good about their latest off-the-wall costume choices. Let's return to this admonition: "A lying tongue hates those it crushes, and a flattering (slippery) mouth works ruin" (26:28). The kind but difficult course is set in being truthful.

"The one who rebukes a person will afterward find more grace than the one whose tongue is slippery" (28:23; see also 29:5). Flattery is particularly devastating because it falsely inflates our egos and sets us up for serious disappointment when the reality check comes. And flattery often comes with emotional strings attached. The flatterer has expectations.

Those who constantly allow their mouths to get ahead of their ears are often called "fools." This is not new territory, but it does move another one of those testing lenses into place for us. Do we make a point of listening, really listening to the person with whom we are conversing? Or are we waiting for the chance to slip in our well-considered comeback? "A fool does not delight in understanding, but in revealing his heart" (18:2; ESV, "expressing his opinion"). "The one who answers before listening — that is his folly and shame" (18:13).

One last checking lens; how does this one sharpen our perception, especially in relation to the previous matter of flattery? "Let a stranger praise you and not your own mouth; a foreigner and not your own lips" (27:2). Perhaps the warning here is a bit more subtle. Strangers rarely flatter. Instead, they are observing something about you, your work, your contribution to a cause, or a myriad of other things, and they are giving an appraisal from what might be a more objective position. Let's say that they have nothing to gain; thus, the assessment is not flattery but outright commendation and admiration. That is preferable to the uncomfortable position into which a boaster places his or her squirming audience. What do I say when that person starts in again on how much she has accomplished for the company? For the team? For the college?

"A crucible for silver and a furnace for gold, and a man by his praise" (27:21). The imagery has to do with refining processes, and I especially love the ambiguity in that last line. Is the testing of this person a matter of evaluating the praise he doles out? We can tell if it is timely, well-placed, and genuine, or if it falls in the hollow realm of flattery. That will reveal volumes about his motives. On the other hand, perhaps the proverb intends to focus on how we respond to praise. Is it with an "aw shucks" type of false humility, or do we honestly acknowledge what that person has observed and then give proper gratitude?

Words at Their Best

I would like to close this chapter on a positive note. How can we really benefit others in our communications with them? Proverbs gives a high profile to encouragement, advice, instruction, and rebuke. Further, the way each of these is delivered makes a good deal of difference.

Words at their best are calm. "A gentle answer turns away wrath, but a harsh word stirs up anger" (15:1 NIV). Counterintuitive as it might be, calmness is powerful—"a gentle tongue will break a bone!" (25:15b). Self-control is essential. "The whole of his spirit (temper) comes out of a fool, but a wise person stills it (temper) behind" (29:11). Perhaps the permission we give ourselves to "vent" is overrated.

Generally speaking, fewer words are better. "When words are many, transgression does not cease, but the one who holds his lips is wise" (10:19). I particularly like the first part of this verse. Often we tend to say more (and more and more) in order to deal effectively with problems. The truth is, however, that we often exacerbate the matter far beyond its original context. "The one who restrains his speech has knowledge; an excellent spirit (characterizes) a man of understanding" (17:27). Finally, here is one of my favorites: "Even a fool who keeps silent is thought to be wise, and the one who holds his lips, discerning" (17:28). This needs no further comment.

There is a small but significant translation issue concerning the Hebrew text of 17:27. For those who follow these matters, the translation "excellent spirit" follows the Hebrew consonantal text that is read (Qere), which has *yekar ruah*. The written (Ketiv) text has *vekar ruah*, "and cool of spirit."

Words at their best are kind, encouraging, and appropriate. (It should go without saying that such words are wise.) "An anxious heart weighs a person down, but a good word makes him rejoice" (12:25). "Pleasant words are a honeycomb, sweet to the soul and healing to the bones" (16:24). When words are said to be appropriate, this implies that they have been carefully chosen for the given situation. It is one thing to mouth a platitude; it is another to take the time to tailor words for this particular loss or that specific hardship. Words aptly spoken are *beautiful*, like priceless gems in well-crafted settings (25:11–12). "A person finds joy in giving an apt reply; and how good is a word spoken in its time!" (15:23).

These words will also be edifying, give sound counsel, stimulate thought, and, when necessary, offer rebuke. We have already observed the value of well-placed reproof. "The heart of a wise person enlightens his mouth, and he adds instruction to his lips" (16:23). The exemplary woman of Prov 31:10–31 "speaks with wisdom, and faithful instruction is on her tongue" (31:26). "Oil and incense bring joy to the heart, and the sweetness of a friend comes from his heartfelt counsel (counsel of his soul)" (27:9).

Good words make us think; they make us reconsider and perhaps revise our opinions. "As iron and iron together, so one person (sharpens) his friend" (27:17). The image here merits an additional observation. When iron is against another piece of iron in motion, sparks often fly. This proverb describes not only placid discourse, but also energetic engagement. It is the disagreement that moves our minds forward, as long as we listen before responding. Finally, rebuke is not easy to give; it takes courage to approach someone who seems to be way too far out on the leash. This example is a rerun: "The one who rebukes a person will afterward find more grace than the one whose tongue is slippery" (28:23).

Words at their best involve confession, an indication of humility and willingness to listen and change. "He who conceals his transgressions will not prosper, but whoever confesses and forsakes them will find mercy" (28:13).

At this point, dear reader, you will be inclined to say "but you forgot to mention 10:21 or 10:32" or any other number of your favorites. That is true! And I urge you to graze through the pages of Proverbs seeking ever more wonderful fodder on which to chew. For now, however, we need to stop. After all, we have gone far beyond the "few words" admonition.

Addendum: Assignments

Let me suggest two "projects" that might be useful after working through this chapter. First, address this set of questions for yourself: In what ways are my words destructive? Whom do I injure and why? What will I do to transform the ways I use words?

Second, choose two or three key proverbs that you want to remember because they will help with the first assignment. Memorize them. My sampling includes the following morsels. I provide the NIV here, for that is the version I used when memorizing them.

When words are many, sin is not absent;
but the one who holds his tongue is wise. (10:19)

Reckless words pierce like a sword,
but the tongue of the wise brings healing. (12:18)

He who guards his lips guards his soul,
but he who speaks rashly will come to ruin. (13:3)

A gentle answer turns away wrath,
but a harsh word stirs up anger. (15:1)

CHAPTER 9

Discipline

Introduction

"The one who loves discipline loves knowledge, but the one who hates correction is stupid" (12:1). Sounds straightforward, doesn't it? In some ways, it is. On the other hand, there are interpretative challenges even in that one verse. Our first exercise will have to do with definition. One Hebrew word, most frequently rendered "discipline" in English, has a wide range of meanings. We will explore them shortly. Some show up without our knowing that it is the same Hebrew word. (This is a standard problem in translation, but it has a high profile with this topic because certain aspects of discipline get uncomfortable public press. Yes, we will address the "rod" proverbs.) Just for the record, the English word "discipline" is also subject to interpretation!

The broad topic of discipline merges with self-discipline, an outcome that parents, teachers, and other authority figures hope for during those long periods of more elementary discipline. The end result of self-discipline is a diligent person who is the antithesis of the sluggard. Proverbs caricatures this lazy idler, but there is a sober tone underneath the humorous poking. These types are dangerous. As we cast our gaze across this swath of representative folks, from the child in need of correction to the recalcitrant sloth, we will discover that we have our interpretive work cut out for us.

What Is Discipline?

The first nine chapters of Proverbs establish the educational context for the book. In this process, the emphasis is on the authority of the father and mother, who are the teachers (1:8; 6:20). Right from the start, discipline is closely associated with knowledge, wisdom, righteousness, justice, and life itself. If that last item sounds radical, we remind ourselves that "the corrections of discipline are the way to life" (6:23b).

The Hebrew word translated "discipline" in Prov 12:1 is *musar*. This term, which is used frequently in Proverbs, can mean everything from instruction, admonition, and correction to chastisement and physical punishment. It all depends on the severity of the circumstances. In other words, none of us escapes discipline, much as we might like to. Worse (or better) yet, regardless of the level at which discipline is meted out and experienced, it is rarely a one-time event. We are slow learners, and repetition is inevitable. So is pain in some form—either physical or emotional—and this varies depending on how receptive a given person might be.

"Strike a mocker, and the simple will learn prudence; rebuke a discerning person and he will discern knowledge" (19:25). Notice who is learning in each of these vignettes. Hardened mockers earn a walloping punishment, but even then they probably will not come around; by this time they are hardwired to scoff at all things good—and especially discipline. Nevertheless, a still moldable bystander may see their punishment and be deterred from making the same poor choices. On the other end of the spectrum are individuals who carefully weigh what is right and wrong. The proverb rightly links their nature (discerning) with what they will do with the rebuke (to discern). When they receive a deserved rebuke, it serves them well. The same vast chasm is obvious between the two individuals described in the following proverb: "The one who rejects discipline despises himself, but the one who hears (and obeys) reproof gains heart (i.e., a full-orbed wisdom)" (15:32).

Here is a test case for interpreting *musar*. As it is used in 12:1, it could simply be translated "instruction," a less painful and more narrowly focused form of discipline. A "disciple," after all, is a student who follows a master's teaching. That fits well with the phrase "loves knowledge," which follows. In this case, when we read this verse, we need not imagine the bizarre prospect of someone actually enjoying a smack upside the head in order to learn. The second part of the verse, however, might make us pause and reassess our initial interpretation just a bit. The person in question "hates correction." Love and hate are the antitheses here, and we would expect their respective objects to be close parallels. Toward that end, perhaps a firmer kind of "discipline" in the first part of the verse fits with the degree of sternness implicit in "correction." Even this one verse may pose some small conundrums.

We can add to this test case—just for fun. (Did I say fun?) Remember that *musar* is used frequently in the book of Proverbs. Here is another instance: "Bring your heart to *musar* and your ears to words of knowledge" (23:12). Okay, the parallel to *musar* in the second part of the verse is knowledge. So, "instruction" sounds like a fitting translation in this context—*until* we arrive at the two verses that immediately follow this one. Because the topics in Prov 22:17–24:34 generally span more than one verse, it is possible that 23:12 serves in some introductory capacity to the two verses that follow it. Wouldn't you know, they wade right into the value of the "rod" as the means of discipline! This is a good segue; let's address the "rod" verses.

The Elephant in the Room and the Rod on the Back

How are we to understand the "rod" of discipline? The expression occurs more than once in Proverbs. Is it intended to be figurative, implying stern discipline indeed but not necessarily physical contact? Or does that rod really mean using a cane or wooden spoon or whatever other instrument your grandmother might have described to you? I say "grandmother" because it seems we have to go back several generations to discover much of this sort of disciplinary action.

The best path into this discussion is to quote all the proverbs that refer to the "rod" and see what the end result is. At that point, even if we do not agree on the nature of the "rod," at least we have marshaled the evidence. Further, that evidence will serve us well as we unpack the real objective, which is to underscore the value of discipline.

Wisdom is found on the lips of the discerning person,
but a rod is for the back of the one who lacks heart. (10:13)

He who withholds the rod hates his son,
but he who loves him seeks him early with discipline. (13:24)

Blows that wound scour away evil,
and beatings the inmost being (lit., rooms of the belly). (20:30)

Folly is bound up in the heart of a young person;
the rod of discipline will drive it far from him. (22:15)

Do not withhold discipline from a young person;
though you strike him with the rod, he will not die.
You, with the rod, strike him,
and his life you will rescue from *sheol*. (23:13–14)

A whip for horses, a halter for the donkey,
and a rod for backs of fools. (26:3)

The rod and rebuke will give wisdom,
but a young person left (to himself) disgraces his mother. (29:15)

At first read, these sound harsh—even tyrannical and outdated. No one, we tell ourselves, is going in this direction for child-rearing advice. As always, however, there is value in slowing down and reading carefully. Above all, love is a major part of the disciplinary process. Not to discipline means, in effect, hating the child. Why? Because the child who runs wild—and that is our natural tendency—heads toward serious danger. Whether we like to admit it or not, evil and folly are part of who we are, and they need to be curbed. *Shevet* is the Hebrew word translated "rod," and it means staff or club, a piece of equipment used to guide sheep and get rid of predators. It is also a figure for God's chastisement when the people are straying—like sheep.

Sheol is a poetic way of referring to the grave; severe discipline exercised early and consistently is designed to prevent the catastrophe of an untimely death. Of course, it is not easy to pick up the chosen instrument of discipline in your home and head for that defiant little rebel. That may be why 23:14 starts with "You, with the rod . . ." We cannot pass this obligation off to someone else if we want what is best for our children. I know; you don't like the scene I have just created. "*My* child is not deserving of smacks. Boys, after all, will be boys; children will be children." But that is just the point. Children left to themselves will grow up to be *big* people with a child's sense of moral accountability. That is not a good contribution to society.

Now, allow me a few additional observations to help this medicine go down more easily. They are posed as a whole series (yes, an impossible list) of conditions. If our home life is shaped by loving and consistent boundaries, if expectations are clear, if we pray that we discipline in love and not in a burst of anger, if we pray for wisdom to discipline with the appropriate measure, if we confess to our children when *we* step over the boundaries that constrain us as well as them, and if we are quick to forgive and embrace repentant children, then we trust in the effectiveness of this process. Tall order? Yes. Did you note the multiple references to prayer?

One more extremely important observation: physical discipline leaves bruises, to be sure, but surface wounds heal. That is not the case with endless verbal abuse. Demeaning and belittling errant children creates irreparable inner damage. Thoughtless and harsh words are no less destructive than ill-administered swats. Just one last reminder: these "rod" verses do not condone uncontrolled and violent outbursts.

The principles that shape discipline in the home carry over to the sphere of national discipline as well. "A wise king winnows out the wicked; he drives the threshing wheel over them" (20:26). Bottom line: evil needs to be addressed. Winnowing means separating and getting rid of chaff—in other words, the useless stuff. Threshing wheels crush. Pretty graphic.

What Does Discipline Accomplish?

In case the paragraphs above have not made the points sufficiently, here is a recap along with several small expansions. The latter address not only that pesky rod that we would like to sidestep but also the additional means of correction mentioned earlier. It is a good thing to have the whole arsenal at our disposal so that, indeed, we don't reach for the club first thing. In fact, children ought to recognize patterns of discipline and know that when we head for the wooden spoon hanging on the wall, they're in big trouble.

Rescue!

Discipline turns a person away from evil and from very serious consequences. To wit, "discipline your son because there is hope; do not get yourself involved in causing his death" (19:18); and "harsh discipline is for the one who forsakes the path; the one who hates correction will die" (15:10). Put another way, if parents don't discipline, we may be assured that God our Father will. It is striking (bad pun) that the very next verse says, "*Sheol* and *'abaddon* (destruction) are before the LORD; how much more the hearts of humans" (15:11).

Because God fully knows us, God's discipline is always entirely appropriate for the occasion. Folly is another way of saying disregard for God's ways. As inherently sinful creatures, we need to have our ways curbed. Death is a part of this, and that is sobering (5:23). Nevertheless, at the end of the day Proverbs also recognizes that some unrepentant persons, when disciplined, grow harder. Their lives close in irreparable tragedy (15:10; 28:9; 29:1).

Example for Others

The disciplined life is instructive. In other words, those around us will see that we refrain from words and actions that are unseemly, and they may take heed. "The one who keeps/guards discipline (shows) the way to life; the one who forsakes reproof causes straying" (10:17).

Self-Discipline

In the best of all possible worlds, eventually we manage to internalize consistent discipline patterns. You know how it works; you hear that voice in your head saying, "Mom would *not* be pleased with that," or "Uh oh; I know where this is headed," and you change course. It is not a cakewalk. One of our translation options for 23:12a reminds us of that: "*bring* your heart to discipline." The subtext here is that the heart does not move in this direction willingly or of its own volition. Nevertheless, embracing the "easier" disciplines spares us from the more painful ones.

"Guarding" or "keeping" instruction/discipline ultimately has everything to do with obedience—namely, submission to principles, rules, and laws that have been set forth for our good. Just in case that makes us chafe, here is a pointed reminder: Jesus "learned obedience through what he suffered" (Heb 5:8 ESV).

Intermission: Chuckling at the Sluggard

Believe me, I have searched for a synonym that captures everything that is wrapped up in "sluggard," but to no avail. "Lazy person" is flat; it has no real character. It is tempting to use "sloth," but this is properly a noun that characterizes the action, or lack thereof, of the sluggard. The problem is that "sluggard" has fallen out of use. Perhaps "couch potato" is the best contemporary synonym, but who knows what kind of shelf life that expression will have? Besides, its context is the lounger in front of a flat-screen TV. The sluggard's style is even more constrained; he or she often simply stays in bed.

As part of the introductory discourses, the teacher/father offers a stinging rebuke wrapped in scathing advice:

Go to the ant, you sluggard; see its ways and be wise.
It has no chief, policeman, or ruler.
In the summer, it prepares its bread;
in harvest time, it stores up its food.
How long, sluggard, will you lie there?
How long before you get up from your sleep?
A little sleep, a little slumber,
a little folding of the hands to continue lying there,
and your poverty will come as one simply walking in,
and your shortage as a man with a shield. (6:6–11)

The same extended observation ("a little sleep, a little slumber . . .") closes the censure of a lazy and senseless person who has not cared for his vineyard but let it go to wrack and ruin (24:33). Although not called a sluggard, a person who sleeps through the harvest is shameful (10:5). It does not take a rocket scientist to put all this together. You don't work, you won't eat. It is a lesson to be learned from watching columns of ants ceaselessly laboring to pull items of food three times their size to their equivalent of a warehouse. Compare that to the sad scene of a dilapidated piece of neglected property.

There are also comical caricatures that are designed to prod with a touch of sarcasm. Because sluggards do seem to sleep interminably (6:9), they are described as hinged to their beds (26:14). Poor things; they just cannot escape. They never seem to master the activities that are part of a basic subsistence routine. In the ancient Near Eastern context, the example is not plowing before the winter. Plowing was a given if any kind of harvest was to be forthcoming (20:4). Translated to a Western, urban couch potato's domain, this might involve not bothering to pay oil, electricity, and phone bills or to continue car registration and insurance. And those don't even take nearly as much work as plowing.

The sluggard has preposterous excuses for inactivity: "There is a lion outside; I will be murdered right in the street" (22:13). To be sure, lions outside were more likely in this ancient context than in our world, but we might surmise that they primarily ranged outside the city boundaries.

Sluggards are constitutionally unable to finish simple tasks, even ones designed to benefit themselves—like eating! "The sluggard buries his hand in the plate; he cannot even return it to his mouth" (19:24, with the same image repeated in 26:15). They cannot satisfy their own cravings, even though craving seems to be a central part of their character (13:4a). This is not a surprise; when what we want is tantalizingly present but always just out of reach, craving is the only way to describe the powerful impulse: "The desire of a sluggard will kill him, because his hands refuse to work. He spends the whole day craving, but the righteous person gives and does not hold back" (21:25–26).

While the images of the sluggard are surely humorous, there is a dark side to this character as well. In fact, sluggards demonstrate serious failings. They are irritants of the worst kind—vinegar to the teeth and smoke to the eyes—to those who must employ them (10:26). They are dangerous; a sluggard is called "one who sinks or is slack in his work," and he "is a brother to the one who destroys" (18:9). Ponder this for a bit. How might it be so? Let's say that a welder involved in a large infrastructure construction project has a habitual lack of concern for good work. We know the tragic results for lots of people when the bridge or building collapses.

Antidote to the Sluggard Sunk in Sloth: Diligence

The Hebrew word translated "diligent" means "sharp" or "keen." That's a good image; it implies moving forward with energy and care. Diligent people work and reap the rewards (10:4b; 12:24a; 13:4b).They conduct their affairs in an orderly manner, evaluating what needs to be done first and then following through with remaining tasks (24:27). They are attentive to all aspects of the work before them. The description of the diligent herdsman is a delight. This person knows the full range of his household and his flocks, and he has a healthy perspective on what lasts and what does not (27:23–27). Mixing in a significant measure of cultural translation, we might reimagine this person as one who knows the state of his investment portfolio but holds it lightly, recognizing that these riches do not last forever. Instead, his real investment is in providing for his family.

This leads us finally to the stunning exemplar of the diligent person—the valiant, strong woman of Prov 31:10–31. If you ever want to feel like a sluggard, just read the heaps of accolades for this woman. We've already visited her in chapter five, so here we simply note that she is precious because she is trustworthy, she works night and day to provide food and clothing for her husband and extended household, and she gets involved in commercial enterprises—buying a field, planting a vineyard, and processing garments. As if that is not enough, her concern extends beyond her own household to the poor at her gates. She is dignified and, in the midst of all her other activity, she speaks with wisdom and fears the Lord.

Recapitulation

Our best takeaway from this chapter is that consistent discipline, unpleasant as it might be at the moment, is *good*. Exercising appropriate discipline draws on our reservoirs of love and wisdom, and our children are the better for it. Receiving discipline appropriately compels us to a posture of humility. There is really no better place to be.

CHAPTER 10

Relationships

Introductory Observations

All of life involves relationships. Just take a random weekday and note which of the following cross your path, either physically or virtually: business associate, mail carrier, roommate, teenage daughter, aged parent, furious boss, childhood friend, recalcitrant student, recalcitrant professor, neighbor with loud barking dog (early in the morning), husband, dentist—and there are countless others. At one level or another, we need to interact with these folks, and in many cases we have no choice as to when, how, or where this will happen. Some interactions are pleasant; some we try valiantly to avoid. Some of us are "social animals" and love every possible context for dealing with people, even those who might be somewhat confrontational. After all, they present a challenging context for honing our social skills, whether it be calling about a dubious bill or chatting over coffee with a potential customer. Others are self-styled hermits—"bless the [fill in the blank] and keep them far from us." (That's a quote from *Fiddler on the Roof*.)

Relationships are profoundly affected by words; thus we are not allowed to neglect all the sage advice from chapter eight. Words and how we use them are also shaped by the kinds of people we are, so we circle back again, this time to character. Who we are in relationship to God is definitive. "The lamp of the LORD (searches) human breath; it searches the inmost being (we know by now that this is 'rooms of the belly')" (20:27). The word translated "breath" here is the same one used in Gen 2:7—God breathed into *'adam* the "breath" of life. In other words, everything about us, the breath that sustains us and the core of our being, is in God's searchlight. That, if you will pardon my saying it, is breathtaking.

Starting Points

"Hatred stirs up strife; but love covers over all transgressions" (10:12). Please slow down again. This is about as basic—and important—as it gets. Our emotions are never in neutral when it comes to other people—those family members, politicians, employees, and dog walkers with whom we come in contact. To be sure, hate and love represent the extremities of the emotional spectrum, but emotions are built right into those "rooms of the belly" of each of us. Thus, we need to be mindful of how we are reacting and whether or not our reactions warrant a bit of transformation. And yes, even those most visceral (we might call them "gut") reactions can stay inside if we shut the doors on the "rooms."

"How," you ask, "can this possibly be done without stifling my true self?" In our environment, which values self-expression above self-control, the advice in this proverb is totally countercultural. It challenges us to "cover" the very serious wrongs that have been done to us; this is a more contemporary way of saying "transgressions." We are not talking here about minor lapses or temporary slights. This is the stuff that underlies anger, makes us harbor bitterness, and creates lasting enemies. The Lord requires us to love sufficiently to cover all of that. Powerful love is necessary to counter the natural anger and hatred that boil up in those kinds of circumstances. Powerful love involves acting, not just feeling. Difficult? Yes, but we are talking about relationships that will either fail or survive (and even thrive).

What might this look like? Here is another perspective, one that highlights the importance of established relationships: "At all times, a friend loves; and a brother (or sister) is born for adversity" (17:17). Love glues friends together through all the vicissitudes of life; family ties run deep. We long for this kind of emotional security, and we will do well to nurture it—actively.

Relationship Spheres

Our task is to chart a course through basic kinds of relationships, ranging from those involving hate-filled enemies to those involving good friends and family. We're going to see that the translation and interpretation of certain key Hebrew words is again a necessary step. First, however, one additional practical suggestion might help. The closest relationships, within our family circles as well as with intimate friends, are the most potentially vulnerable. It makes sense; we spend more time together, and this can be fertile ground for friction as well as fellowship. These bonds need to be guarded, especially from misunderstanding, jokes that are not felt as funny, or taking the relationship for granted.

Who Are Our Enemies and Why Does It Matter?

There are several possible Hebrew words that may be translated "enemy." The most common are "the one who hates" (*soneh*) and "one who is hostile" (*'oyev*). In the context of figuring out *our* enemies, their hatred and hostility have an object, and that is *us*. It seems this would give us every reason to avoid them as much as possible, give them a very wide berth, and maybe even offer a preemptive strike at them before they "get" us. But not so fast.

Jesus' admonitions to "turn the other cheek" and "go a second mile" have roots in the Torah (Exod 23:4–5) and in Proverbs. "When your enemy falls, do not rejoice; and when he stumbles, do not let your heart exult" (24:17). We must keep reading through the following verse: ". . . lest the Lord see and it is evil in his eyes, and he removes his anger from him (your enemy)" (v. 18). In other words, even though the person is actively hostile and has deserved his or her comeuppance, our gloating over this has an odd effect. It is as if part of the punishment was the shame of stumbling, perhaps a public occurrence, and God counts the added humiliation caused by our own reaction as "shortening" the deserved punishment. Instead of celebrating their downfall, we are to love our enemies—and that has yet another unexpected twist in terms of outcomes.

"If the one who hates you is hungry, give him bread to eat; if he is thirsty, give him water to drink; because you will snatch up coals over his head and the Lord will repay you" (25:21–22). Love is demonstrated by helping a hostile person who is in need of basic sustenance. Just to repeat: it does not mean suddenly wanting to embrace that person; it simply means acting to meet survival needs. The second verse has perplexed commentators, and I will not presume to solve the puzzle but will simply suggest this: enemies expect a corresponding hostile reaction—being hit when they are already down—and here is mercy. The coals may symbolize the shock to their system, or they may reflect a humiliation ritual. The latter has been suggested to have a basis in an Egyptian public ritual of carrying coals. Or it might be an added way of providing for the person—not only feeding for that moment but providing fire for continued warmth and food preparation. I am not certain where to land on this one.

What we do know is that the Lord will repay. But what does *that* mean? This verb is related to the well-known word *shalom*, which means more than "peace." It implies that everything will be set right. It is the same word used when a thief is required to pay back in order to restore the well-being of the person who was wronged (Exod 22:3–6). In this case, the person who has broken the circle of anger, hatred, and revenge by acting with mercy may be assured that all will be well.

Neighbors, Companions, Fellows, and Friends

Now we are treading into somewhat murkier territory. The Hebrew word *re'a* seems to cast a very wide net, referring basically to those who have some sort of association with each other. Thus, there are proverbs that use this word and describe bad neighbors, good neighbors, companions, and friends. Good neighbors are indeed friends, and the friend category interfaces with "ones who love." We'll pay a brief visit to each. In addition, a somewhat parallel term, *shakhen*, has connotations of dwelling near or with. Place is important for this association.

Let's confront the "bad neighbors" first. These might better be thought of as "bad fellows," and sometimes they are painfully close, just like neighbors. We are also warned against being one of these types. "Do not devise evil against your neighbor, the one who dwells securely with you" (3:29). The person who deceives his neighbor and then says he was only joking is likened to a madman shooting deadly arrows (26:18–19). We have studied this one in a previous chapter.

Apparently, the business of deception is not a minor lapse; Prov 16:29 presents it in terms of violence: "A violent person deceives his neighbor and leads him in a way that is not good." There is the very real possibility of giving false testimony against our neighbor (24:28–29; 25:18), and this too is deadly, for all the obvious reasons. We hear echoes of our prior study of truth and falsehood.

Less toxic but still in the category of the unwanted neighbor are those who constantly welcome themselves into our homes and, in the process, run the risk of becoming enemies (25:17). Then there is the person whom we have all encountered, perhaps that annoying college roommate. He or she gets up early in the morning, bellowing out "top of the morning to you," singing loudly, and heartily admonishing you not to be late to the 8:00 a.m. class again. It all indeed feels like a curse (27:14).

The hinge between potentially questionable companions and decent friends is illustrated in Prov 18:24. This proverb has its own ambiguities, just as do relationships and their outcomes. I will offer a rough translation. Words that are not in the Hebrew are in parentheses; their presence is already an interpretive move. "A person (and many) companions will be broken apart, but there is a friend who cleaves closer than a brother."

A number of modern translations read "may come to ruin," or something similar (ESV, NIV, NASB, NRSV, Lexham, HCSB), instead of "will be broken apart." The "broken apart" interpretation fits well with the contrasting second part of the verse: "there is a friend who cleaves closer than a brother." Of course, one of the ironies in this language exploration is that the English word "cleave" can mean either slice apart or stick together. The context necessitates the latter. It is the same word used in Gen 2:24: "A man shall leave his father and mother and cleave to his wife, and they shall become one flesh." We see the same word also in Ruth 1:14—Ruth cleaved to Naomi.

> We are going to explore the Hebrew of Prov 18:24 a bit more. "Companions" (re'im) is the plural of rea'. The next word in Hebrew has several significant components. It is a verb form that puns on rea', since it is formed from the same basic consonants. What this verb means, however, is not entirely clear in this context. Its consonants can convey the sense of being evil, when they are combined both in the form of a noun (ro'ah or ra' or ra'ah) and of a verb. If this is the underlying sense, then "come to ruin" is the better interpretation, and many translations have chosen to go this route. (We see the same juxtaposition of this verb with the meaning "come to ruin" and the noun ro'eh, "companion," in 13:20.) Because this combination of letters is also similar to those in the word for "companion" or "friend," several translations follow ancient versions (Greek, Aramaic, Syriac, Latin) and interpret it as having something to do with investing in friendship (KJV, NKJV with footnote, RSV). There is also a third possible meaning, "to be broken apart," though this occurs much more rarely. Nevertheless, it does fit here because this verb form is reflexive. If you are asking what on earth that means, put simply, the action expressed in the verb operates on the subject of the verb. For example, I would destroy my car when I run into a tree. In the process, however, I might also destroy myself. If I were describing this in Hebrew, the latter condition would necessitate a reflexive verb form. In the case of the clause we are looking at in Prov 18:24, it seems that the more companions a friend has, the more likely they are to be separated. Perhaps a poetic subtext is that something unsavory might be part of this as well. I love this stuff, but it is complicated; that's why it is a sidebar!

Good neighbors are friends and are often designated as those "who love." They love faithfully (17:17). They are candid when we need rebuke, even rebuke that wounds (27:6). They know when to keep silent, and they do not shame their friends (11:12). Proverbs advises appropriate treatment of friendships that cross generations, because they are particularly precious. "Do not forsake your friend or the friend of your father" (27:10a). We can imagine contexts in which this gentle reminder is essential. Those who are our parents' age are increasingly vulnerable and lonely as their network passes piece by piece on into glory.

Family Dynamics

Here comes another Pandora's box! Open the family lid and see what bursts out. Honoring parents is a steady theme in Proverbs, and it is interlaced with strong condemnation of those who shame their parents. Honor and disgrace set the contours for a number of these family scenes. Relationships between parents and children can be sources of joy—or not. In addition, the disgraceful wife steadily resurfaces. We do not want to be this woman, or be married to her! We will visit the dynamics among siblings of various stripes; relationships with brothers (or sisters) are tight but sometimes taut.

What It Takes to Be a Parent

Both fathers and mothers serve as exemplars of authoritative teachers (1:8; 6:20), and the father's instruction steadily beckons the young person toward the path of righteousness and away from slippery ways (2:1–8; 3:1; 4:1–4; 5:1, 7; 7:1; 13:1). The subtext here is that we parent and teacher types need to be worth listening to! There is a strong emotional component to these family networks as well. Wise children and those whose conduct is pure (20:11) are a source of joy to parents (23:24–25).

There are also accompanying heartbreaks. "A foolish son is destruction to his father" (19:13a); "a companion of gluttons disgraces his father" (28:7b NIV). It seems that parents end up far too often as targets of their children's active disdain and ill-treatment (23:22; see also 15:20). Why else would we find multiple proverbs warning against evil deeds with which children destroy elderly parents? "The person who curses his father and mother—his lamp will go out in the middle of darkness" (20:20). Robbing parents, and not even acknowledging that this is wrong, is akin to destroying them (28:24). "The one who destroys his father and causes his mother to flee is a son who brings shame and reproach" (19:26).

All of this is beyond reprehensible but sufficiently common that the cluster of proverbs in 30:11–14 that describe "those who . . ." starts with "those who curse their fathers and do not bless their mothers" (30:11). The list is not a pretty one. It continues with those who are pure in their own eyes but not washed of their filth; those whose very facial expressions are shaped by pride; and those who wield swords and knives to devour the poor (30:12–14). No consequences are given because we already should know the end of such godless behavior. But do we? Our culture is riddled with the blatant disrespect for parental authority and values that spirals down into these cesspools. (Simply surf the media outlets that are your territory.) Because this is so, there is merit in revisiting 30:17: "The eye that mocks a father and scorns obedience to its mother will be dug out by ravens of the valley, and the vultures will eat it." In Proverbs, the eye represents a person's character. Utter disdain for parents will be paid back by corresponding shame.

As a welcome contrast at this point, joy and proper pride cross generations. "Children's children are a crown to the aged; parents are the pride of their children" (17:6). We get the first part; all of us have smiled indulgently when grandpa gets his cell phone going and proudly shows the most recent photos of the grandchildren. They are carrying on *his* line, and they are, of course, the best grandkids ever. We are especially glad when this granddad is ours, and the photos are of us! We pause briefly on the second half of the proverb. This is talking about kids—maybe even teenagers, maybe college students—who are *proud* of their parents. That verges on countercultural and is a cause for thanksgiving.

There is more. Rather unlike our Western perspective, in ancient Israel gray hair and age were badges of honor (16:31; 20:29). You might say, "Yeah, right!" But that is because we are fed a daily diet of advertisements from lucrative industries whose express purpose it is to hide gray hair and other signs of aging. How very far we have ranged in so many ways from the fifth commandment to honor our fathers and mothers (Exod 20:12 [11]; Deut 5:16 [15])!

Threats to Marriage Relationships

When errant, under-disciplined children grow up, they end up as the fools so prominently parading through the pages of Proverbs. Worse yet, they bring these disastrous behavior patterns to *their* families. Proverbs contrasts the wife of noble character, who is her husband's crown, with the one who causes shame and is rot in her husband's bones (12:4). What a picture this is! The first wife is a source of joy, beauty, and pride. Women who are wise and prudent are repeatedly honored and are deemed gifts from the Lord (18:22; 19:14). In the second case, however, the husband's very skeletal structure, his substance, is being destroyed bit by bit. Eventually, he will crumple.

Among the less appealing women found in Proverbs is the complaining and quarrelsome wife; she is like constant dripping from a leaking roof (19:13b). Complainers, as we know, really cannot let issues rest. Experiencing one long night of a leaky and loud faucet serves us well at this point. That same image returns with additional wry observations to the effect that dealing with this woman is impossible. It is just as futile to try to hide the wind or hang on to oil as it is to stem the tide of negative words (27:15–16). The best antidote is retreat to a quiet place. Sometimes that is a pretty drastic move. Hunkering down on the corner of a roof (21:9; 25:24) beats staying in the house. We are talking about flat roofs that could be blisteringly hot in the summer or lashed with cold rain in the winter. Still better! Another option was to head for the desert (21:19), a place with sparse provisions but blessed peace and quiet.

At first, we may be amused by these pictures, but after multiple jabs it might get old. We wonder why *she* is so high profile. Why not grumbling husbands, too? Although it might not be entirely satisfactory, here is a reminder. Ancient Near Eastern texts were written with a male audience in mind. Thus, it is first a matter of doing rudimentary contextualization. More to the point, we are all to avoid being generic grumblers and fools — period. It is not a matter of giving a pass to cranky husbands.

Quarrelsome is one thing; seductive is at another level altogether. We have already seen that threat in chapters 2, 5, 6, and 7. Because our moral anchors have pretty much given way these days, we express dismay at the raw force of jealousy as it appears in Scripture. It is bound together with the fury of a wronged husband who will not show mercy (6:34). "Wrath is cruel, anger is overwhelming, but who can stand before jealousy?" (27:4). We try to dial down the rage, but we are obliged again to pause. A marriage vow has been broken, and there are consequences. God is likewise frighteningly jealous when his people break their marriage covenant with him.

It is about time for the contrasting picture, and our wait is worth it. Whoever authored the acrostic poem of Prov 31:10–31 could not say enough about the wife of noble character. In chapter 1, wisdom as the "I-don't-mince-words" cajoler offers everything in her arsenal to keep the young person from stupid choices. Now, this ideal, the completely "whole" woman, is the embodiment of wisdom itself. This woman is so appealing that no one in his right mind would want anyone else for a wife. Every young woman ought to be seeking *how* to get to this point.

Apart from quoting the passage, it is difficult to do it justice, so please open your text and read it along with this summary. Above all, the woman's husband has utmost confidence in her — and it is not misplaced. What a contrast this is to the tragically wronged husband of the adulteress! Likewise, her children are blessed by her constant provision, and they in turn rise up to call her blessed. She does not have to go to the gym to exercise; grinding grain every day and heading outside the door of her house to engage in commercial enterprises are her "treadmill." Fields and the marketplace are familiar turf. She does not seem to need a lot of sleep, and for that we envy her a bit. She stocks the equivalent of a food pantry, and the needy are not turned away. Her words are wise, her instruction is faithful, her demeanor is dignified, and above all, she fears the Lord. It does not get any better.

Lest we be tempted to shrug and say "well, this is just an ideal; it is impossible to lodge it in any kind of reality," we remember that there are a number of challenges in Scripture to live up to an ideal. The most prominent might be, "Be perfect, even as your Father in heaven is perfect" (Matt 5:48).

Siblings

Brothers (and sisters) get somewhat mixed press in Proverbs. There is no filter on the painful realities that sometimes characterize families. These may have to do with greed; all the brothers of a poor person hate him right along with everyone else who is retreating before his pleas (19:7). Experience tells us that money and inheritance lie at the bottom of many long-standing family feuds. On the other hand, the preference of a friend over a sibling may be a matter of simple proximity. When distress arrives in spades, it is better for all kinds of reasons to head next door for help, as opposed to cobbling together travel plans for heading to the other side of the country (27:10b). As we have already noted, a really good friend, one who loves, hangs in tighter than a brother (18:24b).

Looking through yet another lens, we see that offenses between siblings, whatever the cause, are nearly insurmountable. Walled cities and fortresses are the image (18:19). The subtext here might be that we do our utmost to preserve family ties, even though this is not always easy. Perhaps that is because, while we can choose our friends, our sisters and brothers are "ours" by default. Lest this sound as if siblings have landed irredeemably in second place, however, we close with 17:17: "At all times, a friend loves and a brother (sibling) is born for disaster." When the proverbial chips are down, blood is thick. We stick together.

Recap: Threats and Safeguards

With the family at the core of our ever-expanding circles of relationships, we close with several observations directed specifically to preserving family honor, unity, and strength. Critical threats to the family web include those whose feet "rush to evil" (1:16) and whose temptations drag younger family members into lives of rebellious and disobedient behavior, deceit to cover it all up, and contempt for parents. It does not take a rocket scientist to figure out that these choices often have public consequences. These consequences might even move into the legal realm, which ought to cause us to quail, if for no other reason than the overwhelming expense!

Nonexistent moral teaching and sloppy living on the part of parents are recipes for their children picking up the same habits. The one who brings trouble to the home empties that home of anything meaningful (11:29a). Such trouble might arise from greed (15:27a), and we can just imagine all the forms it takes. Internal chaos and long-term damage are fed by repeated arguments and intentional humiliation. This is particularly true in the delicate fabric of the family.

Proverbs counsels right choices and right actions. In the context of the family, two foundational choices will serve us well. The first is consistent, thorough, and loving discipline of children. While Prov 22:6 has often been narrowly interpreted as a promise, it is instead an observation regarding the necessity of a wise and steady hand in guiding a young person on the journey toward adulthood. "Educate a child according to his way," that is, in the way best suited to his or her own abilities and gifts. The consequence of this wise parental investment will be stable members of the next generation who contribute effectively to the best of their ability. The second choice involves grown members of the family. Proverbs enjoins delighted companionship in marriage (5:15–21) as the perfect antidote to temptations from the seductive character of that attractive woman or man at the office, both of whom ruin family loyalty and trust. Now it is up to each of us to choose these paths and walk steadily in them.

CHAPTER 11

Leadership, Justice, Poverty, and Stewardship

Introduction

It seems that we are in an endless political campaign of one sort or another, no matter when and where we live. It just so happens that as I am drafting this chapter, the United States is facing yet another presidential election. By the time the chapter is ready for you to read, that election will be over (and another one will feel as if it is just around the corner). In the meantime, we will have had extensive debate, no doubt far too many accusations made in haste and anger, some honest soul-searching in terms of what is best, and the inevitable spending of vast sums of money to convince us that someone really is the perfect person for the impossible job. I know; I sound cynical.

Nevertheless, here are the routine *and important* questions. Who is qualified to lead and why? What are their deeply held convictions on issues of community well-being? Which communities merit their attention? Do candidates hold to their convictions regardless of their audiences? Are they trustworthy? How do we prioritize our most pressing problems? What is the best path through economic hardship? Who needs to sacrifice? How should we think about national defense? How do we avoid being controlled by polls?

You know that these questions are not limited to the high-profile national election year cycle, and they are not solely lodged in North America. On every continent, they break through the surface of boardroom discussions, union negotiations, religious synods, gatherings of well-meaning volunteers, heads of villages, regular collections of schmoozers at the watercooler, and endless other circumstances. Regardless of the context, here is the problem in an oversimplified nutshell. Whenever we live in community, no matter how small or large, there is potential for friction because we do not all share the same perspectives on how best to flourish. We also do not all bring the same resources to the table. Some individuals seem to like the prospect of holding power, and this carries both good and not-so-good possibilities. More often than not, we rub others the wrong way. When that happens, fur flies, sparks fly, and perhaps other projectiles are in motion as well.

The issues that are central to honest and clearheaded debate about issues of national and community consequence are those that define this chapter. "Righteousness exalts a nation, but sin is a reproach to a people" (14:34). Leadership at various levels defines how we do justice, provide security, and effectively steward our resources, both human and material. Leaders are admonished repeatedly to effect justice for the poor. These are matters of public policy.

Qualifications and Responsibilities of Leaders

Imagine sitting down at the local diner for a breakfast-table discussion regarding ideal leadership. I'm guessing that no matter whether we pulled up our chairs in Kansas, Massachusetts, or Wales, the same basic qualities would surface. We might not envision implementing them the same way, but that is another step. Let's propose character qualities first. As I construct this list, I will confess to putting them in some order of importance as I see it. And that is where we could begin to disagree!

"Honest," we might say. "We want a person of integrity who tells the truth and is concerned for justice." Sounds good. How this broad matter of justice might filter down to individual segments of the population will be an issue for heated discussion as we move forward. Some of us might clamor for righteousness as well, but we have already seen that this trait is subject to misperception and misrepresentation. "Righteousness" is an old word, and besides, there is a growing tendency to separate public from private lives. But never mind. Let's continue our breakfast discussion. Security, both national and local, is front and center. How do we maintain it? How do the right to bear arms and gun control fit in? Economic security counts for something; economic prosperity and national security are intertwined, after all. We also want someone who can hold to convictions in the face of opposition from all quarters. At the same time, however, we really don't want this individual making enemies needlessly. The list might go on, but we are at a good point to see if there is any interface with Proverbs.

Here is what the Proverbs picture looks like. Chapter 16 focuses on kings in the slightly wider context (found in chapters 15 and 16) of the Lord as King. To be sure, many of us have not had "the king" at the top of our governmental structure, but I bet we can make the necessary conceptual transfer. The point is that human rulers should be a reflection of the Sovereign of the universe. That is a tall order. Further, Lady Wisdom claims that rulers reign justly because wisdom is present with them (8:15–16). We could wish that were the case more often!

Truthfulness and Integrity

Truthfulness is a top-level requirement, and it is intertwined with doing what is right and hating evil. In case that did not register, "doing what is right and hating evil" is another way of saying "righteousness." Part of this involves a gut reaction against evil, not a shrug and "whatever." Let us pause over several examples. "Faithful covenant love (*hesed*) and truth keep a king safe; his throne is founded on *hesed*" (20:28). Here is another one: "Lips of righteousness (in other words, those who speak the truth) are the pleasure of kings; and he will love the one who speaks what is upright" (16:13).

Proverbs recognizes the temptation for human rulers to lie—right along with the rest of us. "Just as it is not appropriate for a godless fool (*naval*) to speak too much, so also a leader must not lie" (17:7). The literal rendition of both halves of this verse uses the figure of lips. In the first case, it is "lip of excess." The second figure is "lip of falsehood." Neither sketches a particularly pleasant image, as we imagine flapping lips and the damage they do.

"Divination may be on the lips of a king, but his mouth must not be treacherous against justice" (16:10). What? Run that by me again—perhaps in somewhat different words. The word translated "divination" is generally used in a negative sense in the Bible, but here it might include anything that sounds really like an oracle from God. In other words, this leader is rhetorically persuasive and can sway his audience. We may be familiar with someone of this sort. The point is, his words must not counter true justice or the law.

"Doing what is evil is an abomination to kings, because with righteousness he (God?) will establish the throne" (16:12). This presumes, of course, that the rulers themselves have a solid sense of right and wrong embedded in their hearts. Have you noted that the book of Proverbs does not construct a zone around the king's private life? It is of a piece with his public life; it is a matter of character.

Maintaining Order and Justice

How does a good ruler keep order in a country? Proverbs gives us some brief vignettes, possibly distilled from challenging realities. "When a country transgresses, it has many princes, but a man who understands and knows will (rule) long" (28:2). "A ruler who is excessively oppressive lacks understanding, but the one who hates ill-gotten gain will prolong his days" (28:16). One military coup after another, for example, is evidence that the very fabric of a country has come undone. There is no moral center to hold it together. The second example indicates that oppressive and greedy rulers are evidence that the moral anchor is gone. As an aside, the promise of a long life may have carried more punch in cultures where assassinations of leaders were commonplace. Even a very quick scan through 2 Kings 15, for example, leaves us gasping with horror at one assassination after another. And they were supposed to be *God's* people!

Justice is not only good for the land; it has direct benefits for the ruler as well. This seems so obvious that we find ourselves wondering why Proverbs continues to play this tune. Answer? Because much as we might tell ourselves that we know this already, it has not necessarily penetrated to the point where it has been transformative. Thus, we say it again—and again. "Remove the wicked from before the king. Then his throne will be established in righteousness" (25:5). "A king who is just makes the land secure; but the one who takes gifts breaks it down" (29:4). "If a king judges the poor with truthfulness, his throne will be secure forever" (29:14). We will return to the matter of justice for the poor. In the meantime, having good advisers or counselors also helps. "When there is no guidance, a people will fall, but deliverance comes with much advice" (11:14). Presumably the advice we're talking about here is good!

The additional means for dealing with evil indicate that a good leader does not turn a blind eye to evil or do the classic "wink and nod." "A king sits on his throne to judge; he winnows with his eye all evil" (20:8). He *winnows!* With his eye. And he has the audacity to label evil for what it is. Whew! The winnowing process involved tossing large forkfuls of grain up in the air so that the wind would blow away the useless husks and other debris. In this case, the king's "eye" penetrates through all the rubbish, and it is sufficiently fearsome to send evil scurrying away. Even more aggressive means are sometimes necessary to eradicate the evil that just continues to rear its ugly head. "A wise king winnows out evil people; he makes the wheel run over them" (20:26). Use of this heavy wheel was actually the first part of the winnowing process. A wheel or sledge crushed the grain so that the chaff (so often symbolic of evil) was broken away from the kernels of grain. The procedure was completed as the heaps of crushed material were pitched into the air with the winnowing fork.

Consequences for the People

Depending on the character and actions of the king's subjects, they might expect either his favor or his wrath. Proverbs does not mince words; you did not mess with the king! Apparently, kings were not attempting to keep their poll ratings high by being "nice." Twice the king's anger is likened to the roar of a lion (19:12; 20:2). Outside the confines of the zoo, this experience would send shivers down our spines; the roar meant that prey was in sight, that prey was about to be the next dinner, and it might be us. In the second instance (20:2), we learn that anyone who makes the king angry could lose his life. We might do well to pause and be grateful if we are those privileged ones who do not live under tyranny. "The wrath of a king is a messenger of death, and a wise man will cover for it" (16:14). In a more extended warning, the "son" is urged to fear both the Lord and the king, keeping a healthy distance from those who are disobedient. Why? Because unpredictable disaster can suddenly arise from both the Lord and the king (24:21–22; see also 14:35).

When, however, leaders are pleased with their subjects, it is a source of relief and refreshment. "In the light of the king's face is life, and his favor is like the cloud that brings spring rain" (16:15). The last part of this verse depends on our knowledge of weather patterns in Israel. Spring rains are a particular blessing in the land, adding just one more boost of water to the crops before the dry season sets in.

Proverbs also has advice for us common folk about how to get ourselves on a leader's radar screen. "The one who loves a pure heart and whose lips are gracious—the king will be his friend" (22:11). "Do you see a person who is prompt in his work? He will stand before kings; he will not stand before those who are obscure" (22:29). Let's boil down that list: love what is right; speak well; do your work diligently.

Additional nuggets of common sense are doled out. "Do not honor yourself in front of the king and do not stand in the place reserved for important people. It is better that he say to you, 'Come up here,' than you being humbled before a noble one" (25:6–7). This sounds rather like something Jesus said, doesn't it (Luke 14:7–11)? "With patience an official may be persuaded, and a gentle tongue breaks a bone" (25:15). In the end, however, we are reminded that human rulers are only a small stand-in for the Lord himself. "Many are seeking the face of the ruler, but it is from the LORD that a person receives justice" (29:26).

Justice in the Judicial Systems and Beyond

If you have been reading the examples carefully so far, you already know that justice and concern for the poor were well within the purview of Israel's leaders. We have already discovered that honest court procedures receive specific attention in Proverbs. So do those circumstances in life that potentially rob people of dignity and justice. In other words, Proverbs is again speaking to us—today. Sadly, folks on the margins seem to be special targets for cheating, raw deals, and heavy-handed abuse of justice. What we often overlook as we politicize these issues is the Lord's role as Defender of the defenseless.

"The one who justifies the wicked and convicts the righteous person— both are abominations to the LORD" (17:15). Remember those "six things, no seven" that the Lord hates? It seems that we have an eighth to add to the list. Injustice at every level tears apart the moral fabric of God's world. "Punishment of the righteous is not good" (17:26a; see also 18:5). "A worthless (*belial*) witness mocks at justice" (19:28a). I'll say it again; these seem so obvious, but apparently they need to be said. This in turn says something about persistent shadows in tangled legal systems, no matter when and where we find them.

Oppression and exploitation have consequences. "Do not rob the poor person because he is poor, and do not crush the needy in the gate (i.e., in court), for the LORD will take up their case and will take their lives from those who take from (the poor)" (22:22–23). In case we missed it, the Lord is not about to give a pass to those who kick beaten people when they are already down. *God* is their Defender, and God's judgment will be measure for measure in the most severe terms. Not only does God obligate himself to respond on their behalf; we too are obligated. "Open your mouth for those who cannot speak; do justice for those who are passing away. Open your mouth; judge rightly; defend the poor and the needy" (31:8–9).

Proverbs does not know the category of "innocent bystander." We read: "Rescue those being taken to death; hold back those turning toward murder. If you say, 'Look, we did not know this,' does not the One who weighs hearts, understand? The One who keeps your life—he knows and will return to each person according to what he has done" (24:11–12). This passage has particularly reverberated through the decades since the Holocaust; it has also become a rallying point against those who turn a dull ear to the plight of unborn children. It ought to burst to the surface every time broken and vulnerable people are broken still further.

Community Concerns: Global and Local

Lest we think those horrifying circumstances are outside our borders (wherever those borders happen to be) or from another broken era, we need to look again. The urban gang described in 1:10–19 (see also 2:12–15) is the shadowy but lethal presence behind contemporary urban and suburban tragedies, terrorist attacks, and pervasive fear. These rebels celebrate theft and murder, mock anything that is good, delight in perversity, and entice young adherents to sign up. The same evil paths snake their way through communities over and over again. Injustice runs amok when we lose our sense of moral moorings.

We encounter dubious practices that lie outside the boundaries of the official legal system but that are still influential in matters of justice. In this sphere, Proverbs again tells us what life is like, not necessarily how it ought to be. Even though bribery, for example, is roundly condemned in the Torah (Exod 23:8), the realistic observer knows that bribes, plain and simple, work in the short run. Further, the slippery dividing line between a "bribe" (*shoḥad*) and a "gift" (*matan*) surfaces. Both terms are used in Proverbs.

> The one who profits by violence troubles his house,
> but the one who hates *gifts* will live. (15:27)

> A *bribe* is a stone of grace (i.e., something that has potential value)
>   in the eyes of its possessor;
> wherever he turns, he succeeds. (17:8)

> A wicked person takes a *bribe* from his bosom (i.e., in secret)
> to turn the ways of justice. (17:23)

> The *gift* of a person makes the way wide for him;
> it will bring him before the great ones. (18:16)

> A *gift* in secret will subdue anger;
> and a *bribe* in the bosom, strong wrath. (21:14)

Even a quick read through these examples tells us something else. Though bribes may work and we can gleefully shake hands (in the bosom, of course) over a done deal, there is a longer view that is more in accord with the Torah. We might suspect that this kind of perversion of justice is another matter the Lord hates.

Stewardship of Resources: Wealth and Poverty

Now we turn the lens again, this time peering at justice issues that are particularly bound up with wealth and stewardship of material resources. Proverbs depicts material well-being as a gift from God; it is evidence of God's blessing. "The blessing of the LORD is what enriches, and he does not add trouble with it" (10:22). "A faithful person will have abundant blessings" (28:20a). In the context of God's covenant relationship with his people, blessings and responsibilities intersect. The faithful person will intrinsically have a concern for justice, generosity, and proper stewardship.

Perspectives on Wealth

Wealth is the natural and expected result of diligence, and disciplined work is one consequence of good character. "In all toil there is profit" (14:23a). And "the wealth of a person is precious (and due to) diligence" (12:27b; see also 13:11b). From another angle, wealth grants a sense of security. "The wealth of a rich person is his strong city, and like a wall of protection in his thoughts" (18:11; see also 10:15a for the same sense).

At the same time, wealth can lead as well to unsettling insecurity. After all, those who own elegant and palatial houses install security systems. Some may pretend they do not own any resources, perhaps to avoid an endless stream of solicitors. Proverbs links this pretense with another human foible—pride. "There is the person who makes himself appear rich but has nothing; another pretends to be poor and has great wealth" (13:7). Proverbs also reminds us that material possessions are transitory:

> Do not toil to enrich yourself;
> be restrained according to your understanding.
> Does your eye fly to it (the wealth)?
> It is gone because surely
> it will grow wings as an eagle and fly to the sky. (23:4–5; see also
>   27:24a)

I have purposely translated the section here about "your eye flying" in a rigidly literalist and wooden manner. That's because I want to emphasize the vivid wordplay in Hebrew. When our eyes focus solely on riches, everything else fades before our covetous gaze, and the riches vanish as well. A contemporary illustration—painful for some—might be the compulsion some of us have to watch each adjustment up and down in the stock market. There are seasons when wealth gained does seem to fly away!

In addition to the "long perspective," there is a "deep" one as well. Simply put, there are matters of much greater consequence than the funds we have stacked up in our 401k. "Better is a little with the fear of the LORD than great riches but trouble with it. Better is a meal with vegetables when love is there than a fattened ox in the midst of hate" (15:16–17).

The Double-Edged Sword

So far, so good. Wealth handled with wisdom is a source of security and blessing in ever-widening circles. We know, however, what is coming next. Wealth is also a breeding ground for covetousness. "Covetousness" sounds slightly less judgmental than calling it what it is—greed. The craving for more and more, no matter how much it is, casts a shadow over our enjoyment of blessings, generosity, and security.

"*Sheol* and '*abbadon* are never satisfied, and the eyes of humans are never satisfied" (27:20). Just in case that needs a bit of interpretation, it runs like this. No one ever escapes the grave (the basic meaning of *sheol*). Death will never be full; there is always room for the next victim. What a ghastly image! Likewise, we keep feeding our greedy, insatiable impulses to have more of this and more of that, and those impulses just get fatter and more demanding. They are destructive and ruthless, not least because they rob us of our sensitivity to the suffering of those broken in body and spirit by poverty. A sole focus on wealth, whether from the standpoint of poverty or comfort, can breed moral and spiritual poverty.

The Plight of the Poor

Proverbs does not give much space to describing the physical aspects of destitution, notably gnawing hunger, no place to call home, insufficient clothing, and yawning uncertainty. Instead, it focuses on relational brokenness. As we expect by now, many of the observations are presented as antitheses, and we see even more starkly what is missing for those whose lives are ruined by poverty. "Even by his neighbor the poor person is hated, but many are those who love the rich" (14:20). "Wealth adds many friends, but the poor person is separated from his neighbor" (19:4). The same sentiment slaps him again several verses later. "All the brothers of a poor person hate him; how much more his friends go far from him" (19:7).

There is a further ever-present problem; it is far too easy to abuse the power that wealth brings and to turn it into oppression. "The rich rule over the poor" (22:7a), and "the poor plead with entreaties, but the rich answer harshly" (18:23). We might try to wiggle around this and say we have the underprivileged population's best interests in mind, but that is always a complicated declaration, and I do not pretend to be a political scientist.

Antidotes to Greed and Poverty

During the years that some of us are privileged to enjoy wealth, we have obligations. Possessions are to be used for good, the chief of which is to "honor the LORD with your wealth and from the first of all your produce" (3:9). The consequences are commensurate blessings in fields and vineyards (3:10), images that might be retooled as financial resources with which to help fight hunger, disease, and refugee crises in our social and geopolitical contexts. The case for living with open hands is repeated (11:24–26). These are gifts on loan from the Master of the universe, and thus they must be used in ways that contribute to the well-being of God's creation in its entirety.

As a corollary, when we are faithfully generous, God is not stingy. The one who gives to the poor will lack nothing (28:27a). "Do not withhold good from its (proper) owner when it is in your hand to do. And don't say to your neighbor, 'Go and return tomorrow and I will give to you when you have it with you' " (3:27–28).

At this point, let's revisit an earlier theme. Though they may be abandoned by family and friends—and that is hurtful beyond words—the poor are not abandoned by the Lord. God is not only "present" with them in some way that often defies our ability to make it sound reassuring (as in "the Lord bless you and be with you"—but how?); he is also invested in what they experience. In fact, the Lord takes note of the poor, those who abuse them, and those who rise up to help. No surprise that God has the entire situation well in his purview.

"If a person stops his ears to the cries of the poor, he too will cry out and not be answered" (21:13). This is a sobering principle: measure for measure. "The one who oppresses the poor shows contempt for the One who made him (see also 17:5a), but the one who is generous to the needy honors (God)" (14:31). The first declaration could be scary for those of us who squirm and turn our heads the other way when we are confronted with poverty. Add another factor. "The one who despises his neighbor *sins*, but the one who is kind to the needy is blessed" (14:21). In other words, this also has a *moral* component. It is sin to turn away from a destitute neighbor. Just a reminder that "neighbor" has a wide semantic range. Proverbs also emphasizes the positive motivation: "The one who is kind to the poor lends to the LORD; and he will pay him his reward" (19:17).

As we have seen already, there seems always to be one more angle in Proverbs from which to view the matter at hand. Agur's earnest prayer alludes to another source of tension in regard to possessions:

Two things I ask of you—please do not deny me before I die. Falsehood and lying remove far from me. Do not give me poverty or riches; just let me tear my appointed daily bread, lest I am sated and disown you and say "Who is the Lord?" Or lest I become poor and steal, and so dishonor the name of my God (30:7–9).

When we have all we think we need, it is far too easy to forget it all has come from God. Ingratitude is the next dangerous step. On the other hand, fear of wrenching poverty too easily leads to thievery. Agur prayed to avoid those two extremes; we should as well.

How Can We Possibly Sum This Up?

Nine hundred and fifteen proverbs—a collection that will demand our attention for the rest of our lives. The book of Proverbs has presented a good set of marching orders for our journey. They are terse, clear, and unavoidable. Here are seven: seek wisdom with every fiber of your being; practice righteousness; be truthful; love humility; exercise discipline; serve God and God's people; hate evil.

For Further Reading

Aitken, Kenneth T. *Proverbs*. The Daily Study Bible. Philadelphia: Westminster, 1986.

Camp, Claudia V. *Wisdom and the Feminine in the Book of Proverbs*. Decatur, GA: Almond Press, 1985.

Fox, Michael V. *Proverbs 1–9: A New Translation with Introduction and Commentary*. Anchor Bible 18A. New York: Doubleday, 2000.

———. *Proverbs 10–31: A New Translation with Introduction and Commentary*. Anchor Yale Bible 18B. New Haven: Yale University Press, 2009.

Hess, Richard. "Wisdom Sources." Pages 894–901 in *Dictionary of the Old Testament: Wisdom, Poetry and Writings*. Edited by Tremper Longman III and Peter Enns. Downers Grove, IL: InterVarsity Press, 2008.

Hildebrandt, Theodore. "Proverbs, Genre of." Pages 528–39 in *Dictionary of the Old Testament: Wisdom, Poetry and Writings*. Edited by

Tremper Longman III and Peter Enns. Downers Grove, IL: InterVarsity Press, 2008.

Kidner, Derek. *Proverbs: An Introduction and Commentary.* Tyndale Old Testament Commentaries. London: Tyndale Press, 1964.

Kitchen, Kenneth. "Proverbs 2: Ancient Near Eastern Background." Pages 552–66 in *Dictionary of the Old Testament: Wisdom, Poetry and Writings.* Edited by Tremper Longman III and Peter Enns. Downers Grove, IL: InterVarsity Press, 2008.

Longman, Tremper, III. *How to Read Proverbs.* Downers Grove, IL: InterVarsity Press, 2002.

———. *Proverbs.* Grand Rapids: Baker, 2006.

Murphy, Roland E. *Proverbs.* Word Biblical Commentary 22. Nashville: Thomas Nelson, 1998.

Sandoval, Timothy J. *The Discourse of Wealth and Poverty in the Book of Proverbs.* Leiden: Brill, 2005.

Waltke, Bruce K. *The Book of Proverbs.* New International Commentary on the Old Testament. 2 vols. Grand Rapids: Eerdmans, 2004–5.

———. "The Book of Proverbs and Ancient Wisdom Literature." *Bibliotheca Sacra* 136 (July–Sept. 1979): 211–38.

———. "The Book of Proverbs and Old Testament Theology." *Bibliotheca Sacra* 136 (Oct.–Dec. 1979): 302–17.

Whybray, R. N. *The Composition of the Book of Proverbs.* Library of Hebrew Bible/Old Testament Studies. Sheffield: Sheffield Academic, 1994.

———. *Proverbs.* New Century Bible. London: HarperCollins, 1994.

———. *Wealth and Poverty in the Book of Proverbs.* Sheffield: Sheffield Academic, 1990.

Zuck, Roy B., ed. *Learning from the Sages: Selected Studies on the Book of Proverbs.* Grand Rapids: Baker, 1995.

PART THREE

Coming to Grips with Mortality: Ecclesiastes

The author and reader of Ecclesiastes roam an intellectual landscape that seems overgrown with thickets and brambles. The glum observations of the author are entangled with brash claims that poke us readers like so many thorns. There is no apparent path through the darkened scrub; in fact, at first read, "going in circles" seems to describe this ramble. At the same time, there are occasional clearings into which the sun shines, and we pause, heartened by glimmers of hope and joy. Then we dive back into the underbrush, chopping our way through until we happen upon the next shaft of light from above.

In this biblical book, alternately exasperated outbursts and oddly reassuring affirmations are bound together in a textual briar patch. Scholars differ as to whether the predominantly gloomy outlook is a comfortable fit with theological orthodoxy. After all, "life is frustrating, tedious, and way too short" is not the theme of choice for your normal Sunday morning sermon. Nevertheless, Ecclesiastes unquestionably speaks to these very issues, expressing anguish over the brevity of life, the finality of death, and the pain of incessant injustice. Something about these pained outbursts echoes deeply in our own hearts.

CHAPTER 12

Is What Happens "Under the Sun" Meaningless, Transient, or Elusive?

Basic Questions: Title and Authorship

Figuring out how this book came to be called Ecclesiastes involves a brief line of inquiry. We start with the Hebrew title, Qohelet. (If you are hoping to pronounce this with authority, simply read the "Q" as you would a "K," pronounce the following vowel like "oh," and accent the word's second syllable.)

This title raises several questions. First, who or what was Qohelet? The word is related to *qahal*, which means "assembly" or "congregation." While the word could refer to an assemblage of teachings, such as are collected in this book, it is more likely that Qohelet was a leader who addressed a gathered congregation—in other words, a preacher or teacher. After all, the book is styled as Qohelet speaking (see especially 7:27). In light of what is recorded, however, this would be a rather unusual "sermon" or "lecture"! At any rate, Qohelet gathered the congregation, which in Greek is *ekklesia*—hence, Ecclesiastes.

Can we identify this preacher/teacher before we explore the details of the discourse? There are immediate echoes of King Solomon, the paradigmatic wisdom figure of the Old Testament. Qohelet's wealth and status enabled him to engage in varied projects (2:4–9) that required the kind of wealth that Solomon amassed as a result of commerce and tribute (2 Chr 9). The Hebrew emphasizes that the speaker engaged in all of these ventures "for myself"—nothing altruistic about him. Qohelet chose to investigate "all that is done under heaven" (1:13), and contemplated the potential pitfalls of that choice. Three times (1:17; 2:3, 12), he indicated that his research program ranged into areas of folly as well as wisdom; in other words, he knew it was dangerous but was compelled to understand more, to probe wisdom, and to continue his quest, even though despair lurked at every turn.

This sense of compulsion offers us another possible connection with Solomon as we encounter him in the historical books. There we see that a significant part of Solomon's utter foolishness was manifested in the realm of international politics. He married foreign women as political capital (1 Kgs 11:1–8), and they were his downfall. This sounds dismally parallel to Qohelet's treatment of women (2:8). This is a character lapse to which we will return.

On the political front, Qohelet was called "son of David, king in Jerusalem" (1:1) and "king over Israel in Jerusalem" (1:12). He referred to himself as being wiser than anyone who had ruled over Jerusalem prior to his time (1:16; see also 2:7, 9). The last reference might include non-Israelite kings if we make the Solomon connection. Otherwise, David was the only prior king "over Israel in Jerusalem," not much of a boasting point for Qohelet's claim to be "wiser than anyone" before him.

So far, we have trained our sights on Solomon but, as with many of our scholarly pursuits, there are questions. Here are just a few for now. After the first two chapters, the allusions to Solomon disappear, leaving the figure of the author more distant and shrouded. What happened to the imposing regal figure? And why? Further, while almost all of the observations, sober reflections, and pieces of advice come from an autobiographical posture ("I saw," "I declared," "I tested"), the first and last chapters of the book speak *about* Qohelet in the third person. Not only that, these beginning and end points attribute to Qohelet the unforgettable "Vanity of vanities! . . . All is vanity!" (1:2; 12:8 KJV, ESV). Does this literary masterpiece embed the memory of Solomon's wisdom in a later philosophical treatise?

Taking up another lens, the Hebrew word *qohelet*, which appears only once in the book apart from the aforementioned framework, is a feminine noun form, accompanied by a feminine singular verb. " 'See, this I have found,' said (feminine singular verb) Qohelet (feminine noun)" (7:27a). Now, *what* Qohelet found we will save for later. At this point, we will simply ask if there might possibly be intended parallels with the public and challenging preaching of Lady Wisdom in Prov 1:20–33.

A final arena for questions: the Hebrew vocabulary and grammar used in Ecclesiastes are noticeably different from the Hebrew of other biblical texts. Just what this means is not clear. A number of scholars have suggested that it reflects Aramaic influence, and indeed Aramaic was the lingua franca along the eastern Mediterranean Sea from the seventh century BCE onward as both the Neo-Assyrian and Neo-Babylonian empires made their presence felt. Others note that the text possibly includes some Persian loanwords. Persian dominance in this same region likewise did not start until the middle of the sixth century BCE. Specifically, Cyrus the Great issued the decree to send the Jews back to their land in 539 BCE. Solomon, on the other hand, ruled in the tenth century BCE. Having said that, these language cultures did not abruptly arise in the sixth century, and we ought not rule out possible language imports earlier. Even if the final composition of Qohelet was significantly later than Solomon himself, his figure does hover over our interpretation. See Daniel C. Fredericks, *Qoheleth's Language: Reevaluating Its Nature and Date* (Lewiston, NY: Edwin Mellen, 1988).

The Key Hebrew Word

"Vanity of vanities" is indeed the signature phrase, even though few of us twenty-first-century readers really know what "vanity" means, at least in this context. To remedy this, translators have produced an assortment of contemporary renditions, among them "Meaningless! Meaningless! . . . Utterly meaningless! Everything is meaningless" (NIV) and "Absolute futility . . . Absolute futility. Everything is futile" (HCSB).

But here it becomes perplexing. Labeling something "meaningless" or "futile" presumes a negative value judgment. It implies that the "something" in question could just as well not exist; it has no purpose. Few of us rest comfortably with that comprehensive assessment of our own lives, and yet that seems to have been the steady drumbeat of Qohelet. Yes, there are times when we reach that point, but is this what our *preacher* was really saying—over and over again? Was Qohelet a cynical curmudgeon, or do these outbursts point to something far more compelling?

The key Hebrew word is *hevel*, and it appears in some form thirty-eight times in the book. Its literal meaning is "vapor" or "breath"—an exquisite metaphor as Qohelet systematically linked it with just about every conceivable aspect of existence, good and otherwise. Every endeavor is like a breath; it is transitory—here and gone. The superlative form (*hevel havalim*) defines the framework of the book (1:2 and 12:8). Right from the start, Qohelet nailed the existential problem—anguish at the disappearance of the seemingly substantial aspects of life that end up being so painfully temporary. This is also how he wrapped it up.

Imagine a puff of breath on a cold day; you see it for an instant and then it is gone. What sobering associations are we to make with *hevel*? It is certainly fleeting; so is life. Under most conditions, breath is invisible. Likewise, most lives do not make indelible marks, epitaphs notwithstanding. In fact, Qohelet bemoaned the fact that there is no memory of those who have gone before us, nor will we be remembered by those who follow (1:11). We try to capture the details of our daily lives in writing; for example, we think we will preserve the deep emotional involvements about which we journal and reflect endlessly. But no one will read these writings—and we might well be embarrassed if they did. Even writing itself does not assure remembrance and continuity. Surely, this is a recipe for despair; Qohelet had it right.

At the same time, breath is necessary. To live, we must keep inhaling and exhaling. And with each steady breath, there is hope; breathing implies a perspective that *includes* the future. Furthermore, life has a predictable pattern that can cultivate quiet confidence. We will return to this, but for now we simply note the web of complications surrounding just one word. Maybe we are not to dismiss the repetition of *hevel* as simply a dark foil of futility and emptiness against which the rest of Scripture is to be read.

Obviously, no matter how we choose to interpret *hevel*, there is not a single English word that sufficiently conveys all the embedded implications. Furthermore, *hevel* is a noun, whereas many of the interpretive suggestions reshape it as an adjective. In other words, the insubstantial *nature* of breath itself characterizes even those most apparently *substantial* aspects of our existence. This is an existential collision!

For now, I am content with "transient" and "elusive" as interpretations, but there are others we must explore at least in passing. Michael Fox has landed on "absurd,"[1] and Robert McCabe has proposed "frustratingly enigmatic."[2] Think carefully for a moment: these translations are interpretations that move to a level beyond the basic meaning of "breath" or "vapor." They suggest an intellectual and emotional response to the perception that everything is fleeting.

What, after all, does the "absurd" look like to us? It taxes our cognitive patience. Our carefully woven webs of rational coherence are torn apart. The image that comes to mind is an exquisite spiderweb ripped to shreds by the thrashing tasty morsel caught in it. The web has worked, but it is also destroyed and simply has to be woven again—and again and again. We struggle to find logic and reason in the whole process but, as Fox notes, absurdity is based on contradictions. Claiming that something is "absurd" is ultimately a protest against God.[3] Or take McCabe's expression. "Enigmatic" might be manageable as a concept, but few of us live comfortably with enduring perplexity. Enter our emotions; we find it unbearably frustrating not to plumb the circumstances of our lives to their depths and finally understand. In fact, Eccl 3:11 gets at this very point; God has planted eternity (*'olam*) in our hearts but we cannot figure it out. We will have more to say about this passage later.

For the time being, however, let me backtrack a bit and make a brief case for "elusive" as a possible foundational interpretation of *hevel*. The puffs of vapor I noted above are not only here and gone. Even while they remain briefly within eyeshot, they defy any attempt to corral them into one place. So also the mind-boggling array of activities and possessions that Qohelet deemed *hevel*. It is no accident that another favorite expression of Qohelet is "chasing after the wind." That would be a frustrating, and possibly embarrassing, exercise. Try it.

If "vanity of vanities" has so shaped our cultural connection to Ecclesiastes, where did this expression come from? A simple explanation runs like this: the Latin Vulgate translated *hevel* as *vanitas*, "emptiness," which is clearly echoed in English "vanity," even though we rarely mean "emptiness" now when we use that word. In the Septuagint, we find *mataiotēs*. That is the same word Paul used in Rom 8:20 to describe the excruciating frustration the entire creation experiences in its bondage to decay.

Recurring Expressions

Like *hevel*, the phrase rendered "chasing after the wind" has sufficient ambiguity in Hebrew to tantalize our imagination. It may be translated "striving after the wind," "desire of the wind," "shepherding the wind," or "vexation of the spirit." These translations reflect two expressions found in Ecclesiastes, each of which uses a different but related Hebrew word in conjunction with "wind/spirit" (*ruah*). The central element in both expressions, however, is wind. This image is a perfect parallel with *hevel*, understood as breath. *Hevel* often occurs in conjunction with *ruah* in the text.

Wind defies in every way all attempts to overtake or master it; so also breath and vapor show themselves to be utterly elusive. Together, these are apt metaphors to describe life itself, as we try to capture the present and find that it simply slips past us. In fact, all human and animal life forms have the same *ruah* (3:19–21), and it is lost with death.

Two Hebrew expressions add to our picture of wind blowing every which way. They are *ra'yon ruah* (1:17; 4:16) and *re'ut ruah* (1:14; 2:11, 17, 26; 4:4, 6; 6:9). See Michael V. Fox, *A Time to Tear Down and a Time to Build Up: A Rereading of Ecclesiastes* (Grand Rapids: Eerdmans, 1999), 42–48. Several observations are in order. First, the initial words in the two phrases seem to be related; at least Hebrew lexicons put them together. Nevertheless, the three-letter verbal root from which both Hebrew words are built has a range of meaning, including "to shepherd," "to associate with," "to desire," or "to strive or long for" (BDB, 945–46). That is a lot of latitude. Second, it seems that the image disappears after the first half of the book, sort of like the wind dying down. In its place, there are two new expressions; one is a reference to not being able to rule the wind/spirit (8:8), and the second is "knowing the path of the wind" (11:5).

Once we have breath and wind blowing and swirling about, then we can bring the studied eye of the observer to the scene. Qohelet repeatedly said "I saw" (sometimes translated "I have seen"), and he frequently followed that declaration with "under the sun" or "under heaven." His was an honest perception of the way things are as we experience them with our feet planted firmly on the ground. This is the world of nature and especially of human nature. It is our fallen world, currently in "bondage to decay" (Rom 8:21). That means it is rotting away—transience with a vengeance.

Qohelet wove together these recurring expressions: "I have seen all the deeds that have been done under the sun, and see here, all are *hevel*, and chasing after the wind" (1:14). Both sun and wind appear early in the poem in chapter 1. "The sun rises and the sun sets, and to its place it hurries, rising there. It (the wind) goes to the south and turns to the north; round and round the wind goes, and on its rounds the wind returns" (1:5–6). This effectively sets the stage for recurring observations of the natural realm.

In the meantime, the complex and often perverse functioning of this world is troubling, and Qohelet turned it over and over in his mind: "I said in my heart . . ." He spoke frankly in terms that sound pessimistic, wounded, and even fatalistic. What he pointed out is disheartening; in fact, it is downright depressing to see wickedness in the place of judgment (3:16), oppression (4:1), evil done "under the sun" (4:3), and a lonely man who was never satisfied (4:7–8). And those are just the beginning.

Qohelet also felt the weight of what he saw. In fact, he called it "an (evil) task that God has set on humans in order to occupy them with it" (1:13; see also 3:10). Foremost in his perception was the toilsome labor to which humans are subjected. The Hebrew term (*'amal*) suggests back-breaking agony as the lot of the children of Adam and Eve. In fact, the connection with the curse on the ground in Genesis 3 practically slaps the reader in the face. The term *'amal* occurs in Ecclesiastes almost as frequently as *hevel* (thirty-five times). We are not to miss the utter paradox. Even grueling labor is—well, it is like a breath.

In this context, rich with allusions to a creation marred by painful toil and suffering, the author occasionally poses the rhetorical question "what profit . . . ?" or "what gain . . . ?" or "what advantage . . . ?" For example, "What does a man gain from all his labor at which he toils under the sun?" (1:3; cf. 3:9; 5:15). In any human economy, labor ought to bring reward. It's not so easy, Qohelet said. He declared the "profit" nonexistent: "everything was *hevel*, a chasing after the wind; nothing was gained under the sun" (2:11b). He maintained that all achievement is motivated by envy; it is simply *hevel* and chasing after the wind (4:4). Wisdom fares only somewhat better in this "profit" business; the observations are mixed. "Wisdom is more profitable than folly, just as light is better than darkness" (2:13; note also 7:12). But "what advantage has a wise man over a fool?" (6:8a).

Nevertheless, Qohelet did not allow his reader to wallow endlessly in an Eeyore mindset. One last recurring expression is vital to our own pursuit of wisdom. In the midst of *hevel*, chasing, profitless labor, and the "under the sun" perspective, it is God's gift to be able to "eat, drink, and find satisfaction" (2:24; 3:13; 5:18; 8:15). Our poet yanks us back to a counterintuitive reality, insisting that joy is equally important. This enjoyment rises through the clouds of *hevel* with the claim that delight is found only in God—"without him, who can eat or find enjoyment?" (2:25); "be happy and do good" (3:12). Qohelet urged the immediate appreciation and enjoyment of what is present and known, wholesome advice in light of the uncertainty of all that is yet to come.

Temporary Conclusions

Just like *hevel*, our conclusions for the moment are like vapor; they are temporary and subject to the press of additional exploration. Nevertheless, to this point we have noted the light and fleeting nature of breath and vapor, and the impossibility of chasing it. The contrast with heavy labor, pain, and frustration is formidable. And this becomes part of the overarching structure of the book, to which we now turn.

CHAPTER 13

A Masterpiece of Literary Structures

Introduction

With *hevel* and "I saw under the sun" firmly in our minds, now we venture farther into the text to explore the artistry that makes Qohelet's "sermon" so compelling. We start with the superlative expressions of anguish—*hevel* in the extreme—that bookend Ecclesiastes (1:2 and 12:8). These bookends are further joined by additional matching features, each of which we will explore.

In Ecclesiastes, the phrase "under the sun" is periodically and momentarily eclipsed by acknowledgment of what "God has given." These acknowledgments are what I like to call conceptual counterpoints. To wrap your mind around this phrase, think of your good friend listening to you complain for an extended time and then saying, "but there *is* another way to look at it." We'll come back to this just as Ecclesiastes does—repeatedly. That's how counterpoints work.

There seems to be a slow evolution of thought throughout the book. You may ask, "Doesn't every book, except for perhaps a select few, have developing thoughts?" To be sure, but here is the point for Ecclesiastes. As Qohelet relentlessly pursued his investigation, he moved from overwhelmingly negative attitudes at the outset to a more balanced outlook. It was not an easy path, and there were twists.

Finally, there are three delightful poems in the book, and poetry has structure. We'll savor especially the "time for everything" masterpiece that both reassures and unsettles (Eccl 3:1–8).

The Bookends

Now is the time to introduce the literary term *inclusio*. It is obviously related to "include," but we cannot stop there. In the context of Ecclesiastes, it means that a key element at the beginning of this literary masterpiece is mirrored at the end. We often use the term "closure." Think of an *inclusio* as a two-part literary pattern that brings closure by reminding the reader of the issues at the beginning that got this underway in the first place. It is a common characteristic of poetry from the ancient Near East. This is the place to visualize again our pair of bookends, one at the beginning and the other at the end of Ecclesiastes.

Ecclesiastes has a "thick" *inclusio* with three distinct parts both at the beginning and at the end. Here's how it works. The introduction (1:1) briefly mentions Qohelet, son of David, king in Jerusalem. The epilogue (12:9–14) is more expansive and describes Qohelet's teaching, careful reflection, and writing skills, while poking a bit of fun at the never-ending nature of the "academic" pursuit (12:12b). Both of these (1:1 and 12:9–14) are observations about Qohelet from an outsider, written in the third person. This pair of reflections constitutes the first part of the *inclusio*.

Moving inward from these remote endpoints are the superlative framing phrases ascribing the impermanence of vapor to all human endeavors: all is utterly *hevel* (1:2 and 12:8). We have talked about that already; this is just a reminder, and it is the second part of our "thick" *inclusio*.

Take one more step inward. Right next to the anguished sighs about *hevel* are two remarkable poems (1:3–11 and 12:1–7). Both echo themes from the tragedy of Genesis 3 as they frame Qohelet's intellectual pursuit. This is the innermost section of our three-part pair of bookends. As we explore these poems further, you will want to have your Bible open. It will make the next paragraphs more meaningful.

The heaviness of living in a fallen world presses in with the very first question: what is gained by hard labor (1:3)? Why not just curl up and ignore it all? Weariness and endless toil are clear reflections of the curse pronounced on the ground and on human effort (Gen 3:17–19). Sun and wind, both recurring themes in Ecclesiastes, appear to ride an endless merry-go-round. The intrinsic lack of satisfaction and constant desire for "something more" are pitted against monotony from every perceivable direction. Finally, the ultimate insult to the rigor of laboring through life is the oblivion that death brings. Memory, one of our most precious gifts, is gone—"to dust you shall return" (Gen 3:19).

At this point we uncover a subtle counterpoint of sorts. To be sure, it is so subtle that you might say I have entered into the land of wishful thinking. But let me try it on you. Yes, the repetitive nature of existence could lead to *ennui*, a word that captures the wholesale lethargy accompanying our state of mind when we are only partially engaged. Or it might be frustrating—caught in the same hamster wheel forever with no exit. Nevertheless, there is something stable about it, and stability is a gift in the midst of tumult. There come points where we actually crave routine.

That the natural world is indeed predictable has a degree of assurance in the face of uncertainty, especially the uncertainty associated with death.

This initial poem is mirrored by the masterpiece at the end. From the vantage point of pleasant light and vigorous youth (11:7–9), Qohelet's audience is urged to think ahead to the test that is old age (12:1–7). None of it is pretty—no gentle rocking chairs and cups of tea here. No, navigating through physical disintegration is a grim task, and it only goes one direction. No pleasure is found in these long days. Metaphors sear the picture into our minds. Vision dims into darkness, limbs once strong give way, teeth fall out, hearing fades, sleep escapes (12:2–4), all desire is gone, and terrors invade because of frailty (12:5). The vessel bearing life is shattered and "the dust returns to the earth as it was" (12:7a; cf. Gen 3:19). Even so, at this extremity Qohelet extended a profound source of hope; the spirit goes into the care of God who gave it (12:7b).

Conceptual Counterpoints

As we have already noted, there is a constant counterpoint in Ecclesiastes. First, we read the complaints about a transitory and pain-ridden life "under the sun," with its vexation, frustration, failure, despair, bewilderment, and injustices. Did you get it? There is a lot to trouble us "under the sun," and Qohelet never minced words. He faced it all head-on. On the other hand, he did not allow his readers to ignore the divine Presence. There are those fleeting moments when the presence and participation of God in the world are profoundly evident. Qohelet kept coming back to them, usually after the most outraged expressions of dissatisfaction. Just note the placement of the following passages in the context of a twelve-chapter book: 2:24–26; 3:11–17; 5:1–7, 18–20; 8:12–17; 9:7–9; 11:5; 12:7, 13–14. And if you are really into exploring, read them. You will find the same refrain echoing through the text. Here is its first appearance: "There is nothing better for a person than that he eat and drink and see the good in his work. I've also seen this; that it is from the hand of God. 'For who will eat and who will find enjoyment apart from me?' " (Eccl 2:24–25). Or consider 5:18–20 [17–19]:

> Look at what I've seen—that it is good and appropriate for a person to eat and drink and see good in all his work at which he labors under the sun, the number of the days of his life that God has given to him. For that is his portion. Thus, every person to whom God gives riches and possessions and empowers him to eat from them, to take up his lot and to rejoice in his labor . . . this is a gift of God. For he will not

remember much the days of his life because God keeps him occupied with joy in his heart.

So, back and forth, back and forth. This is conceptual parallelism or counterpoint on a large scale, with the themes repeated over and over, just like breathing (*hevel*). And this overarching literary structure helps to convey the message that is also clearly present in the words. Heartache, despair, and pain are more prominent because they make up the majority of each person's experience; they create a steady and sometimes overpowering rhythm. Nevertheless, God *gives*, and what he gives is sufficient.

Evolution of Thought

Interwoven with the oscillating counterpoints, Qohelet slowly, sometimes haltingly, moved from raw anguish and self-absorption at the outset to a more mature outlook toward the end. Here is what he sounds like in the early chapters:

> With great wisdom is great anger, and the one who adds knowledge adds pain. (1:18)

> And I, I hated all my toil. (2:18a)

> I turned and I saw all the oppressions that were done under the sun and the tears of the oppressed, and there was no one to comfort. (4:1a)

Continuing on his exploratory journey, Qohelet detoured into the space occupied by the house of God (5:1–7). It was a sobering visit; above all he was impressed with the need to keep his mouth shut, particularly in the matter of making vows to God. It is a fool who approaches God with no sense of remorse over evil and with an excess of words. Qohelet twice used the figure of dreams to illustrate the dangerous potential toward sin that lies in an excess of words. The parallel is compelling; dreams come and go haphazardly and are beyond conscious control.

The text is particularly emphatic about vows, words uttered with moral intent in the presence of God, and the necessity of carrying through on them. Recognizing that God is actively and personally responsive to words, Qohelet's advice is simple and profound: listen, and fear God. That is sufficient.

What happened after this house-of-God visit, however, is equally striking. Qohelet's initial perceptions of transience, of wind and vapor, developed another very real dimension. Now, he saw evil; sometimes he called it "sickening evil" (5:13, 16 [12, 15]; see also 6:1–2). This observation is not absent earlier (see 2:21), but here it surfaces as a contrast to God's presence, and the emphasis intensifies: "This is an evil . . ." (9:3) and "There is an evil . . ." (10:5). Death lurks behind this evil, and our customary avoidance of death will not do. "The day of death is better than the day of birth; it is better to go to the house of mourning . . . for this is the end of all humankind, and the living will set it on his heart" (7:1b–2). Contemplating death and mourning is better than the frivolity in which the author had also engaged. Naming "evil" is a moral obligation, neutral objectivity is distinctly out of the question, and the end of the matter is the basic need to fear the judgment of God (Eccl 8:12; 11:9; 12:13–14).

But here is another "nevertheless." Along with his long, hard look at death, Qohelet seemed more and more capable of standing back, folding his arms, and taking verbal potshots at fools and their ill-fated enterprises (7:1–12; 10:1–20). His stinging observations sound a good deal like the proverbs we have studied. Many of Qohelet's proverbs are evaluative; recognition of something that is "better" implies the ability to discern between good and evil. The memorable word pictures and tidbits of advice encapsulate keen comments about nature and human nature. The fool is prominent, illustrating characteristics to avoid. Reversals and ironies abound, chance is acknowledged, and yet there is also some degree of predictability in cause-and-effect sequences. There comes a point, however, beyond which advice and observation cannot penetrate. The mystery of God's creation is likened to the miracle of life ("bones") developing in a mother's womb (11:5). Humankind is given the mandate to be active stewards of creation in spite of the fundamental inability to predict or control the outcomes of those endeavors (11:6).

In sum (for now), Qohelet moved from self-absorption to fear of the Lord, from frustration at life's vexations to common sense.

"For Everything a Season"

In the sidebar, you can see the poem in 3:1–8 as it appears in the oldest complete manuscript of the Hebrew Bible. As you look at this and I venture into an explanation, keep in mind that we read Hebrew from right to left. On the right-hand side, we encounter each of the defining events that shape the development of this poem. We might think of these as bullet descriptions. As we read, they are our first impressions and they are constantly changing and modulating. In the left-hand column is the repeated word for "time," alternating with "and time." It is the constant. In between is an empty, undefined interval. Even this visual impression is compelling.

	לַכֹּל זְמָן וְעֵת לְכָל־חֵפֶץ תַּחַת הַשָּׁמָיִם:
עֵת	לָלֶדֶת
וְעֵת	לָמוּת
עֵת	לָטַעַת
וְעֵת	לַעֲקוֹר נָטוּעַ:
עֵת	לַהֲרוֹג
וְעֵת	לִרְפּוֹא
עֵת	לִפְרוֹץ
וְעֵת	לִבְנוֹת:
עֵת	לִבְכּוֹת
וְעֵת	לִשְׂחוֹק
עֵת	סְפוֹד
וְעֵת	רְקוֹד:
עֵת	לְהַשְׁלִיךְ אֲבָנִים
וְעֵת	כְּנוֹס אֲבָנִים
עֵת	לַחֲבוֹק
וְעֵת	לִרְחֹק מֵחַבֵּק:
עֵת	לְבַקֵּשׁ
וְעֵת	לְאַבֵּד
עֵת	לִשְׁמוֹר
וְעֵת	לְהַשְׁלִיךְ:
עֵת	לִקְרוֹעַ
וְעֵת	לִתְפּוֹר
עֵת	לַחֲשׁוֹת
וְעֵת	לְדַבֵּר:
עֵת	לֶאֱהֹב
וְעֵת	לִשְׂנֹא
עֵת	מִלְחָמָה
וְעֵת	שָׁלוֹם:

The poem starts with the extreme points of our existence, birth and death, neither of which is subject to my control or yours. It ends at a similarly overwhelming place: wars scar whole continents and cultures, while peace is elusive—perhaps like *hevel* itself. In between these endpoints is a remarkable structure. (Engage in the sidebar exercise at the end of this chapter in order to explore further this exquisite verbal architecture.)

Events parallel to starting and stopping life follow the opening volley—planting and uprooting, killing and healing, breaking down and building up. We plan these enterprises; they are intentional actions. What's more, life's experiences are balanced, and both good and evil are to be expected. But just note: in the poem, these good and evil counterpoints are not presented with uncompromising rigidity. In fact, positive activities quickly come to be overshadowed by negative. Killing and breaking occupy the first place in their pair structures. There is something potentially unsettling about that, and it continues into the sphere of our emotional responses. Weeping and mourning take precedence over laughing and dancing. Is it because life's dark places so overshadow the bursts of joy? Chapter 7 will suggest that as well.

Many of these "times" are characterized by mundane and seasonal choices that unfold on the home front and in the fields. Such activities as planting crops, constructing stone homes and walls, mending, and looking for lost items were the substance of village life in the ancient Near East. We have our own counterparts. They might include raking leaves and cutting the grass, surviving the morning and evening commutes, and fixing the leaky faucet. These routine activities, however, are sandwiched between the stark reminders of life and death, war and peace. Those are uncompromising.

A Resting (and Restless) Point

The poem ends; seasons and times are duly noted and some sense of stability, even if tentative, is gained. But now there is another wrinkle. God has made everything lovely in its *time*, and there is a profound sense of *eternity* planted deep in the hearts of humankind (3:11a). We sigh audibly in relief; time and eternity are drawn together in our hearts—a mystery, to be sure, but one that reassures.

One problem: it is impossible to *know* anything beyond the present; neither the past nor the future is really accessible (3:11b). The disappointment is palpable, and these issues of time are not left alone. Our poet returned to them later in this chapter and beyond as well. Nevertheless, transcending temporal uncertainties is a clarion call to trust God and to act in accordance with belief in God's providential ordering of events. The premise that what God does will endure forever (3:14) introduces a forceful moral component into the way humankind chooses to deal with the vicissitudes of life; people are to fear God because the injustices of all time, past, present, and future, will be brought to judgment (3:15–17). That prepares us for the next chapter.

Try an exercise and "map" the positive and negative valences in the poem in Ecclesiastes 3. It might look something like the following chart, although I suggest it with caution because it does introduce a rigidity into the poem that is likely not intended. Explore the changing positions and connections among each element. Note that the most "extreme" points at the beginning (birth) and end (peace) frame the entire poem as ultimately positive.

First Position	*Second Position*
To be born (+)	To die (-)

Actions

To plant (+)	To uproot the planted (-)
To kill (-)	To heal (+)
To break down (-)	To build (+)

Emotional Responses

To weep (-)	To laugh (+)
Mourn (-)	Dance (+) [*different Hebrew forms from the others in the poem*]

Actions

To cast away stones (-)	Gather stones (+)
To embrace (+)	To distance from embrace (-)
To seek (+)	To lose (-)
To keep (+)	To cast away (-)
To tear (-)	To sew together (+)

Intentional Choice and Emotional Response

To keep silent (?)	To speak (?)
To love (+)	To hate (-)

States of Being (macro-level)

War (-)	Peace (+)

CHAPTER 14

Coming to Grips with Mortality

Reminders

So far, we have *hevel* as a defining motif. It is joined by allusions to life "under the sun," the pursuit of wind, and matters of profit. All of those themes recur, like waves beating against a shoreline. We have observed toil and labor, residue of the Genesis tragedy. Evil is everywhere, and it is felt! At the same time, a slight turn of the head and we are prodded toward enjoyment. How does all this come together? Does it?

We poked our way through layers of the text and found balance and symmetry, especially at the beginning and the end of the book. The swinging pendulum of the "time" poem in chapter 3 reminded us of steadiness, at the same time that it nudged us toward a bit of uncertainty. Of course, using the term "pendulum" is an anachronism, but an apt one. The "back and forth" movement captures the counterpoint that we all experience in our travels through life. That oscillation is also captured in the larger pattern found throughout the book. Our major time and energy investments in life have a decidedly grim note to them, and the author reminds us of that again and again. Nevertheless, those reminders are punctuated by glimpses from above. Now, we are going to probe each of these further.

What Is Qohelet's Crisis? A Summary

Here it is in a nutshell: no human enterprise, no matter how earnest and valuable, is sufficient. "Sufficient for what?" you might ask. Just wait; that's part of what we need to address. In the meantime, however, ponder this brief summary of our lives "under the sun."

First, the more knowledge and wisdom we acquire, the more anger, vexation, and pain accompany them, especially because wisdom is not always appreciated. Next, we expend a lifetime of effort, but we have to abandon the very things we strive for. Third, contrary to our culture's incessant messages, pleasure provides no lasting satisfaction, and yet the desire for pleasure seems insatiable. Fourth, the injustices of life are inescapable. Related to that, what good does it do to try to be righteous? The wicked seem to prosper quite nicely.

Here is the capstone: death threads its way through Qohelet's reflections. Everything we deem substantial is but breath, and with death even that breath vanishes. Even though we long to make a mark in this sad world, in the face of inevitable death lasting personal importance is highly unlikely. There will be an antidote to this crisis, but that does not reduce the impact of the blows, especially as they come one after another. We will address each of these in the order in which they first appear in the book.

Unpacking Details: Knowledge and Wisdom Have Limits

Qohelet's opening observation is this (1:13): in order to keep humans occupied, God laid an "evil task" on us. Whether we translate the adjective as "evil" or soften it with "heavy," it still may rattle our comfortable theological cage. We need to clarify this declaration a bit. Is the "task" solely the pursuit of wisdom, or does it include the whole of "what is done under heaven"? Let's presume for now that it is the more narrow focus on wisdom. The same sentiment is echoed in 3:10–11—God has given a task to humans to keep them busy. That task is dealing with the frustration of having knowledge of the fabric of the created order but not having the capacity to put it all together.

> It will be helpful to explore just briefly the range of possible translations for the Hebrew word *ra'*. Its basic meaning is indeed "evil," a strong word that carries moral connotations. Depending on the context, this term may be rendered as "trouble," "disaster," "distress," or "calamity," and it can be both a noun and an adjective, just as "evil" is in English.

It is ironic, isn't it? Wisdom and knowledge are tantalizingly present, almost within our grasp. Almost, but not quite. Instead, they remain just beyond our reach; they are deep, profoundly deep. In fact, Qohelet used the expression "deep, deep" (7:24) with regard to this quest. We'll get there eventually, but for now chapter 1 requires more attention. Some things are irreparably twisted (1:15). We can see distortions but are incapable of intervening. Shortly thereafter, Qohelet landed anger, anguish, and pain right at the doorstep of increased knowledge and wisdom (1:18).

We understand this; consistent attention to the world outside our own small spheres is deeply troubling. Part of us wants to turn off the news.

After the introductory first chapter and the description of his own pursuits in 2:1–11, Qohelet adopted a rather suspicious ambivalence in regard to wisdom. Agreed, it is better to be wise than foolish, just as it makes more sense to walk in the light than in the dark (2:13–14). That's pretty obvious. Nevertheless, something more ominous was on Qohelet's mind:

> And I said in my heart, "What happens to the fool will also happen to me. Why have I become more wise?" And I said in my heart, "This also is *hevel*." For there is no memory for the wise or the fool that is lasting. Already in the coming days, everything is forgotten, even how the wise dies with the fool. (2:15–16)

The counterpoint continues. Wisdom and knowledge keep company with joy, and all are gifts from God (2:26). And yes, a significant contrast between humans and animals centers on intellect. Nevertheless, Qohelet prodded his audience back to a grim reality. Both humans and animals have the same breath, and when it is gone they end up as dust (3:18–20). To be sure, wisdom with poverty trumps an old and foolish king (4:13). Perhaps this is a veiled allusion to Solomon as he ended his reign far removed from his earlier wisdom.

Indeed, wisdom is protective (7:11–12), gives strength (7:19), and enhances the person who possesses it (8:1, 5). But Qohelet's ambivalence surfaces again. Wisdom is best found in the house of mourning; attending funerals helps us regain a proper perspective on everything (7:4–5). Further, wisdom is fragile; "oppression drives the wise into madness" (7:7). At this point, we are reminded of 1:18—the more wisdom and knowledge, the more anger and pain.

In the face of wisdom's apparent inaccessibility, Qohelet tried another approach. He set himself to the painstaking task of documenting everything (7:23–25). The relevant word is *heshbon* (vv. 25, 27; see 9:10 and a related word in 7:29), and it indicates a thorough tally. But even that failed! Qohelet was no further ahead. He seemed to pause and revisit his previous thoughts: proper times, ignorance of the future, fleeting thoughts on wickedness and justice (8:6–14). He tried once more to sort it all out. "I set my heart to know wisdom . . . [but] man is not able to figure out what has been done under the sun; in all that man labors to seek, he will not find. And if a wise person says he knows, he has not been able to find out" (8:16–17).

One final volley at wisdom: every advantage that might be expected from ability, brute strength, well-honed intellect, and elusive wisdom is eradicated by "time and chance" (9:11–12). To twist that knife in the open wound, Qohelet told a story (9:13–18). Once upon a time, there was a poor but wise man whose wisdom actually saved a threatened city. We're not told how. In fact, all we learn from this story is that the poor man's wisdom was despised and he was forgotten. What irony! Oh yes, wisdom is better than the powerful instruments of war, but the story ends on an enigmatic note: "but one person who sins destroys much good" (v. 18).

Substantial Investment in Work Vanishes

As I mentioned above, the Hebrew word for really grueling labor, 'amal, rivals hevel for the number of times (thirty-five) it occurs in the book. The paradox of calling heavy labor a mere breath stops us in our tracks if we are reading attentively. 'Amal is also linked with "chasing after wind" (2:11; 4:6), an equally arresting image to join with heavy labor. Again, Qohelet did not mince words. "I hated all my labor at which I labored under the sun" (2:18). Eight times the word appears in a repetitious pair such as this; even the repeated words feel heavy.

All aspects of life are evil and a vapor, because that for which we labor passes out of our control, a crisis of significant proportions (2:19–22). No wonder Qohelet continued to ask "What's the use?" or "What gain?" as he talked about work (1:3; 3:9). The emotional anguish associated with the entire enterprise is overwhelming. Tainted motives, envy, and lack of contentment prompt all human achievement and drive a person to end-less striving (4:4–8; see also 6:7). And yet the fool who does not work but folds his hands is one who "devours his flesh" (4:5). Relentlessly, Qohelet pressed the point. Insatiable desire, ever-increasing consumerism, and hoarded wealth only bring despair because we take nothing from our labors past the threshold of death (5:10–17 [9–16]; see 6:1–6). It is all a "sickening evil" (5:13, 16 [12, 15]; 6:2), utterly destructive when the fabric of our very being has become entangled with greed.

Before we labor on, we should remind ourselves of the counterpoints that shape this entire book. Labor is also a good and satisfying gift from God, and joy accompanies it (2:24–26; 3:13; 5:18–20 [17–19]; 8:15).

Pleasure and Joy Are Also Transitory

Given our cultural emphasis on leisure, we might be inclined to place pleasure firmly in the sphere of relaxation and rest. Qohelet, however, pursued pleasure actively; this does not sound like a leisurely endeavor.

So what *is* pleasure? Is it different from joy? Some of us are suffi-ciently influenced by C. S. Lewis' *Surprised by Joy* that we separate them. We presume that joy comes unexpectedly and is a more profound experi-ence, while pleasure is more superficial. But not so fast. A single Hebrew word means "pleasure," "joy," and "gladness," and it shows up in Eccle-siastes in both positive and not-so-positive contexts. For example, Qohe-let tested and pursued this positive experience energetically. At the same time, he was skeptical, knowing pleasure ultimately fails (2:1–2, 10–11). He said that the heart of fools is in the house of pleasure (7:4). Neverthe-less, there is nothing better than to enjoy life and work, bread and wine (2:24–26; 3:12, 22; 5:18–20 [17–19]; 8:15; 9:7; 10:19; 11:8). This kind of plea-sure is therapeutic. In fact, it is a command: "Be joyful (or, take pleasure), young man, in your youth . . ." (11:9). Always the same word.

The shallow side of this pleasure can manifest itself in foolish laugh-ter. "Laughter is madness" (2:2), vexation is better than laughter (7:3), and the laughter of fools is like crackling thorns under a pot (7:6). Just for the record, folly occasionally has a sobering intersection with Qohelet's inces-sant pursuit of pleasure (1:17). One sphere in which this might be more evident is our relationships. Qohelet was muted in this regard, but realistic. Companionship is essential (4:7–12), but relationships can be bitter (7:26).

Injustice and Oppression Loom

The matter of injustice was a bit of a latecomer to Qohelet's observa-tions, but it vexed him increasingly, especially since he saw it invading every sphere. The deadly specter of evil lurks around every corner in his discussion. As goods and produce drift away from our control, it is a "sickening evil." These are the words of a consummate realist. Wicked people often prosper in the present; that is injustice (3:16).

The same observation surfaces again in conjunction with inadequate court procedures: when the sentence against an evil person is not ex-ecuted quickly, then human hearts are filled to do evil (8:11). In the mean-time, Qohelet probed more deeply. Injustice and oppression don't just happen; they are intentional and systemic. Insatiable greed at every level is the culprit (4:1–2; 5:8–10 [7–9]).

To be sure, in the wider time frame, God will judge both the righteous and the wicked, even though human judicial systems fail miserably (3:17; see 8:12–13). That judgment, however, is in the future. And speaking of divine justice, there is one more consideration. Add to human injustice the occasions where humans are "robbed" when God gives humans ev-erything that seems valuable but takes away their lives before they can enjoy the accumulation of goods (6:1–2). This too is *hevel* and leads to the crux of the human crisis—death.

The Culprit Is Death

Each of Qohelet's observations has as its backdrop the inescapability of death. The same grim encounter overtakes the wise and the foolish, the righteous and the wicked (2:14–16; 9:1–3). Not only do all of these die; they are not remembered (cf. 1:11). Humans as well as animals all return to dust (3:18–20). After being given the mandate to care for the earth (Gen 2:15), being reduced to dust was a searing reminder of the corruption of sin and death (Gen 3:17–19).

Find Annie Dillard's *Pilgrim at Tinker Creek* and read the chapter entitled "Fecundity." The parallels with Qohelet's sentiments about death are striking. How would you characterize the despair expressed in both of these texts? At the same time, note the differences, particularly in terms of Dillard's apparently jaded view of God. By the way, please read further in Dillard. It is a bit unfair to her to read only this one chapter!

Our view from under the sun was unsettling enough; now the contrasting shroud of darkness lowers an even heavier burden (2:13–14; 5:15–17 [14–16]; 6:4, 12; 11:8; 12:2). Even though there is a suitable time for everything (8:5–6), no one has any power over the day of death (8:8). In other words, the steady pendulum represented in chapter 3 stops midswing. The images of active life—the cord that binds, the bowl and pitcher that carry sustaining water—are shattered (12:6). And we have no idea when this grim event will be marked on our calendars. Time and chance happen to everyone (9:11).

There is an end to all passion and activity, and the destination is *sheol* (9:6, 10). This utterly dismal prospect and the terrible uncertainties prompted ambivalence in Qohelet's own reflections. At one point, he declared that the dead and unborn are better off than the living because they do not need to live with evil (4:2–3), but he countered his own claim later on: life is better because, cruel as it might be, the living still have memory, deep emotions, companionship, and the prospect of personal engagement (9:4–6). There is one added benefit: wisdom is found in the presence of death (7:1–4).

One more point for now. Yes, all living creatures came from dust and to dust they will return (3:19–20). Qohelet went on to ask: Who knows the ultimate end of the spirits of these creatures (3:21)? The question remains unanswered in this context, but the reader who ventures back to Genesis and follows the trajectory of the biblical narrative toward its final dramatic end *does* know.

Response to Crisis: Justice and Hope in Judgment

This chapter has dealt with crisis—our crisis as humans in this broken world. Thus, just as Qohelet did, we pause for this brief reminder. We neglect the radically altered perspective we gain in God's presence to our peril. Because Qohelet's world was intolerably dark, the faint glimmers of light when God is mentioned are all the more compelling. God *does* supply what humankind needs, notably time and stability (3:1–14), knowledge, work, pleasure, and relationships (2:24–26; 4:9–12; 5:18–20 [17–19]; 9:9). Oddly, we can rest in our own inability to understand the work of God, because *it is his work*; he is the Maker (11:5). So we do our work faithfully and trust his sovereign hand to oversee what will be successful.

In spite of egregious injustices in this temporal sphere, God's justice will, in the end, set those things right (8:10–14). In the meantime, Qohelet issued a call to execute justice where possible (8:11), enjoy God's gifts responsibly, and bear in mind the disciplining prospect of judgment (11:9). At the crux of this counterpoint lies the ultimate paradox. Unassailable hope and meaning are found in the prospect of judgment. Nothing is trivial, no injustice will be overlooked forever, and fear of the Judge will be the best security (3:17; 12:13–14).

Michael Fox has addressed the conceptual frameworks of wisdom, labor, and joy, noting that a sage would seek sensory experience as a path to insight. Thus, it is no surprise that Qohelet set out on the quest he described. His "heart" had a central role in his initial investigations and perception in 1:12–2:26 (*A Time to Tear Down*, 77–78). After that, its role diminished.

CHAPTER 15

Ecclesiastes Conundrums

Introduction

This is an exploratory chapter. In fact, it stakes out the same kind of adventure in which Qohelet himself engaged. He took on the knottiest issues in life and seldom arrived at satisfactory solutions. That did not preclude his trying. In this chapter, we will do the same with several interpretive challenges that simply defy resolution; that is what a "conundrum" is. And yet, because we have the same inquisitive spirit as Qohelet, we are drawn to them. I will suggest various lenses through which to view these passages, without presuming to give the last word.

Both puzzles appear in chapter 7, which, as we have already seen, starts with entirely counterintuitive proverbs that front-load encounters with death. In fact, everything associated with death is stated here to be better than the usual joys of life. That said, we are led on a brief trek past crackling thorns, foolish laughter, madness, and bribes (7:6–7). Qohelet offered a gentle rebuke to those who think the current generation is beyond help: "Don't say, 'Why were the earlier days better than these?' It's not from wisdom that you ask that!" (7:10).

With this we are ready, more or less, for the next challenges. Our investigation of each passage starts with a relatively literal (and admittedly awkward) translation, interspersed with brief notes along the way to explain specific translation choices and the initial implications of those choices. Following that, we will explore additional possibilities in terms of interpretation.

First Conundrum: Can We Be "Too Righteous" (7:13–18)?

It will work best if we tackle this passage in smaller bites. Here are verses 13 and 14.

(13) Look at the work of God; for who is able to fix what he has twisted?
(14) In a day of good, be in (that) goodness, and in a day of evil, look;
This, side by side with this, God has made so that man would not find anything after him.

In the Hebrew of verse 14, there is a difference in the forms of the word for good—*tovah* (feminine) and *tov* (masculine). I have chosen to indicate this distinction by using "good" and "goodness." Altogether, it sounds pretty existential—just enjoy that day by being "in" it.

The evil day, however, is a different story; the tone changes. The message seems to be, "distance yourself when you consider an evil situation, since you cannot do anything about it." It is a reprise of what we have already encountered. God planted a sense of the transcendent and eternal in our hearts, but we cannot fathom them from beginning to end (3:11). Now we are reminded that good and evil days come when and in whatever order God determines. This also sets the stage for what is to come.

(15) Everything (*'et-hakkol*) I have seen in my fleeting days:
there is a righteous person perishing in his righteousness,
and there is an evil person (whose life) is prolonged in his evil.
(16) Don't be righteous to an excess and don't become overly wise;
why be appalled?
(17) Don't be evil to an excess and don't be a fool;
why die when it is not your time?

Raise your reading antennas just a bit and notice that the two warnings about not being righteous or evil to an excess are exactly parallel. We'll return to the implications of this seemingly unorthodox admonition shortly. In the meantime, unlike the caution against being overly concerned with wisdom (whatever that might suggest), "don't be a fool" is not qualified at all. It is a flat-out warning and a no-brainer. One more matter for now: the consequence for dabbling in excesses of righteousness and wisdom is horrified confusion—"Why be appalled?" I have chosen that interpretation over a second possibility that has to do with self-destruction, but it is a difficult choice. Both are viable translations, and "why destroy yourself?" does respond directly to the sobering observation of a righteous person perishing in his righteousness (v. 15b). Nevertheless, "appalled" or "horrified" or "dumbfounded" fits better in light of Qohelet's ongoing critique of wisdom. Think back to 1:18—wisdom

and knowledge mean more anger and pain. In contrast, evil and folly
lead to death—period. There are no questions in that realm.

(18) It is good that you grasp this one,
but also from this (other) do not rest your hand,
because the one who fears God will go out with all of them
   ('et-kullam).

"This . . . also . . . this" is verbally parallel to verse 14. Go back and look
at the literal rendition. "All of them" echoes "everything" that Qohelet
saw (v. 15). In each set, the words are the same. The words for "everything" and "all of them" look different because the latter has a suffix
attached. Our question is this: Are these verbal similarities intended to
guide our interpretation?

Let's now return to the whole passage. Qohelet's statement in 7:15a
sets the stage. "I have seen *everything* in my fleeting days." "Everything"
included the apparent injustice of the righteous being cut off while the
wicked live happily on. This was really troubling; it always has been and
will be. As a result, Qohelet offered up practical warnings that respond
to this ugly problem. As he stated the first set, however, it sounds well
outside the boundaries of orthodoxy, particularly if we read it as advis-
ing moderation in our quest for righteousness and wisdom, and in our
indulgence in sin! Put another way, the sage's advice seems to be, "avoid
extremes on both ends of the moral spectrum, but minimal righteousness
and wisdom are acceptable along with a small degree of sin." Probably
that is not the best interpretation.

Should we try again? Perhaps we ought to interpret the clause as an
admonition against *self*-righteousness. After all, that is a snare that traps
each one of us more often than we might like to admit. There is, however, a small problem. Get ready; it's time for a Hebrew lesson that will
eventually land us in grammar. The Hebrew word *tsaddik* does not mean
"self-righteous." It simply means "just," "righteous," and "ethical," both
in relationship to God and with others. To get "self-righteous" out of this,
we need to presume that the adverb translated above as "to an excess"
is conceptually connected to the adjective "righteous." If we read it that
way, this might be a caution against an overly positive self-perception
that is deeply linked with pride.

Walter Kaiser has offered an interpretation of this as excessive public
righteousness, describing "a multiplicity of pseudoreligious acts of sanc-
timoniousness; ostentatious showmanship in the art of worship; a spirit
of hypercriticism against minor deviations from one's own cultural norms,

which are equated with God's righteousness; and a disgusting conceit and supercilious, holier-than-thou attitude veneered over the whole mess" (Walter C. Kaiser Jr., *Ecclesiastes: Total Life*, Everyman's Bible Commentary [Chicago: Moody, 1979], 85–86).

What if, on the other hand, we were to link the warning against *excess* directly and solely with the verb "be"? In other words, arrogant self-perception is not the target of this admonition, even though a self-righteous posture is indeed utterly unbecoming. Instead, this warning is directed to those who emphasize *acting* as they perceive "righteous people" ought to act — *"being"* in that sense. This may sound as if I am splitting hairs, and perhaps that is the case. Nevertheless, it could be an important distinction if it serves as a warning against *working* at righteousness excessively, perhaps to burnish our own medals. We can only begin to suggest scenarios where this plays out. One might be the quest to achieve power, rarely a benign motivation no matter what the context. Another might be the ever-present human tendency to live according to checklists of "good things to do." The negative possibilities here are sobering. Whatever the presumed goal, however, the real end is utter frustration, because perfection in righteousness is forever beyond human capacity.

Even though the initial "prompt" has to do with righteousness, Qohelet saw the same kind of problem with the quest to achieve wisdom. He already said that we can never plumb the depths of wisdom. In the meantime, viewing oneself as wiser than others is not advisable. In this case, the form of the Hebrew verb permits the interpretation "don't make or perceive yourself too wise." The bottom line is this: it is possible to strive for righteousness and wisdom with entirely the wrong motives.

We feel on much surer footing with the flat-out counsel against wickedness and folly that follows it. Given the second part of verse 15, relatively mindless persons *could* anticipate that possibly, just possibly, they could live on for a good long time in spite of wholesale wickedness. Qohelet slapped that thought down flat. Fools and evil people, he knew, die before their time.

We have not quite wrapped this up. The "conclusion" in verse 18 is ambiguous; neither of the options to be grasped and held onto is named. The most positive way of reading this sets righteousness and wisdom at those two poles; we are to hold onto both. To bolster that, verse 19 praises wisdom, and verse 20 presents an honest reflection about righteousness that fits well with the observation that attempting to achieve perfection is a lost cause even before we start. This line of interpretation sounds promising except that it leaves out that bewildering closure: the person who fears God will "go forth with all of them." All of what? Does it refer to everything that Qohelet had observed? Read literally, it seems to acknowledge more than two options. The lack of clear resolution is more in keeping with the overall perplexing tone of the book. Perhaps one application of this is the realization that choices will never be easy—for all kinds of reasons.

Second Conundrum: Wisdom and "The Scheme of Things" (7:23–29)

We have already visited parts of this passage in our earlier tour through Qohelet's observations about wisdom. Qohelet lamented the inaccessibility of wisdom. It is distant; it is too "deep, deep" for anyone to find it (vv. 23–24). Against this backdrop, Qohelet was driven to seek order. He meticulously sifted the data one item by one.

> (25) I turned, I and my heart, to know, and to explore,
> and to seek wisdom and a rational explanation;
> and to know wickedness, folly, and the recklessness—madness.

Yes, this is an awkward translation, but it helps us see something important as we venture farther into our problem passage. In regard to his search for wisdom, Qohelet was focused; he wanted to know, explore, seek, and construct paradigms for understanding. I have chosen to translate *heshbon* as "rational explanation" because it implies a paradigm that is logically constructed and that works to explain observed phenomena. In contrast, the words related to foolish wickedness tumble onto the page in excess. Any logic is shattered in the presence of recklessness. As before, these declarations signal a foray into the dark side of folly and madness (see 1:17 and 2:12), but now Qohelet linked them with wickedness. It is ominous, and we wait with some uneasiness for the results.

The interpretation of the Hebrew words here is especially challenging, as two of them (*heshbon* and *sikhlut*) appear only in Ecclesiastes. They both have related Hebrew forms, however, that help us. *Hashav* means to "reckon" or "count," suggesting that Qohelet was conducting a comprehensive investigation, compiling all the data. The second word, *sikhlut*, has a number of cognate forms, all of which mean "folly."

(26) And I am finding more bitter than death the woman who is
  a trap;
her heart is netting, her hands are fetters.
A good person before God will be rescued from her,
but the sinner will be trapped by her.

The multiple references to all kinds of folly, possibly joined with the
known excesses of the Solomon figure, may have prompted these rueful
observations. They acknowledge the horrifying bondage of relationships
with evil partners. The more a creature struggles to escape a netting or
a snare, the more entangled it becomes. We might revisit our spiderweb
and look closely at the pathetic morsel buzzing futilely in the sticky snare.
So also with people. Avoiding this trap is utterly dependent on our relationship with God. Otherwise, the end is not pretty.

(27) "Look, this is what I have found," said Qohelet.
"(Adding) one to one to find a rational explanation,
(28) which still my soul has sought but not found.
One man from a thousand I have found,
but a woman among all of these I have not found.
(29) Only see, this (that) I have found—
that God made 'adam right in relationship to God (yashar),
but they have sought many rational explanations."

Qohelet's final findings were pretty slim, and they are couched
alongside affirmations about what he did *not* find. These latter manifest
themselves in several arenas. First, exceedingly few people pass muster—
one man out of a thousand and no women. We are not certain about the
characteristics that qualified that one man to be noted. It does not necessarily have anything to do with rightness or morality, even though some
translations presume a direct linkage both with the appalling woman
of verse 26 and the specific attribute of "rightness" to 'adam (v. 29). The
repeated declaration about finding (vv. 27 and 29), however, seems to
ask for a refocus. Thus, this passage as a whole and verse 28 in particular
may not be prematurely dismissed as misogynistic; other factors seem
to be at play.
  Let's explore them a bit further. The fatal attraction of an evil woman
interfaces with all kinds of references in Proverbs to prompt the tragic
reflection of verse 26. It also interfaces with the life experiences of biblical
figures who were lured into those traps. Moreover, implicit in verse 29 is
the tragedy of the fall. Ecclesiastes echoes and re-echoes Genesis. In the

beginning, God's image-bearer was in right relationship with God (*yashar*), but the "wisdom" offered by the serpent lured both Adam and Eve onto their own paths toward what they perceived as knowing good and evil. Interestingly, in Gen 3:6, the word describing Eve's perception of the tree is not the standard Hebrew word for wisdom. It is more focused on insight and enlightenment.

We will make one more Genesis connection as we explore these observations: as a result of Adam and Eve's disobedience, Eve heard a somber pronouncement: "Your desire (*teshuqah*) will be for your husband, but he will rule over you" (Gen 3:16b). The Hebrew word *teshuqah* refers to a grasping and clutching desire. It is used only three times in the Hebrew Bible. Consider its parallel use in the very next chapter of Genesis, where God warned Cain that "sin desires to have you but you must rule over it" (Gen 4:7b). Adam and Eve's relationship would be characterized by self-centered striving on the part of both of them. That may be the wretched backdrop to Qohelet's observations about women.

But back to what Qohelet did not find. It seems his attempt to find a rational explanation (singular) fizzled entirely. It might be like our contemporary scientific attempts to come up with the "theory of everything." So far, that lies beyond our capabilities. Qohelet's end point was disheartening, but there was no other option for him. We settle for what we can get—multiple partial explanations. Too often those partial explanations move into the realm of one form of idolatry or another. We are predisposed to worship whatever we can wrap our minds around rather than the Master of the universe (Rom 1:21–23). That, of course, is utter folly. The perversity of the human heart and mind complicates existence exceedingly; the ambiguity of Qohelet's observations about his findings reinforces that conclusion.

Conclusion

We have reached the end of our own pursuit of rational explanations for Qohelet's conundrums and have found that there are still unresolved puzzles. That is not a bad place to be because we will continue to return to read and reread, to explore and seek. May Qohelet's relentless quest compel us to press on as well! It will be a good thing that we go well fortified, for the book of Job is next.

For Further Reading

Allendar, Dan P., and Tremper Longman III. *Bold Purpose: Exchanging Counterfeit Happiness for the Real Meaning of Life*. Wheaton, IL: Tyndale House, 1998.

Boda, Mark J., Tremper Longman III, and Cristian Rata, eds. *The Words of the Wise Are Like Goads: Engaging Qohelet in the 21st Century*. Winona Lake, IN: Eisenbrauns, 2013.

Brindle, Wayne A. "Righteousness and Wickedness in Ecclesiastes 7:15–18." *Andrews University Seminary Studies* 23 (1985): 243–57.

Crenshaw, James L. *Ecclesiastes*. Old Testament Library. Philadelphia: Westminster, 1987.

Dell, Katharine J. *Interpreting Ecclesiastes: Readers Old and New*. Critical Studies in the Hebrew Bible 3. Winona Lake, IN: Eisenbrauns, 2013.

Eaton, Michael A. *Ecclesiastes*. Tyndale Old Testament Commentaries 16. Downers Grove, IL: InterVarsity Press, 1983.

Fox, Michael V. "The Meaning of *Hebel* for Qohelet." *Journal of Biblical Literature* 105 (1986): 409–27.

———. *A Time to Tear Down and a Time to Build Up: A Rereading of Ecclesiastes*. Grand Rapids: Eerdmans, 1999.

Fredericks, Daniel C. *Coping with Transience: Ecclesiastes on the Brevity of Life*. The Biblical Seminar 18. Sheffield: JSOT Press, 1993.

———. *Qoheleth's Language: Re-evaluating Its Nature and Date*. Lewiston, NY: Edwin Mellen, 1988.

Garrett, Duane A. *Proverbs, Ecclesiastes, Song of Songs*. New American Commentary 14. Nashville: Broadman, 1992.

Gordis, Robert. *Koheleth, the Man and His World: A Study of Ecclesiastes*. 3rd ed. New York: Schocken, 1968.

Kaiser, Walter C., Jr. *Ecclesiastes: Total Life*. Everyman's Bible Commentary. Chicago: Moody, 1979.

Kidner, Derek. *A Time to Mourn and a Time to Dance*. Downers Grove, IL: InterVarsity Press, 1976.

Longman, Tremper, III. *The Book of Ecclesiastes*. New International Commentary on the Old Testament. Grand Rapids: Eerdmans, 1998.

McCabe, Robert V. "The Message of Ecclesiastes." *Detroit Baptist Seminary Journal* 1 (1996): 85–112.

Murphy, Roland E. *Ecclesiastes*. Word Biblical Commentary 23A. Dallas: Word, 1992.

Provan, Iain. *Ecclesiastes, Song of Songs*. NIV Application Commentary. Grand Rapids: Zondervan, 2001.

Schwab, George M. "Woman as the Object of Qohelet's Search." *Andrews University Seminary Studies* 39 (2001): 73–84.

Scott, R. B. Y. *Proverbs, Ecclesiastes: A New Translation with Introduction and Commentary*. Anchor Bible 18. Garden City, NY: Doubleday, 1965.

Seow, Choon-Leong. *Ecclesiastes: A New Translation with Introduction and Commentary*. Anchor Bible 18C. New York: Doubleday, 1997.

Sneed, Mark R. *The Politics of Pessimism in Ecclesiastes: A Social-Science Perspective*. Ancient Israel and Its Literature 12. Atlanta: SBL Press, 2012.

Whybray, R. N. *Ecclesiastes*. Old Testament Guides. Sheffield: JSOT Press, 1989.

Zuck, Roy B., ed. *Reflecting with Solomon: Selected Studies on the Book of Ecclesiastes*. Grand Rapids: Baker, 1994.

PART FOUR

Wisdom and Suffering: Job

"Humans are born to trouble as surely as sparks fly upward" (Job 5:7 NIV). These are the astute words of Eliphaz, one of Job's well-meaning friends. The observation is on target; as long as a fire continues, sparks blaze upward, are extinguished, and a new shower erupts. Likewise, as long as life continues, it is fraught with difficulties. In Job's case, however, it was not a mere shower of sparks; his life itself resembled a blazing inferno.

We encounter Job coming to grips with the nature of his God, who, in Job's experience, attacked him without cause and then maintained a stony silence. We also encounter him in the unenviable position of rejecting the well-meaning advice of three notable men who had come a good distance to comfort him through his ordeal. They were increasingly insulted and insulting as Job continued his plea of innocence. You and I, dear readers, also know the contents of the first two chapters. As a result, we also have much more troubling theological questions to engage. They have to do with the purposes of God. As those chapters make crystal clear, it was God who initiated the processes—all of them—that culminated in Job's intense suffering. Many other things are not necessarily clear, but God's apparent culpability is, and that is sobering in the extreme.

Our questions have to do with life, death, destructive and gratuitous evil, God's wisdom and sovereignty, God's integrity and faithfulness, and humans' equally important integrity and faithfulness. They also touch on goodness, covenant, sin, pain, prayer, intercession, accusation— the list can go on and on. And it does.

An integral part of our exploration has to do with the text itself. We wrestle not only with theological and ethical questions but linguistic and literary ones as well. They all interface as we probe the words of the book's characters that shed light on our own responses when we find ourselves in the position of Job, Eliphaz, or Elihu.

CHAPTER 16

The Array of Issues Confronting the Interpreter of Job

Overview: Where Are We Going First?

The host of interpretive issues that arise in conjunction with this towering narrative can be overwhelming. The temptation is to skip a chapter earmarked "interpretive issues" and head toward the greener fields of application. "How *should* I respond when I am suffering as Job did?" "Is it wrong to question God?" "How do I counsel friends whose lives have fallen apart for inexplicable reasons?" Let me encourage you, however, to hang in for this chapter. The lessons we glean from the book may have a good deal to do with how we knit together the book's challenges. Toward this end, we will engage the following basic concerns.

First, we want to grasp the structure and general contents of the entirety of Job because many of our additional questions build on our ability to recognize discrete sections. This is easier said than done, however. In fact, many readers eagerly engage the first two chapters, tiptoe through the third, glaze over by the end of the sixth, and resurface in time for part of God's responses and the seemingly reassuring closure in chapter 42. This temptation to "get through" the text is not only a modern one. As it turns out, the ancient Greek translations of Job are noticeably shorter than the Hebrew text. Perhaps they too struggled with the same challenges in confronting the overwhelming volume of words (and really difficult ones at that). Nevertheless, the whole is a monumental work of art, and we want to absorb it all.

There is some discussion as to why the text of Job in Greek is abbreviated. Perhaps it was a product of translators wrestling with the meaning of words that were already challenging because they were used so seldom. One option: bypass them. On the other hand, it might have been a concern that readers would falter along the way. After all, this is a lot of poetry that seems repetitive on the first read. In chapters 22–31, just about one-quarter of the text is missing in the Greek version. At the same time, there are several significant additions in the narrative portions of the book. The terse admonition of Job's wife in the Hebrew text, "curse God and die" (2:9), is embellished. According to the Greek rendering, she asked Job why he was waiting so long; he was suffering and she was reduced to being a wandering servant. Instead, she urged him to "say some word to the Lord, and be done." The end of the book is likewise expanded. Following the notice that Job died, "old and full of days" (42:17), the Greek text added an assurance; Job would rise again with those whom the Lord would raise up. Just for good measure, it closes by indicating that this man is described in "the Syriac book," which locates Job in the regions of Idumea and Arabia and appends some genealogical records. See Choon-Leong Seow, *Job 1–21: Interpretation and Commentary*, Illuminations (Grand Rapids: Eerdmans, 2013), 6–9.

With the comprehensive structure of Job firmly in mind, we will next explore whether or not the book's recognizable sections were initially intended to be read together. Perhaps they were originally discrete units from different time periods and contexts. Are we missing something if we don't delve into the possible separate sources underlying this text? Or are we missing something if we do? That pursuit is wide-ranging; as we will see, it is not just a matter of two or three distinct segments. The language differences and conceptual shifts among some sections further complicate the issues. These might suggest separate dates for the narrative framework, the poetic compositions, and the final compilation. In conjunction with these questions, we will take a brief detour into the wider cultural context of the ancient Near East, in which there are vaguely parallel treatments of the ubiquitous problem of human suffering.

Undergirding all of these matters is the tangle of theological challenges. In light of our firm knowledge of God's covenant-keeping faithfulness, what do we make of the God who intentionally afflicted Job?

Structure and Brief Summary

The Narrative Introduction (chs. 1–2)

Here we meet Job, whose blessed existence and stellar character landed him in an unwelcome spotlight. He was the subject of an extremely troubling exchange between God and the *satan* ("adversary") regarding his motives for fearing the Lord. The reader is privy to two scenes that Job never saw. In each of them, God challenged the *satan* to "consider" Job. In turn, the *satan* challenged God to take away the blessings he had given him and see if Job would still be God-fearing. To the reader's horror, God turned the *satan* loose on Job, imposing only minimal boundaries. We will consider the identity of the "adversary" in the next chapter.

Job's Initial Outburst (ch. 3)

In revulsion at his worsening condition, Job could restrain himself no longer. He cursed the day that he was born, wishing it out of existence. He longed for the rest that death affords.

First Cycle of Dialogue (chs. 4–14)

Evidently stung by the force of Job's initial outcry and increasingly strident responses, each of the three friends took it upon himself to bring Job around, to cajole him, to corner him, and to redirect his dangerous thought patterns. Job, riled in turn by their thinly veiled accusations, and loathing his condition, alternately derided them as useless and charged God with being a sovereign despot.

Second Cycle of Dialogue (chs. 15–21)

In the second cycle, each friend waxed eloquent on the terrible end awaiting the wicked, their possible intent being to scare Job into a proper attitude of repentance. Darkness, terrors, and calamity await those who are truly wicked. The friends did not name Job in their descriptions; they did not need to. Each response from Job was increasingly vehement as he tried to break through their stagnated worldviews, describing to the best of his ability God's vicious attacks against him.

Third Cycle of Dialogue (chs. 22–27)

In this go-round, the composure of the friends disintegrated, each of them responding in a different way. Eliphaz turned to direct, cruel, and false accusations, followed by the boilerplate call to repent in order to enjoy God's beneficence again. Bildad's feeble attempt started with extolling the grandeur of God in the heavenly realms, but it quickly degraded to calling humans worms. Zophar wisely said nothing. In Zophar's place, we have Job growing more loquacious and bold, alternately longing to find where God had gone and acknowledging the mystery of God's ways, affirming his own uprightness, and picking up the same threads of the friends in terms of what ought to happen to the wicked.

"Where Shall Wisdom Be Found?" (ch. 28)

At this juncture, there is an interlude. Either it was Job's taking a deep breath to regain his perspective after the torrent of words and thoughts, or the narrator has called for a needed pause in the drama. The quest is for wisdom, which is recognized as exceedingly valuable but also as eluding all attempts to comprehend it.

Job's Self-Vindication and Self-Incriminating Oaths (chs. 29–31)

Likely in response to Eliphaz's harsh accusation (ch. 22), Job set the record straight in terms of the socially responsible actions he performed prior to plummeting to his current circumstances. Then, in a daring move, he took a series of oaths against himself, all following the pattern, "if I have done . . . then let me suffer the appropriate deserved consequences for that action." In effect, although he did not call on the name of the Lord, this was his summons; God would have to respond.

Elihu Enters the Fray (chs. 32–37)

We are, however, kept in suspense for six chapters as a new voice entered, and it was not a timid voice. We will explore the nature of Elihu's role at length, but suffice it to say here that he certainly made himself heard, expressing his anger at Job as well as the friends for not doing justice to the difficult issues. In addition, he took it upon himself to adjudicate some of the fine points of the arguments. His real contribution, perhaps unbeknownst to him, was setting the stage for the appearance and voice of the Lord.

"Then the Lord Answered Job" (chs. 38–41)

Finally, the Lord responded. Perhaps it would be better to say that the Lord appeared, majestic and overpowering with his questions about Job's own lack of power and knowledge. Job's plight was not at all in the script of God's remarkable discourses about his created order. God spoke twice, separated by a brief utterance from Job. God's second set of questions challenged Job to "be God," and then escorted Job into territories inhabited by Behemoth and Leviathan.

Job and God Respond: Narrative Epilogue (ch. 42)

Overwhelmed—but we don't know exactly how—Job affirmed God's absolute power and inaccessible wisdom. Then, in a stunning turnabout, God rebuked the friends, elevated Job, doubled all the possessions of which he had been robbed, and gave him seven sons and three daughters.

Of One Piece?

Relationship of the Prose Introduction and Epilogue to the Poetic Core

The book of Job contains a number of literary features that have caused a majority of scholars to see it as a composite of some sort. Most notable is the apparent incongruity between the narrative framework and the poetry, which is some of the finest but most difficult in the Hebrew Bible. Job's character as described by God (Job 1:8; 2:3) seems inconsistent with his turbulent speeches. How could the pious and accepting Job of the prose narrative be the same anguished and angry Job who unleashed torrents of accusations against God? In addition, the covenant name YHWH (Lord), a name that appears regularly in the prose framework, does not appear in the cycle of dialogues, apart from Job 12:9. Instead, *'el* and *'eloah*, generic words meaning "God," are used almost exclusively throughout the poetry. Further, there is an apparent contradiction between God's speeches in chapters 38–41, which effectively put Job in his place, and God's affirmation of Job at the expense of his friends in the final chapter (Job 42:7–8).

Some readers have claimed that both the twofold restoration of Job's property and the birth of ten additional children subvert the entire point of the dialogues. Notably, the *satan*, the real adversary of Job, did not reappear fully vanquished at the end. Instead, Job appeared to be subdued by his own Adversary, whom he perceived to be God. These issues are challenging in the extreme. There is much more to be said in response to each of these, and we will get there—all in due time! Even if the prose and poetic materials were two disparate texts later brought together, at some point this dissonance needs to be addressed.

For extensive surveys of the challenges to the unity of the text and cogent responses, see Edouard Dhorme, *A Commentary on the Book of Job*, trans. Harold Knight (Camden: Nelson, 1967), lxi–cxi; and John E. Hartley, *The Book of Job*, NICOT (Grand Rapids: Eerdmans, 1988), 20–33. Among those who read the text as composite are Marvin H. Pope, *Job: Introduction,*

Translation and Notes, AB 15 (New York: Doubleday, 1965), xxi–xxii; H. H. Rowley, *The Book of Job*, NCB (London: Marshall, Morgan & Scott, 1976), 8–18; and David J. A. Clines, *Job 1–20*, WBC 17 (Dallas: Word, 1989), lvii–lix. Generally, recent scholarship has focused on the value of reading the book as a whole. As examples, see David Noel Freedman, "Is It Possible to Understand the Book of Job?" *Bible Review* 4 (1988): 26–33; Carol A. Newsom, *The Book of Job: A Contest of Moral Imaginations* (Oxford: Oxford University Press, 2003), 16; Robert S. Fyall, *Now My Eyes Have Seen You: Images of Creation and Evil in the Book of Job*, NSBT 12 (Downers Grove, IL: InterVarsity Press, 2002), 19–20, 71; Yohan Pyeon, *You Have Not Spoken What Is Right About Me: Intertextuality and the Book of Job*, SBL 45 (New York: Lang, 2003), 54–56; Steven Chase, *Job*, Belief: A Theological Commentary on the Bible (Louisville: Westminster John Knox, 2013), 5; and Seow, *Job 1–21*, 26–38. These represent only a small sampling.

Additional Literary Complexities

Even within the poetic materials, there are complications. What appears to be the dissolution of the dialogue in the third cycle has prompted numerous commentators to reposition segments of those chapters. We will unpack the suggestions in a subsequent chapter. As the third cycle stands, Bildad's words were feeble at best; Zophar had clammed up by this time. Did his words get lost? Did Job overpower both of them, sarcastically stating their pieces for them? Or did he wave them off with one hand while he continued to look at the problem from all angles himself? Chapter 27 is attributed to Job, but it certainly expresses a wide range of opinions, some of them sounding suspiciously like Zophar's.

Was the wisdom poem in chapter 28 "original" in whatever sense we mean that word? Was Job its author? Or did a later narrator insert this as a "breathing space" after the increasing intensity of the verbal battles that preceded it?

The utterances of Elihu, seemingly characterized by different structural, stylistic, and linguistic features, have been labeled a later addition. It seems Elihu used a lot of words that have an Aramaic flavor to them. Because Aramaic was the international language (sort of the way English is now), we might think that Elihu was not only younger than Job and the friends but also more cosmopolitan and widely traveled. To make sure everyone knew that, he laced his speeches with the latest idioms. This matter of Elihu's speeches representing a separate and later source is not an interpretive "done deal," by the way. We will explore it further in the chapter devoted to Elihu.

God's verbal assault on Job is also puzzling. Why is it divided into two sections, and why do both of them appear so ill suited to the deep concerns that Job expressed throughout both the dialogues and his subsequent monologues in chapters 29–31? And why did God's second discourse apparently range into the realm of mythology?

In the interests of forging ahead, let me make a fledgling proposal regarding the integrity of the book. If we presume a composite text from varied periods of time, we may be overlooking the richness and depth of living characters wrestling with the realities of debilitating suffering, destructive misunderstandings, and a seriously fractured relationship with God. Already in the narrative of chapters 1 and 2, for example, the reader discerns Job's profound fear of God that placed him in the role of an intercessor (Job 1:5). That fear dovetailed with his affirmation of God's sovereign hold over all circumstances of life (Job 1:21; 2:10). These convictions continue to manifest themselves through the rest of the book, gaining an existential reality when uttered from Job's crucible of suffering. Reading the text as a whole, the anticipated tensions that accompany long-term grief and suffering are echoed in the lengthy poetry; the dialogues and monologues are necessary for Job to work through the crisis. In that regard, Seow has suggested that the book intentionally subverts the classic lament form because here *God* is the enemy, not the one to whom Job appeals for help (Seow, *Job 1–21*, 54).

When?

Our question is purposefully vague. When did Job live? When were parts of the book written? When did the book reach the form in which we read it now?

We start with the epic narrative about a character named Job. Presuming for now that the account reflects a historical figure whose story gained entrance into the traditions of Israel at some point, when might he have lived? As we will see in the next chapter, Job's age suggests that we are to be thinking of the patriarchal period—in other words, about five centuries before God made the covenant with Israel at Mount Sinai. According to Ezek 14:14, 20, Job's reputation for righteousness had become part of Israel's national narrative; he was right up there with Noah and Daniel (Dan'el in the Hebrew text). Note that both Noah and Job were outside "covenant Israel," and Dan'el may have been as well. Just for the record, Ezekiel's barb is coated with an ironic tip; righteous foreigners trump idolatrous covenant people.

Dan'el was a known mythological figure in an Ugaritic epic "The Tale of Aqhat," dated to the middle of the second millennium BCE. The main question is whether or not this mythical figure was known for the righteous character to which Ezekiel appeals. While there is a brief allusion in "The Tale of Aqhat" to Dan'el sitting at the gate and judging the causes of the widow and the orphan (*ANET*, 151), this is a minor element within the metanarrative of that text, which does not seem to focus on righteousness! In other words, the jury is still out as to whether Ezekiel was alluding to the Dan'el in the Ugaritic tale, to biblical Daniel, or to someone else. Fortunately, our primary subject is Job, not Dan'el.

At the same time, however, the poetic exchanges portray all of the disputants as being steeped in what Israel would affirm as the doctrine of retributive justice. When someone was disobedient, there was punishment in store; if a person obeyed the word of God, blessing ensued. While these just consequences were standard fare in the ancient Near East, they were also hallmark covenant sanctions. Job's worldview as expressed in the poetic dialogues was shaped within this framework of divine justice. That was why he continued to agonize over the cause(s) of his plight. Therefore, we might lodge a good part of the final form of the book of Job under the umbrella of Israel's covenant relationship with the Lord.

The case is strengthened by the appearance of the divine name YHWH (Lord), which is God's name as he was in relationship with his people. Its significance was revealed at Mount Horeb (Exod 3:14–15) at least four centuries later than the patriarchal period. Given the tenuous existence of Israel in the land during the periods of the judges and early monarchy, a literary product such as the book of Job probably did not emerge until the united monarchy at the earliest, that is, during the tenth century BCE. One additional theological connection might help. The affirmation that the Lord was the King, Creator, and Israel's Redeemer resonates with Isaiah, the towering eighth-century BCE prophet during the reign of Hezekiah (Job 19:25; cf. Isa 41:14; 43:14; 44:6, 24; 49:7). Some refer to the verses just cited as part of "Second Isaiah" and assign to them a date several centuries later. I do not think that is a necessary conclusion, but either way the point stands; the poetry in Job reflects Israel's covenant traditions.

What might we then suggest? It is no surprise that the nagging problem of suffering would be the subject of a range of literary endeavors from the ancient Near Eastern cultures. For example, a poem from Mesopotamia, apparently dating to several centuries after 1000 BCE, depicts the plight of a sufferer and his dialogue with a companion. We have our

own cultural icons, people who have triumphed over exceedingly difficult tragedies and whose stories become part of our culture's language.
If we are "journaling types," we have likely done the same for ourselves.
It seems to be in the human DNA to record anguish as part of the effort
to triumph over it.

For an accessible rendition of excerpts from "A Sufferer and a Friend in
Babylon," see Victor H. Matthews and Don C. Benjamin, *Old Testament Parallels: Laws and Stories from the Ancient Near East*, 3rd ed. (Mahwah, NJ:
Paulist, 2006), 239–44. This is also known as "The Babylonian Theodicy"
(*ANET*, 601–4). The sufferer pleads for help in understanding his plight. He
is especially troubled because he has lived well—praying and fasting—but
the divine assembly has not seen fit to bless him. To the contrary, they have
abandoned him, and he questions their capability to maintain any kind
of order. The friend alternately reproaches the sufferer for wrong-headed
thinking and urges him to seek the gods even though they are, in the end,
unreachable.

In similar fashion, perhaps the narrative of a man named Job was
deeply embedded in ancient Near Eastern cultural lore and came to be
preserved within the developing Israelite sacred literature. In this regard,
it was unlike other parts of sacred Scripture, much of which was revealed
from God through the prophetic voices. Nevertheless, it was perfectly
positioned and adapted to serve the purposes of God's Spirit in addressing the universal problem of human suffering. As Israelites adopted the
story, poems that may have been part of the original oral tradition, or
that were perhaps added later, served as the vehicle for exploring all the
facets of this deepest of human conundrums. Since we have already mentioned the eighth-century court activity in conjunction with our study of
Proverbs, this literary process may have transpired during the reign of
Hezekiah, if we want to take the Isaiah connections to heart. That part is
hypothetical. What we can say is that the richness of the poetry and the
theological daring in Job far outstrip the extrabiblical examples. That is as
it should be; this is, after all, the word of our all-knowing and absolutely
sovereign God.

To be sure, there are scholars who date the text later. The sixth century BCE, a time of national upheaval and crisis, has been a high-profile
suggestion in more recent works. This presumes, however, that the narrative of an individual named Job was primarily a vehicle for a larger
sociocultural commentary. That seems potentially reductionistic, and it
does not recognize that human suffering crosses all time boundaries.

Seow notes a wide range of dates for the book of Job, but suggests that the earliest date would be the sixth century BCE because of the mention of the Chaldeans (1:17). He establishes links with Jeremiah (also sixth century) and Second Isaiah (Seow, *Job 1–21*, 40–42). Representative of the more sociopolitical approach to dating the final composition of the book of Job are Chase, *Job*, 5; and William P. Brown, *Wisdom's Wonder: Character, Creation, and Crisis in the Bible's Wisdom Literature* (Grand Rapids: Eerdmans, 2014), 68.

Moving Forward

I hope your literary and theological appetites are whetted. In the next chapter, we are plunging into the most challenging questions that great minds have ever engaged.

We have only to watch or read of the documented atrocities that have shattered millions of lives even in the last century to have our faith in our fellow human beings (and perhaps God as well) shaken to the core. Words fail us as we try to frame the question: How can humans be so utterly vile? What is the nature of this palpably revolting thing called evil? Later on in these chapters on Job, we will refocus on this conundrum through a literary lens. At the beginning of our study of the evil world in which Job finds himself, however, we are compelled to revisit Genesis 1–3. Yes, Eden may seem an unlikely place to turn, and yet it is there that we first encounter the "knowledge of good and evil"—lodged in the fruit of a tree. It is ominous because it is linked with a prohibition and the specter of death (Gen 2:9–17), and all of it is under God's sovereign dominion. Because of our familiarity with the narrative, this all has a benign shroud over it. Perhaps that needs to be ripped away as we begin to see that choice of Eve and Adam for what it was. At the same time, our Creator initiated and reigns over all of these processes, a fact articulated by Isaiah: "Forming light and creating darkness; making *shalom* and creating evil, I the LORD do all of these" (45:7). One last connection for now: the six days of creation of Genesis find a parallel in the six "scenes" of Job 1–2. Was it intentional on the part of the author? It is impossible to say, but we do not want to miss the connection; both narratives carry us behind the veil of experiential knowledge (Samuel E. Balentine, *Job*, SHBC [Macon, GA: Smyth & Helwys, 2006], 25–28).

CHAPTER 17

God and the *satan* (Job 1–2)

Introduction

Before we tackle the theological enigmas of these two chapters head-on, we need to meet Job. He was, by all accounts, a formidable character, and it was his integrity and fear of the Lord that set this drama in motion.

The Setting: Where and When

Our narrator immediately "locates" Job. As we have noted, he was geographically outside the covenant community of Israel. That is a significant datum. At this point, it would be helpful to access a map that includes the regions around ancient Israel. The "land of Uz" seems to have been in Edom; we get a clue in this regard from Lam 4:21a ("Rejoice and be glad, daughter of Edom, dwelling in the land of Uz"). Further Edom connections surface in the genealogy of Esau, the father of the Edomites. Eliphaz, one of Job's "friends," was also the name of the first son of Esau (Gen 36:9–10), and much further down the line Uz is listed as a descendant of Seir, who lived in that region (Gen 36:28; 1 Chr 1:42; see also Jer 25:20). Edom was south and east of the Dead Sea and was later characteristically an enemy of God's people. There's a long history there, but it lies outside our pursuit. Some have suggested Aram to the northeast as an alternative location (citing Gen 10:23 and 1 Chr 1:17). The main point, however, is that Job was not living in what we identify as geopolitical Israel.

We might further surmise that Israel as a national entity did not yet exist at Job's time. Here's a possible clue: if we jump to the end of the book, we discover that Job lived a good long time—140 years—*after* his terrible ordeal. Given that at the beginning of the book he was already a senior member of the community with ten children, we might calculate that his total years were somewhere in the vicinity of two hundred—that is, if we read the numbers literally. Some are not inclined to do so. Nevertheless, this figure does parallel the ages of the patriarchs—Abraham,

Isaac, and Jacob—and suggests that the reading audience might view Job and the patriarchs as roughly contemporaneous. An approximate date for the patriarchs would be the first part of the second millennium BCE. That gives the necessary leeway for some disagreements on how to figure out when Abraham, Isaac, and Jacob lived. Just for the record, there are scholars who presume the book as a whole does not reflect a historically grounded narrative. In their assessment, Uz is a mythical location and the characters likewise the stuff of imagination.

A Man of Character

Job was a person of comprehensive well-being, both materially and spiritually. Both aspects are important. When all of his possessions were stolen, slaughtered, or otherwise destroyed, it was an enormous loss. That was on top of losing his ten precious children. The numbers associated with his children and his possessions could be stylized, as the pattern of seven plus three applies to both sons and daughters, as well as sheep (seven thousand) and camels (three thousand). In addition, the multiples of ten are also evident in the five hundred oxen plus five hundred female donkeys. The key point, however, is that Job was extraordinarily wealthy—"blessed," in the accusation of the *satan*.

Second, Job's character was above reproach; he was "blameless, upright, feared God, and shunned evil" (1:1, 8; 2:3). After this description was provided by the narrator, it was repeated by God—twice. The Hebrew words translated "blameless" and "upright" do not imply "sinless." Job did not make that claim for himself. Instead, his life was characterized by consistent integrity in every sphere. He was a blameless person of upright social standing. He had a finely tuned moral compass, knowing evil and avoiding it. In addition to this repeated, fourfold superlative, Job's healthy fear of the Lord resulted in his sacrificing burnt offerings on behalf of his children, just in case they might have ruptured their relationship with God (1:5). Job was, in effect, the priest for the family as he made intercession for them. This is vitally important as we seek to understand Job's complaints and pleas.

The words Job uttered in conjunction with his regular sacrifices for his children are of interest: "it may be that my children have sinned and 'cursed' God in their hearts." The Hebrew word translated "cursed" here is actually *barakh*, which generally means "to bless." See also 1:11 and 2:9, where we encounter the same usage. It likewise appears with the same meaning in 1 Kgs 21:10, 13, where a man named Naboth was framed by Jezebel. This horribly wicked woman arranged for Naboth to be falsely accused, directing men to say that he had "cursed" God and the king. Both this case and the case of Job and his children involved words uttered against God, something so unseemly to the authors of these texts that they possibly could not bring themselves to write the word for "curse," and instead counted on the readers' ability to read between the lines.

The Rest of the Cast

"The Sons of God"

As the curtain veiling the scene in heaven is lifted for us, the "sons of God" had come to stand in the presence of the Lord. Although here they were just part of the backdrop, the role of these celestial beings is a bit complicated. They reappear as a celestial chorus in Job 38:7—"... when the morning stars sang together and the sons of God shouted aloud." In the days before Noah, "sons of God" took "daughters of men" and the result was catastrophic (Gen 6:1–4). However we identify them in that context, we surmise that their activities were unsavory in the extreme. The freedom they exercised in the days before Noah may reverberate into this introductory scene in Job, for a troubling personage roamed freely in their midst.

The *satan*

That troubling character was the *satan*. Just a word of explanation is in order at this point. Many modern translations (for example, the ESV, NIV, NRSV, HCSB, NASB) translate this with the proper name Satan. This has undoubtedly been done under the influence of the New Testament, where the archenemy of everything good is named; he is Satan, the devil, making his initial appearances in the temptation scene (Matt 4:1–11 and parallels) and ferociously waging war in the heavenly realms until his demise (Luke 10:18; Rev 12:7–9). In the Hebrew Bible, however, his identity is less specific. The Hebrew word *satan* means "adversary" or "accuser," and it generally occurs with a definite article: "the adversary." (I have chosen not to dignify this creature with an uppercase name; whoever he is, he does not deserve that recognition.)

This adversary/accuser had the freedom to roam the earth and enter the presence of God. While this might be unsettling, another angle on the matter is that he had to "roam" in order to know what was occurring; God, on the other hand, simply knew—and knows. The nature of the *satan*'s role in this opening scene is somewhat ambiguous. It appears that he set out to accuse Job as an underhanded way of really accusing the Lord in whose presence he stood.

A survey of additional appearances of the word *satan* in the Hebrew Bible may help us work through further implications of his role here. Sometimes this word refers to a human who served in a potentially adversarial role (1 Sam 29:4; see also 2 Sam 19:23; 1 Kgs 5:18; 1 Kgs 11:14, 23, 25). On other occasions, the one called *satan* was in heaven as an opponent. Zechariah was shown the *satan* standing to the right of Joshua, the high priest, in a position to accuse him. Notably, however, that accuser was firmly rebuked by the Lord (Zech 3:1–2). An accuser (no definite article in this case) incited David to number the people of Israel (1 Chr 21:1). His appearance adds a new dimension to the same narrative as we read it in 2 Samuel 24, where we are told that the Lord incited David. Chronicles is a later rendition of the narrative; perhaps this reflects a paradigm shift as God's people intentionally distanced the Lord from evil. The same indefinite form appears in Ps 109:6: "Let an accuser stand at his right hand."

The Lord

It was the Lord who initiated a conversation that radically altered Job's existence. He intentionally drew the adversary's attention to Job and was, as we shall see, unquestionably in control of both exchanges. That will necessitate our taking a good hard look at what might have been the divine purposes underlying apparently unconscionable actions. It will not do simply to say that God gave the *satan* permission. While that is true, it sidesteps the larger issue—I repeat: God initiated the entire process.

God also set conditions that made Job's suffering even more unbearable. The adversary was not allowed to take Job's life. That meant that Job was hanging on the cusp of life and death, in extreme agony. They did not have the advantages of morphine back then. Job repeatedly questioned the nature of his God; we will as well. One more thing that we must say: in this picture, God and the entirety of his creative wisdom were vulnerable to attack by the adversary. That too was part of God's sovereign design and is remarkable beyond words.

The Drama Gets Underway

First Challenge and Counterchallenge

"Have you paid attention to my servant Job? There is no one like him." And God went on to praise Job's character, echoing the same fourfold affirmation of the narrator. What a terrifying thought! Job's extreme integrity made him the ultimate target. We might initially conclude, along with Eccl

7:16, that it is safer (from our thin perspective) to be lukewarm God-fearers and only mildly righteous persons. It depends on our definition of "safe."

In the meantime, the accuser seized the opportunity right away, pointing out that any half-wit could figure this out. God was not getting "free" worship from Job; Job was good for what he got out of it. In other words, the adversary first impugned Job's character and then, in the next breath, God's design for a just world. God had made a fence around everything that was Job's. A contemporary counterpart to this kind of thinking might be that insidious sense of "Christian entitlement"—freedom from suffering and reward in the here and now for the arduous and self-sacrificing task of "being good."

The *satan* followed this observation with his proposal: "Take away everything that marks Job as one of the relatively few blessed individuals in this miserable world, and see what he does then. My money is on the side that he will curse you." Some have interpreted this in terms of a great "wager." If Job caved in, the accuser would win. If Job remained faithful to God, God would win. Given, however, the pivotal role of the accuser and the constant reminder that God is Judge and King of God's universe, this is better seen as a trial. But who was on trial, and what was the nature of the accusation?

At first, we presume Job was the one on trial and that the *satan*, serving in the capacity of prosecuting attorney, was after him. Would Job remain faithful? What would that mean in his circumstances? Does "faithful" mean he followed the counsel of his friends, whose advice sounded God-fearing but moved suspiciously into the same realm as the accusation of the *satan*? It seems that Job was getting a truly raw deal, as no one showed up to defend him.

What if, however, God and his design of the entire created order were on trial? To wit, is the very fabric of the universe, with its complex of moral, supernatural, and physical dimensions, flawed? Does that design manifest divine wisdom or does it manifest self-serving divine desire for worship that has gone awry? God certainly demonstrates his power; that is not the question. The more basic questions have to do with the wisdom, faithfulness, and goodness of God. No matter how we frame these questions, the sobering thought at this point is that an innocent person would suffer egregiously in order to move the trial ahead no matter who was in the dock. God orchestrated it to be so.

While it would be an endless task to enumerate powerful treatments of innocent suffering, among the most compelling for me have been Elie Wiesel's *The Trial of God* and the PBS documentary *God on Trial*. Both reverberate with the horror of the Holocaust. Another equally gripping perspective on the tangle of moral issues surrounding innocent suffering is Shushako Endo's *Silence*. That will be enough for now.

The narrator masterfully avoids assigning responsibility; the *satan* was given free rein to attack everything that belonged to Job—family as well as possessions. This permission was given by God, and it was a response to the accuser's incitement that God stretch out his hand and strike. We remember that God was the one calling the shots and that God, whether we find it comfortable or not, was where the buck would stop. In the end, the notion of God's comprehensive sovereignty is more assuring than the prospect that there are things and/or persons outside God's control. Even without knowing the drama in heaven, Job worked his way toward this point as well. The question remains, however, as to what God's good purposes might be in the face of every devastating circumstance that we encounter.

Disaster Falls

For Job, those circumstances followed one upon the heels of another: raiders from Sheba who fell upon and killed Job's herdsmen and cattle, fire that fell from heaven and devoured both flocks and shepherds, Chaldeans who likewise raided, and a monstrous desert wind that struck the four corners of the house in which Job's children were feasting. It fell, killing them all. We have an ominous foreshadowing with the description of Job's children eating and drinking on "the day" (1:13); the final messenger used the same words to describe the scene when the tornado struck their gathering (1:18–19). Through the entire news report, the Hebrew repeats the verb "fell"; these were catastrophic losses and devastation, beyond human comprehension. The Hebrew verb accompanying "great wind from the desert" is feminine, as is the Hebrew word for "wind" (*ruah*). A quick refresher on Hebrew grammar: nouns in Hebrew are either masculine or feminine, and the verbs and adjectives associated with them match that gender. In this context, however, the next clause begins with a masculine verb, perhaps implying that *God* "touched" the four corners of the house. Each of the four messengers reported with numbing rhetoric, a pattern that underscored their terror: "I only, I alone have escaped to tell."

The "fire from God" that *fell* from heaven (1:16) could be that messenger's way of saying this was the hugest lightning strike he had ever seen, or it could intimate his perception that they had experienced something supernaturally off the charts. The *satan* worked his malicious schemes through human enemies as well as "natural disasters." Desert raiders were anathema for wealthy pastoralists such as Job. The same pattern afflicted biblical tribes during the period of the judges; Midianite raiders terrorized Israel in a huge swath from the Jordan Valley south and west to Gaza on the Mediterranean coast (Judg 6:1–6).

Job's First Response

In the face of these losses, Job got up, but he did not shake his fist at God. Instead, he tore his cloak and shaved his head in mourning for his children. Those were intentional and prescribed actions that were part of lamentation. They were not hysterical outbursts. Once prepared, he fell to the ground in worship. Just as the disasters had fallen, so Job fell. His words have resonated through centuries: "Naked I came out from my mother's womb, and naked I shall return there. The LORD has given; the LORD has taken away. Blessed be the name of the LORD" (1:21). Nakedness is a metaphor for utter vulnerability, expected only at the extremities of life. Job acknowledged this ill-timed vulnerability, but he affirmed God's role as blessed Sovereign. The word is indeed "blessed" but we wonder if we are supposed to connect the subtext that we have already noted in terms of this word's double meaning (see above).

The main point is that Job did not sin or charge God with anything untoward (1:22). The meaning for *tiphlah* ("untoward") is uncertain, but the word seems to have a sense of the unsavory or offensive. Thus, if the accuser was out to indict Job for self-serving motives, he came up short. Bereft of everything, Job worshiped God. The question remains whether the matter of God's design had fared as well.

As a follow-up to the recommendation above regarding *God on Trial*, let me suggest reading through the Mourners' Kaddish, the Jewish prayer uttered on the occasion of death and remembrance of the dead. The words in parentheses are recited by the gathered congregation.

May his great name be exalted and sanctified (amen)
in the world that he created as he willed.
May he cause his Kingdom to reign in your lives and in your days,
and in the lives of all the house of Israel,
quickly and soon.
And say: amen.
(May his great name be blessed forever and ever.)
May the name of the Holy One (blessed be he)

> be blessed, praised, glorified, exalted, lifted up,
> honored, upraised, and lauded;
> above all blessing and song,
> praise and consolation that are spoken in the world.
> And say: amen.
> May there be great peace from heaven,
> and life upon us and upon all Israel.
> And say: amen.
> The One who makes peace in the high places,
> May he make peace for us and for all Israel.
> And say: amen.
>
> In the context of our study of Job, it is worth noting that the final lines of the Kaddish are drawn from Job 25:2b.

The Second Round

It seems that a gathering of the heavenly hosts in God's presence was a regular occurrence. On this given day, however, there was a notable difference. While the "sons of God" stood before God as usual, the accuser was in their midst "to stand before God." The expression is repeated; the *satan* was a presence to watch. The dialogue proceeded as before, until God added the following: "and [Job] still grasps on to his integrity even though *you have incited me against him* to swallow him *without cause*" (2:3b). This last statement is breathtaking. God handed responsibility for Job's unfortunate straits back over to the *satan*. At the same time, God acknowledged his own culpability in the disasters unleashed against Job without cause. To be sure, the adversary's wicked incitement was the result of a much more profound theological and ethical challenge—to wit, why are good people good? Both God and the accuser had a stake in that question.

In response, the *satan* conceded that there are boundaries; certain strong people can handle all sorts of distress except their own weakness and pain. He thus challenged God again to stretch out God's hand, but this time to strike Job, his bone and his flesh, the very essence of Job's physical frame and being. The agony would reduce Job to reviling (the word is again *barakh*) God to his face. Both "hands" were involved—God's and the adversary's—as God gave Job into the *satan's* evil hands. This time, the adversary did not use intermediate forces; he went forth and afflicted Job from bottom to top. God did set a boundary, but it was in effect a very cruel one. Job's life had to be preserved, which meant interminable suffering without the release of death.

What was the nature of Job's affliction? The Hebrew is *shehin ra'*—some sort of terrible inflammation. There are echoes of the plague of boils (Exod 9:8–11)—the same word is used—and even more of Deut 28:35, which states that when Israel was disobedient, among the welter of divine curses would be "painful boils [*shehin ra'*] . . . from the soles of your feet to the top of your head."

Our horror at Job's intolerable situation grows. We're not the only ones; Job's wife weighed in as well. But what did she say? Did she start with a question ("Are you still hanging on to your integrity?") for which there was an unwritten follow-up question ("whatever for?")? Or was it an admonition to "hang on to your integrity, Job; it's all you've got right now"? It could be either in the Hebrew. We can try to figure it out from the context, but that does not immediately clarify the matter. Her next utterance is "bless God and die!," possibly implying "stay strong to the very end but get it over with." Or did she really say "curse God and die!"? It's that word *barakh* again. If she intended the latter meaning, her advice played right into the accuser's hand, even though she would not have known that that was the case.

It is not until we tackle Job's response to her that we can sort it out a bit more: "You are speaking like one of the godless fools" (2:10). The demand that he curse God and die would fit the pattern of an utterly godless person. As we noted in our study of Proverbs, there are different words in the Hebrew Bible for a variety of foolish types. The worst one is the *naval*, and Job put her in that category.

Pressed to this extreme, Job's reaffirmation of God's sovereignty was even stronger. He not only accepted God's giving and taking away; that fit the previous context, in which he lost everything. This time, from his visceral and comprehensive pain, he acknowledged God's prerogative to dole out evil. He had it right; the evil afflictions were mediated by *satan* but were in God's design. To the credit of Job's wife, she did not walk out. How do we know that? Job later bewailed the fact that his affliction was so ghastly that the stench overwhelmed his wife (19:17).

Even more to Job's credit, he did not sin "with his lips." This last phrase has prompted some to suggest that the torrent of words that would soon spill out was brewing in his heart. The question will be if these words were in fact "sinful."

In the meantime, it is of more than passing interest that the name Job may be related to the Hebrew word for "enemy," and Job was the "enemied one" (Seow, *Job 1–21*, 58). The Hebrew consonants are similar. Needless to say, that has all sorts of possibilities in this context fraught with ambiguities.

Friends and Comforters

News of Job's misfortune came to Eliphaz, Bildad, and Zophar, and they journeyed to be with him, intent on being sources of comfort and moral support in mourning. Their mourning practices were unusual by our standards. Not only did they weep loudly and tear their garments, they also threw dust "onto their heads heavenward" (2:12). We leave this narrative introduction with Job hunkered down on an ash heap in silence, surrounded by these three friends who were too appalled—and respectful of his extreme suffering—to speak.

CHAPTER 18

The Character of Job on a Trajectory: Wrestling with His Own Mortality and God's Sovereignty

Introduction

In this chapter, we follow Job from his silent brokenness through the increasingly volatile exchanges with his friends/counselors/would-be comforters. He dared to say things about God that shocked them and that perhaps make us pause as well. Although the friends get their full-fledged turn in our next chapter, here we begin to hear them "speak," because their claims were part of the backdrop for Job's outraged responses. As we will see, he dismissed them quite quickly and focused on other issues related to his suffering. Foremost was coming to grips with God's apparent responsibility for his ceaseless and senseless pain. We will cycle back in a subsequent chapter to unpack at greater length what Job said about the God who had become his Adversary.

Job's Initial Outburst

As the prologue drew to a close, Job acknowledged that all he had was from the hand of God, and that God could both remove all of the bounty and bring calamity (1:21; 2:10). He did not lose sight of the fearsome side of God's sovereignty. In his extreme circumstances, he was learning to hold the things of his life with a gentle grip. His wife, on the other hand, demonstrated the all-too-common attitude that the *satan* had anticipated Job would manifest. For her part, when ill came, there was nothing else to do but curse God and die (2:9). Job would not give in so quickly.

Instead, he cursed the day he was born! At the precipice between life and death, his torment was excessive and seemingly interminable. How could he continue to exist in that state? What could possibly be a way forward? His choice was a grim one; he turned into the dark. Night, darkness, cloud, and deep shadow were the forces that he implored to overwhelm the light and the day of his birth, and not just the day of *his* birth but the birthing of the entire creation. The multiple words for black and ominous darkness force us toward that realm along with Job; it is inescapable.

Job's agony and despair led him temporarily to those places he knew were aligned against God. In creation, God had brought light and order from darkness and the void (Gen 1), but Job sought to undo that ordering. His seven curses are a fractured mirror of the seven days of creation. He begged day to turn to utter darkness and night to be "barren," with the intent that night would no longer give birth to day—ever.

Job ventured even farther into the shadows by invoking those who had the courage to wake up the chaos monster, Leviathan. The watery depths represented disorder and chaos to Job's contemporaries. The ancient world knew well the appeal to supernatural forces. In their minds, it would be no surprise that the mythic and powerful Leviathan was there. If Job were to awaken its dreaded power, God would need to subdue it again. While this desperate call for Leviathan is an adumbration or foreshadowing of God's spectacular description of that creature (ch. 41), here Job's focus was squarely on cursing the day of his birth and all days with the frightful assistance of Leviathan.

Job would also have the brilliant morning stars darkened (3:9; see 38:7), adding to his appeal to undo all creation. The initial part of Job 3 is a dark counterpoint to the creative processes that God would celebrate in chapter 38. The reverberations with Genesis 1 are also unmistakable. The prospect that there might actually be a response from dark powers to this plea is horrifying.

The Hebrew words for "day" (*yom*) and "sea" (*yam*) are similar and when they are plural (*yamim* and *yammim*, respectively), they sound alike. Likewise, "those who curse" (*'orere*—the singular is *'orer* and the object is the day) and "the one who rouses" (*'orer*, with the object being Leviathan) sound similar. There was an ominous unifying thread between rousing Leviathan from the chaos of the sea and effecting a curse on all days, all time. In an eerie way, Job's series of curses, which one scholar has called "counter-cosmic incantations" (Hartley, *Job*, 91), reached blindly for the realms to which we as readers were privy in chapters 1 and 2. They also pointed forward; those cosmic realms are fully on display in God's response in chapters 38–41. We will read much more about Leviathan! Faint adumbrations of God's majestic tour are woven into each of Job's sometimes tentative, sometimes furious verbal outbursts.

Nevertheless, Job did leave the dark shadows of that other world and instead took up questions. "Why?" and "Why not?" are laced through his troubled words. Why was he still alive? Why did he not die? Why was life given to one "whom God has hedged in?" (3:23). What an irony! The *satan* accused God of putting a "hedge" around Job that protected him (1:10). Job perceived God's "hedge" as an incomprehensible obstacle, all of it making him "shriek" and "growl" (3:24), both more vivid translations than the "sighing" and "groans" of the NIV, ESV, NASB, HCSB, and NRSV. He longed for the rest that death brings to every person, from kings of the earth to stillborn infants, from the wicked to the weary (3:13–17).

The way to death, however, was a scene of prolonged misery. Light was not a welcome guest for Job; he asked why it must invade his miserable existence. It exposed the jagged edges of hurt and pain. The darkness of death would provide a cushion. It would be like drawing the curtains closed. Job not only waited for darkness; he dug for it (3:21). It gives us the sense that he would have dug his own grave if that would get this over with faster. Bitterness and misery were his life; he would meet his grave with excessive joy. But how could there possibly be anything right about that?

In another horrible irony, God had attested to the fact that Job feared him; Job now declared that what he had feared had come in full force. He had lived his life in dread of doing something that would displease God. To avoid any potential consequences of God's anger, he even made sacrifices on behalf of his children, just in case they slipped up (1:5). That unnamed dread now gave way to the experienced horror of his living hell. No peace, no rest, no quietness, only turmoil. To this his friends were compelled to respond. And this was only the beginning!

Job as Respondent

Eighteen chapters are devoted to Job's remarkable speeches. After affirming his submission to what he recognized as God's prerogatives (1:20–22 and 2:10), his devastation went on for months (7:3), and it was comprehensively excruciating and revolting (7:5). He ranged from deep hurt at his friends' lack of compassion and understanding to sarcastic rejection of their attempts to advise him. Although he repeatedly expressed his disappointment with his friends (6:14–27; 12:2–5; 13:2–12; 16:2–5; 19:2–6, 21–22; 26:2–4), most of his words either were addressed to God or protested the horrifying condition into which God had brought him.

Job had a lot to say about *words*. The brevity of his life compelled him to speak (7:7–11). Words were the only vehicle he had for presenting his case, and he needed to be heard. Through words he articulated his longing and expressed his steadily diminishing hope. Through words he took his friends' elementary declarations about God, mostly designed to herd him back into the corral, and built from them truly formidable statements about God's nature. Job never lost his theological insight. In fact, it was sharpened in the crucible. Some of his words were painfully awkward and incomplete. We understand; trying to speak eloquently from depths beyond depths is well-nigh impossible. His friends, by way of contrast, could all have won public speaking contests for style.

Job's apparently morbid vexation sent his friends into paroxysms of rebuke. In response, Job's tone turned sarcastic and bitter (12:2–3). He reproached his friends for their increasingly useless and destructive words, but after a few volleys each time, he pursued more troubling issues. Where was God? Why? Why? Why? His early longing and pleading for death gave way to a fierce fight for his life and for his reputation, shaped with judicial metaphors. This would be a lawsuit if he could just get God to be present. After all, it was God's injustice that Job experienced. His concern was whether he could articulate his case in an effective manner or whether the divine deck was already too stacked against him. Job's words to God were in turn pleading, accusatory, and audacious. At times, he spoke about God instead of to God, possibly too demoralized to keep asking for restoration when it was evidently not in the cards. No doubt we can relate. There are times when prayer appears to fail. Above all, Job's responses are not static or one-dimensional. Neither are ours in the face of ongoing and inexplicable misery.

The First Cycle of Dialogue (chs. 4–14)

Responses to Eliphaz

Initially, in response to Eliphaz's attempt to console and cajole him, Job acknowledged that he had spoken rashly (6:3), but nevertheless justified this. His friend's pronouncements about God did not fit his experience and simply sounded glib. Job said so, and he said why. Eliphaz had admonished him not to despise the discipline of the Almighty (5:17). Some discipline! Job said the arrows of the Almighty were in him, they were poisoned, and God's terrors were against him (6:4). But here is an interesting twist. Job also preferred death over the possibility that he might betray trust in God, remarkable in any circumstances but especially when he acknowledged that *God* had reduced him to sitting helplessly in pain on the ash heap.

Oh, that my request might come, that God would grant my hope, that God would be willing to crush me, that he would loose his hand and violently cut me off! Then I would yet have my consolation, and I would respond[1] even in unrelenting anguish—that I had not denied the words of the Holy One. (6:8–10)

He had enjoyed a living and loving relationship with God, and that whole framework *sustained* him, at least for a while.

Job posed angry criticisms of his friends, ratcheting up the emotional tension. They were unreliable. Their inability to treat him, or anyone for that matter, with love (*ḥesed*) was because they had abandoned the fear of the Almighty. This captures our attention for several reasons. If we are truly to love our neighbors, it seems we must have our relationship with God in order first. Further, Job's pious friends continued to urge *him* to develop a more keenly tuned fear of God. In fact, they tried all sorts of angles on this as the three sets of dialogues went on. Right away, however, Job nailed them—*they* were the ones lacking in fear of the Lord. Instead, they were more afraid of what demands Job's situation might make of them (6:21–23). Would they be required to "post bail" or pay bad debts? Those might be our contemporary equivalents.

In spite of Job's deep desire to be faithful to God, he wrestled with dwindling hope. His daily existence was heavy bondage, the agony dragged on, nights seemed endless, and his body was ravaged (7:1–5). He was painfully aware that his life was fragile, like the threads on a loom, and that it was coming to an end with little hope (7:6).

> This arresting image of the fragility of both hope and a thread is also a wordplay. The word commonly translated "hope" (*tikvah*) has as its verbal root *kavah*, meaning "to wait for." A related word, *kav*, means "line," perhaps with the sense of being stretched and in tension. *Tikvah* also means "thread" or "cord" in at least one passage. Rahab of Jericho put a *tikvat ḥut* in her window, as directed by the Israelite spies, in order to make certain her life was spared (Josh 2:18–21).

Job's observations of the world around him—a cloud disappearing (7:9), a person who never comes home again (7:10)—were the basis for his understanding of the finality of death. *Sheol*, the grave, was a familiar part of his vocabulary. Job "loathed his life"; he said this three times (7:16, 9:21, and 10:1). He talked about his misery. He talked about dying. All he had left was his ability to speak. Not knowing how long he would live, he was compelled to talk. We will find as we look back through the lens of chapter 42 that what Job said was not dismissed by God as wrong or improper. That is a tremendous encouragement when our often inarticulate railings are interpreted as violations of propriety.

Job sidelined the friends. Why be bothered with useless drivel? His torment was too extreme. He addressed God, returning to the image of the sea and the sea monster (7:12) to which he had already appealed (3:8). His thoughts slipped into frightening realms in the face of overwhelming despair, fear, and insecurity. Job accused God of unpleasant visitations (7:13–14) so terrifying that Job would rather have God leave him alone. Through Job's vivid descriptions, we catch the faintest glimpses of what would be fully unveiled in God's glorious appearing. At this point, however, we see a different and deeper perspective on Job's dread of the Almighty, one that stymied his ability to talk clearly about it. "My whole being (*nephesh*) would choose strangling; death, rather than my bones. I despise . . . . I would not live forever. Cease from me; because my days are a breath" (7:15–16). The last word is *hevel*, reminiscent of Ecclesiastes.

In what has been called a parody of Psalm 8, Job accused God of oppressive and relentless attention. "What is man that you make him great and give your heart (attention) to him? You visit him every morning and examine him every instant" (7:17–18). Stop it, Job said, at least until I can "swallow my spittle" (7:19). At the same time, he begged God to pardon his sins.

With poignant longing, Job intimated that when God *would* care enough to search for him, it would be too late (7:21). These were not distant third-person ruminations; some Job directly addressed to God. At the same time, Job did not employ the traditional language of prayer, where brokenness is expected to elicit God's compassion. His experience told him otherwise. Questions boiled to the surface again: Why? What? And why? They were interrupted by Bildad.

Putting Bildad in His Place

Bildad's boilerplate declaration about God's anticipated response to a blameless person (ch. 8) prompted the equivalent of "I hear you" from Job. Then Job went on to issues that mattered more, the first of which was the prospect of a dispute with God; the word *riv* implies a lawsuit (9:3). While his friends continued to enjoin prayer and repentance, Job moved steadily in the direction of a confrontation over injustice. That this was impossible did not faze him (9:14–20); what did he have to lose at this point? Job struggled to understand himself at the same time that he wrestled with God's character.

> If I justify myself, my mouth brings me evil;
> I am blameless (*tam*), but he (or "it") made me crooked.
> I am blameless; I do not know myself; I despise my life.
> It's all one; this is why I said, "the blameless and the evil he de-
>   stroys." (9:20–22)

Ironically, *tam* means "whole" or "complete," while Job was speaking as a completely shattered person. At the same time that he could not
define his own moral stance, he also found God morally ambiguous. And
it got worse for Job; he declared that God mocked the despair of the innocent and perverted justice. "If not he, then who is it?" (9:23–24).

Job also trumped Bildad's focus on God's sovereignty with his own
account of God's raw power, far in excess of anything that was possibly on Bildad's radar screen. Job heaped up seven vivid descriptions,
one after the other, to proclaim God's supreme dominion, but in each
next breath, he declared the divine action to be unsettling in the extreme
(9:5–10). His affirmation of God's wrath bookends this section: God over-
turns mountains in his anger (9:5); and even the helpers of Rahab, from
the same chaotic spheres as Leviathan, cower under God's anger (9:13).

Job had a full and healthy view of God's sovereignty; in fact, what he
said on this subject is not so different from what God himself would say
in chapter 38. The problem for Job, however, was that God's indescrib-
able power was unleashed against him, crushing him and needlessly
multiplying his wounds (9:17). Job felt unqualified to address God, either
with regard to power or justice; nevertheless, he did! "*You* are dipping
me in a pit, and my garments will abhor me . . ." (9:31). But then, perhaps in apprehension, Job backed off briefly: "*He* is not a man like me . . .
that we could come together into judgment" (9:32). "Oh," Job said, "if
only we had an arbiter between us!" We will return to that longing. In
the meantime, his days continued to hurtle away—like a runner, like an
eagle swooping down on carrion (9:25–26).

Circling back, Job requested that his divine Opponent articulate the
charges against him, bitterly asking God if he enjoyed oppressing and rejecting him (10:2–3). In tones of perplexed outrage, he directly questioned
God: Why did you shape me so carefully, just to destroy that product of
your creativity (10:8–12)? These questions reverberate into our own experiences. Why have you trapped me in a body that is wracked with pain, that
does not move when and how I want it to? I'm an artist; why can't I see any
longer? Or hear the notes I want to compose? Why have you isolated me?

Job's testimony to God's gift of life (10:12) gave way before the continued onslaught from God, who stalked him and reduced him to shame.
He wished he had never been born—or had gone straight from womb to

tomb (10:18)—and pleaded with God to turn away from him so that he might have a fleeting moment of joy before the utter darkness of death. His description is chilling:

> Before I go—and do not return—to the land of darkness (*hoshekh*)
> and the shadow of death;
> a land of darkness (*'ephatah*) like the gloom of night (*'ophel*);
> the shadow of death where there is no order
> and it (light) shines like *'ophel*. (10:21–22)

And Then Zophar

How was it possible to respond to that? Zophar tried, but following his exhortation (ch. 11), Job directed another sarcastic jab at his "wise counselors": even animals, he said, know what the friends had been going to such lengths to say (12:7). In fact, all nature knows the sovereign working of the Lord and needs only to be asked in order to divulge these truths (12:8–10). Here again we are treated to a brief adumbration of the forthcoming terrestrial "field study" (chs. 38–41) in which God affectionately described a whole array of his wild creatures. Just a note: this context contains the only use of the divine name, YHWH (LORD), in the poetic dialogues (12:9).

Job pressed on to declare that these truths are not just found in nature. Human experience and long tradition foster wisdom, even though it ultimately belongs to God (12:11–13). At the end of the day, God upends all the sociopolitical contexts that purport to be hothouses for nurturing wisdom. Persons of high position and repute are brought down, and it is because God determines to accomplish this. The characteristics that define social status are removed; counselors, judges, kings, priests, advisers, elders, and nobles are all humiliated, and their plans come to nothing. God has his way with everything and everyone, leaving a swath of destruction (12:14–25). Having said all this, however, Job did not throw up his hands and say "whatever!" in the most injured of postmodern tones. He refused to abdicate.

Instead, Job continued to retool his words for the legal realm. In the process, he taunted the friends (12:2–3). If they would keep silent, that would be wisdom for them; as it was, they were caught in a growing web of lies and deceit. He pressed on, building a courtroom scene for his audience. He would speak to the Almighty and take up his case with God. In his view, the friends were not just uttering useless words; they were false *witnesses*—in fact, false witnesses who spoke deceitfully *for God* (13:2–9). Job warned them against "showing partiality" to God (13:8, 10 NIV, ESV). The Hebrew interpreted as "show partiality" here may literally be

rendered "to lift up the face." In the very next verse, the same word recurs;
God's "lifting up" ("splendor" NIV; "majesty" ESV) would terrify them
(13:11). Their deceitful attempts to defend God were paltry by comparison.

Making his case *now* was essential as there seemed no firm possibility
of hope beyond the grave (13:13). The traditional translation of 13:15a is
"though he slay me, yet will I hope in him" (NIV), but there are alterna-
tives: "If he were to slay me, I would have no hope," or even more drama-
filled, "Behold, he *will* slay me; I have no hope."

It is worth pausing to unpack the different options for translating 13:15a in
order to see what they contribute to our understanding of Job's dilemma.
In some few passages of the Hebrew Bible, there is a difference between
what is "written" (as reflected by the consonants that are preserved in the
text) and what is "read" (as reflected in notes along the side of the text that
indicate how the word in question has traditionally been pronounced). This
is one such passage. What is *written* in the second clause is "I have no hope."
It involves a negation (לֹא, pronounced "lo"). In this case, the text indicates
that Job believed God would kill him and that he was simply waiting for
that to happen. On the other hand, what is *read* here is לוֹ ("for him," also
pronounced "lo"), which produces the meaning "I will hope/wait for him."
Either *could* fit the slightly wider context. Job had just said, "Why do I take
my flesh in my teeth and my life in my hands? Behold, he will kill me . . ."
(vv. 14–15a). This seems to indicate that he anticipated dying soon; in other
words, "I have no hope." But on the *other* hand (turning it around again),
he continued by saying, "Surely, I will defend my ways to his face; and this
could be deliverance for me, because no godless person would come before
him" (vv. 15b–16). The upshot of what he said indicates that he did expect
to die as a result of his calamity (v. 19b) but that he determined to have his
case in order before that happened. It may help to remind ourselves that
Hebrew thought generally focused on this life rather than on speculations
about the world to come. The challenge is to figure out what Job said for
"this life." Just as an aside, Job did not use *tikvah* ("hope") here. The concept
of "hope" is built into the verb "to wait for."

Job's explicit request for an audience with God was part of a second
challenge: "Distance your hand far from me, and do not torment me
with your terrors. Summon and I will answer, or I will speak and you
will respond to me" (13:21–22). This was bold, but it was not the end.
Job went on to accuse God of *hidden* hostility (13:24) and harsh punitive
measures (13:27). Again, we are reminded of the possible implications of
Job's name—"the enemied one" (cf. v. 24).

The blunt bottom line at the end of the first go-round was this. Humans die; that's it. A dead person is like a dried up riverbed (14:11). The dead do not rise again or awake, even when the heavens vanish; in fact, death is an endless sleep (14:12). For a moment, Job shook himself out of this pessimism and longed to be hidden temporarily in *sheol* until God's wrath had swept over. His deep emotional, gut-wrenching cry was that God would then care enough to call out for him, to long for Job, and that his transgression and sin would be sealed and covered over (14:13–17). But that yearning was fleeting on Job's part, and he knew it was futile. There was no hope for revival after death—ever. God wears away hope. In fact, God destroys what hope there is, and humans are left with their own pain and mourning (14:18–22). It does not get much worse than that.

The Second Cycle (chs. 15–21)

Job's tone changed in the second round. He did not address God with the same mixture of confusion, longing, hope, and hopelessness. Instead, responding to Eliphaz's assurance that the *wicked* writhe, that they are marked in anguish, and that the destroyer is against them, Job said (in essence), "Oh really? Let me run this scene by you again." He lashed at God with brutal honesty: "Surely now I am exhausted; you have devastated my entire company" (16:7). *God* was his adversary who had assailed him, torn him, shattered and crushed him, cast him into the clutches of wicked people, and attacked him repeatedly (16:7–14). This was the work of an enemy, someone out to destroy him, and Job put it in no uncertain terms. What is astonishing is that this broken person continued, up to a point, to plead *with God*: ". . . as my eyes pour out tears to God" (16:20b). He appealed to the earth (as a witness) and to a *witness* in heaven (16:18–19). Who this witness might have been and how Job processed all of this will merit much fuller exposition in a forthcoming chapter.

After his fierce accusations, Job was spent. He ceased to beg for God's attention, almost as if he had given up on that project. His words were a sea of pain, despair, injustice, dishonor, and horror at the hand of God. He surged up momentarily, challenging his opponents to try again (17:10), but it was just a breath, and he subsided again. His brokenness drove him back to contemplating the darkness of the grave, with the rotting and corruption of the flesh on which worms feed. This would be home and these would be family:

If I hope for *sheol* as my house, if I make my bed in darkness, if I say to the pit "you are my father" and to the worm "my mother" or "my sister," where then is my hope? Who will see my hope? Will it go down into the bars of *sheol*? Shall we descend together into the dust? (17:13–16; see also 21:26)

After another salvo from Bildad (ch. 18), Job cried: "Have pity on me, have pity on me; you are my friends! For the hand of God has struck me" (19:21). This "hand of God" trapped him in a net, walled up his way, stripped away his glory, broke him, dashed his hope, and kindled wrath against Job (19:6–12). Where could he turn? God had removed all his social supports; relatives, guests, friends, servants, and even his wife avoided him when they saw him coming (19:13–20). All viewed him with disgust or hostility, most likely because his extreme suffering made them quite uncomfortable in their relative ease.

Futile and damaging words continued to strike him. As a rejoinder, he asked that *his* words be written—for posterity. It is in this context that he burst out with his belief in a kinsman-redeemer whom he would see. However we understand that declaration—and we will explore it at length—it rang with hope even in Job's isolation.

Each friend had heaped up his assurances as to the fate of the wicked. Exasperated after Zophar's contribution (ch. 20), Job said, in the simplest terms: "I've seen otherwise. The wicked continue to prosper all their lives; they never reap the consequences of their evildoing. They are strong and secure. God should deal out justice to them as they deserve. Instead, everyone simply dies. Everything you have said is *hevel*." That is a very abbreviated version of chapter 21.

The Third Cycle (chs. 22–27)

Of the three cycles of dialogue, this is the most challenging one. We can understand why; there is only so much we can say about the same things unless we venture into unlikely places. It is evident that each of the speakers had come to the end of himself, and so had Job. No doubt horrified, he heard outright false accusations from Eliphaz (ch. 22), who presumed himself a "comforter." We will explore shortly just how this rhetoric may have functioned. Nevertheless, Job's tone was less strident. More pressing was his own pursuit of God's elusive presence: "Oh that I knew I would find him . . ." (23:3). He wanted to present his case, to be sure (23:4), but he also just wanted to find God. It sounds like a game of hide and seek, but a very serious game: "I go forward, backward, left and right, and I never grasp him or see him" (a condensed rendition of 23:8–9). Fleetingly, Job expressed another glimmer of hope: "For he knows my way; when he has tested me, I shall come forth as gold" (23:10).

That would be especially true because Job continued to affirm his own uprightness (23:11–12). At the same time, his words still echoed with fear and darkness in conjunction with God's presence (23:15–17).

Job undertook to untangle for himself the truths about the fates of wicked and righteous people. He had heard enough from the friends; he also knew his own traditional wisdom as well as his experience. All of the possible perspectives came crashing together against each other. This was not an academic discussion. It had everything to do with Job's own integrity; he had to sort it out to make sense of his existence. If not he, who would? Evil people were unjust, particularly in their abuse of the poor, whose destitute conditions Job described at length. The real injustice, as Job called it, was that God did nothing about these abuses (24:1–12). Equally troubling, murderers and adulterers roamed at night, doing their evil in the dark (24:13–17). Nevertheless, Job also knew the answer of the traditionalist—"they'll get their due"—and in the end, he affirmed it. Even though the mighty seemed secure, they too would vanish, having been cut off like so many heads of grain (24:18–24).

It was another moment of transition for Job in his constantly dynamic thinking, one that was interrupted by Bildad, who failed even more miserably than before to make a meaningful contribution. Job pounced on Bildad's brief allusion to God's peacemaking presence in the heavens (25:2). After a sarcastic jab about how helpful Bildad's counsel was, Job unleashed a vibrant description of what God *actually* does in those heavenly realms. Some of his discourse described the visible heavenly realms—the sky—but he ventured much farther. "The dead are in deep anguish, those beneath the waters and all that live in them" (26:5). *Sheol* and *'abbadon*, the abode of the dead, were exposed and vulnerable in the blinding light of God's presence (26:6). The sea, the scene of primordial chaos, was stilled by God. *Rahav*, a symbol of that chaos and closely linked with the serpent, was overpowered by God (26:12–13). Job knew that this was just the beginning; the rest was incomprehensible, and we are allowed only faint whispers (26:14). So much for benign, one-line descriptions of God's power, as Bildad would have it. Nevertheless, we pause momentarily. With this discourse, Job again remarkably ventured along the edges of those realms that would come bursting back to him in the torrent of words from God.

Let's presume for the moment that Bildad's somewhat awkward declaration followed by Job's dismissive response interrupted the turn in Job's reflections that we saw at the end of chapter 24. If that is so, then Job picked up that same theme again in chapter 27, further developing it as he struggled for satisfactory closure in the face of apparent moral chaos. He vowed by the God who had made his life bitter that he would not speak falsehood just to make others happy, that he would maintain his own integrity, and that he was righteous according to all the metrics he knew. And then he affirmed what the friends had said all along—and what traditional theology maintained. The end of the godless, in spite of appearances, would be at the hand of God. Their punishment would be accompanied by unimaginable terrors (27:13–23). God would not hear the cries of the wicked; the wicked would not call out to God because they had no relationship with him, a state entirely in contrast with Job's own experience.

And that is where we will leave it for now, except for two observations. First, Zophar apparently had nothing further to say, at least not as the third cycle is structured. Second, Job continued to talk about, rather than to, God. Perhaps it was his way of responding to the distance he was experiencing from the divine side.

> I have made the case that Job's wide-ranging reflections in these last chapters are not at all out of character for one who continued to wrestle as he did. Nevertheless, scholars differ in their assessments. For an overview of possible reconstructions of the third cycle of speeches, see Samuel Rolles Driver and George Buchanan Gray, *A Critical and Exegetical Commentary of the Book of Job*, vol. 1, ICC (New York: Scribner's Sons, 1921), xxxvii–xl; Hartley, *Job*, 24–26; and H. H. Rowley, *Job*, 170–79. Because chapter 27 sounds like a recapitulation of orthodoxy, some suggest that it was originally spoken by Zophar but that the designation was lost. It could also be that Job was so vexed by the friends that he pretty much co-opted both Bildad's and Zophar's speeches. Knowing what they would say, he took their words and lobbed them back in their face(s). From a literary perspective, perhaps the author deliberately dissolved the last cycle into a "confused tangle of incoherent voices—a formal way of paralleling the argument of Job that the hedge against chaos had given way and that disorder and evil in the world make clear understanding impossible" (J. Gerald Janzen, *Job*, IBC [Atlanta: John Knox, 1985], 172).

An Addendum: Job's Conviction Regarding His Own Sin

We want to linger on Job's apparent perception of his sin. The questions always come up: How could Job be "blameless" as he is described in the prologue? No human being is without sin; what is the point of that description? And how did Job view himself if he protested so much about his innocence? The Hebrew word translated "blameless" is *tam*. We have already seen that it does not imply sinless perfection. It may better be understood as describing a "person of integrity."

The best approach is to summarize what Job himself said. He cast about searching for the reasons for his predicament, repeatedly returning to the possibility of his own sin (cf. 13:23–26). In fact, he agonized over it, mindful that God was watching. After the "parody" on Psalm 8, which he started with "What is man that you make him great and give your heart (attention) to him . . . ?" (7:17), Job pleaded with God to look away (7:19). "I have sinned (or 'if I have sinned'), what will I do to you, O Watcher of humankind (*'adam*) . . . ? Why do you not pardon my transgression and take away my iniquity . . . ?" (7:20–21). Job's plea for pardon presumes his sense of guilt.

At the same time, Job entertained the notion that God was determined to find him guilty even if he was not (9:28–31), that God planned ill against him. "You seek out my iniquity and search for my sin, although you know I am not guilty" (10:6–7). After his description of God's artistry in forming him (10:8–12), he raised the same troubling issues again. "If I sin, you watch me and do not acquit me of my iniquity. If I am evil, woe to me! But I am in the right. I cannot lift up my head, filled with disgrace, but look on my affliction" (10:14–15). This is the real anguish of a person wrestling with his sometimes inexplicable nature. Job was at a loss to know whether he was guilty or innocent because shame was so bound up with his suffering (10:15).

Nevertheless, his conviction grew that he had been wronged, especially in light of the evidence that his life presented (23:11–12; 27:1–6; chs. 29–31). This desire to realize justice turned his focus from the allure of death to the demand for vindication. Each of these issues will surface again as we explore further Job's troubled relationship with God. Now, however, we turn our attention to the friends.

CHAPTER 19

Great Doctrine Misapplied

Introduction

Job's friends are often summarily dismissed as having little concern for the depth of his suffering, and as being far too quick to condemn him on the assumption that his afflictions were the result of sin. While it is true that their theological pronouncements did not fit Job's circumstances at all, it is equally true that they shared a traditional sense of divine justice, a justice without which the moral nature of the universe would be turned upside down. Put in simple terms, it went like this. If you are good, it is appropriate that you receive good in return; if you are wicked, watch out!

The friends manifested an abiding concern to defend this system of divine retributive justice, which in their minds was under attack with every utterance of Job. It is also the case that they had traveled great distances to be with Job, had mourned the terrible transformation that had taken place, and had spent seven silent days with him. Job's last word in his opening monologue (ch. 3) had been "turmoil" (*rogez*). The friends were compelled to offer their best assistance. One more thing: unbeknownst to them, their arguments were wholly supportive of the adversary's claim right from the beginning. Job was only good because he expected good in return.

They spoke in turn, starting with Eliphaz the Temanite, who was very possibly the senior member of the delegation. Each received a response from Job. Eliphaz and Bildad the Shuhite spoke three times; Zophar the Na'amatite limited himself to two lectures. The discourses of each are magnificent poetry through which emerge the personalities of the individuals. Their peculiar quirks grew increasingly pronounced as their frustration levels rose following each outburst of Job. All were galled at the fact that Job did not respond "properly" to their wisdom, and Job was equally frustrated that they had not really heard him.

The First Cycle of Dialogue: A Defense of God's Justice

In the first cycle, each friend appealed to a source of authority outside himself. For Eliphaz it was a whisper couched in a numinous and terrifying night "vision." Bildad's source of authority was long-standing poetic tradition, and Zophar appealed to mystery.

Responding to the agonizing outcry of Job, Eliphaz's very first words reminded Job of how he had helped those in need. That would have been a wonderful encouragement to Job, except that Eliphaz used his words as a backdrop for a biting criticism. It ran like this. Although Job had helped others, Eliphaz suggested that he could not handle his own trouble well. Needless to say, this was unkind in the extreme. Job, who had just confessed his fear and dread, was told that his "fear" should be his confidence (4:6).

Eliphaz reaffirmed the stability of the moral realm; those who are innocent do not perish, and those who are evil will reap the fruits of their actions. In the course of articulating this, however, he repeatedly circled back to fear. It seemed to attract him like a magnet. He described the plight of fearsome lions, using five different words for the creatures. His appeal to the hair-raising supernatural visitation was the stuff of nightmares, causing him trembling and terror. A spirit (or wind—*ruah*) slipped past his face, and a voice came from an unidentifiable form. It declared that no mortal could possibly be righteous before God and that humans are mere dust—crushed, broken, and soon to perish forever (4:16–21). "Man is born to trouble" (5:7).

Job's sole recourse was obvious to Eliphaz. He counseled Job to appeal to God, who cares for all of humankind, who thwarts the wicked, and who protects the needy. Eliphaz extolled the value of God's discipline and correction, and promised deliverance from evil, famine, war, and destruction. Job and his descendants would be blessed (5:17–26). Comprehensive, to be sure! Just for the record, Job followed Eliphaz's advice; he appealed to God, and he made his case in no uncertain terms.

In closing, Eliphaz assured Job that his words were true, and he admonished Job to apply them (5:27). Unfortunately, Eliphaz himself misapplied them, making them a most insidious kind of falsehood. Each promise, albeit well meant, no doubt severely wounded Job in light of what had happened to him. Imagine being in Job's place and having someone assure you that your dwelling would be secure, nothing of your property would be missing, and your children would be many (5:24–25). Something about that might sound hollow at best.

By the time Bildad spoke, Job had responded to Eliphaz's promises of God's goodness. *His* experience was that God's terrors were marshaled against him (6:4), which hardly appeared to be good. He wanted to die. It may be that Job's confrontational tone prompted Bildad's somewhat less gentle approach! Bildad commenced with, "your words are a mighty wind" (8:2). While this may simply be an insult, the image also conveys an undercurrent of potential danger; Job's words could be damaging. Bildad took it upon himself to quell any verbal mischief with a harsh and personalized statement of the retributive principle: "If your children sinned against [God], he sent them into the hand [power] of their transgressions" (8:4). This suggested that Job's intercession for his children (1:5) was ineffective. Bildad's subsequent promises of restoration sounded hollow after that blow.

At least Bildad did not pride himself on his own wisdom (8:8–10). Instead, he invoked long-standing tradition and the value of learning from the forefathers. He also had a poet's sensitivity to the moral lessons inherent in nature. Just as plants cannot grow without water, so the godless have no hope. Even though they may look good for a time, when uprooted their lives wither away, and any support they seek is as fragile as a spider's web (8:11–19). Like Eliphaz before him, Bildad affirmed that God's justice means that the blameless person is favored by God and those who do evil are not. Job had no quarrel with the truths that his friends articulated (9:2); they simply did not apply to his current situation.

When his turn came, Zophar acknowledged that Job had not been adequately answered by the friends' theological expositions of God's justice. His attempt therefore moved somewhat toward the perspective that God himself would present at the end. Zophar wished that God would speak (11:5), noted that wisdom is complex (11:6), and asked if Job could comprehend the unknown (11:7–9). Obviously, the answer was no. If Zophar had stopped at that point, he might have made progress, but he too felt compelled to call Job to repentance and to promise him all the brightness, peace, and security that seemingly attended those who walk with God. There is an irony in the fact that his affirmation that God's ways are hidden is followed by his own clarity in speaking for God.

Round One summation: the wicked are punished, the righteous are rewarded, and the friends relatively tactfully slipped Job into that formula. Their problem was, however, nailed by Job. "Will you speak wickedly on God's behalf? Will you speak deceitfully for him?" (13:7). The friends responded with seasoned formulas. Moving beyond these seems to have made them uncomfortable. It all sounds far too familiar; we find ourselves facing these temptations as well.

The Second Cycle: The Wicked
Have Every Reason to Fear

By the time the friends started in again (ch. 15), Job had turned *his* attention almost entirely to God and the comprehensive nature of God's sovereignty. Job longed for some kind of communion with God but saw little hope of this. Instead, his consistent experience was that God overpowers humans. Responding to these rather suspicious sentiments, each friend waxed eloquent in the second cycle on the terrible end awaiting the wicked, intending to scare Job into a proper attitude of repentance. Eliphaz boldly questioned Job's wisdom, piety, devotion, and general integrity. He claimed that the wisdom of the aged and tradition were on "their side" (15:10). In a line that must have been a bitter thrust, he prodded Job, asking if the "consolations" of God were not enough (15:11).

After this head-on attack, Eliphaz reverted to his previous theme (cf. 4:18): if God places no trust in his holy ones, how much more corrupt are humans, "who drink up evil like water" (15:16b)! On this basic premise he built the next segment of his case, a focused description of the fate of those who practice evil. As before, Eliphaz exploited fear and terror as he described the tormented state of the wicked (15:20–26). Even though the evil person appears to be well off, this will not last: "the breath of God's mouth will carry him away" (15:30c). According to Eliphaz, evil is at the core of human DNA: "conceiving trouble and giving birth to evil, and their womb prepares deceit" (15:35).

At the outset of Bildad's second response, he seemed to rebuke everyone for the stalled dialogue. The second-person pronouns are plural (18:2–3). Nevertheless, the most recent speaker was Job, and Bildad refocused on Job in verse 4: "(you are) tearing (your)self apart in your anger; is the earth to be abandoned because of you?" He then devoted his entire discourse to the darkness, terrors, and calamity that await those who are truly godless. He warned Job of impending entrapment:

> For he is sent into a net by his feet, and into its webbing he
>   wanders.
> A trap seizes him by the heel; a snare holds him fast.
> His cord is hidden on the ground; his trap lies in his path. (18:8–10)

Bildad's vivid imagery of constant terror and descent into nameless oblivion was intentionally horrifying. Death was a gruesome stalker after its prey and would consume the disintegrating body.

His calamity is ravenous;
disaster is ready for his falling.
It consumes pieces of his skin;
death's firstborn consumes his limbs. (18:12–13)

Equally faithful to the pattern, Zophar also indulged in a long recital about godless, covetous, and proud people who have oppressed the poor and have grown rich at their expense. As Zophar saw it, the end of every evil person was sure.

His bones are full of his youthful vigor,
but with him it will lie in the dust. (20:11)

The poison of serpents he will suck;
the tongue of an adder will kill him. (20:16)

When he has filled his belly,
he [God] will send against him his burning anger,
and rain down upon him his blows. (20:23)

Heaven will expose his guilt;
the earth will rise up against him.
A flood will expose his house,
rushing waters on the day of his wrath.
This is the portion from God of the wicked person,
the heritage appointed by God. (20:27–29)

In the course of his lecture, Zophar did let slip a significant part of his problem with Job: "I hear instruction that shames me" (20:3a). Perhaps we are reading thinly veiled undertones of wounded pride.

Each of the friends exposed the inherent weaknesses of evil people. Though the wicked appeared invincible, they were rotten at the core and God would destroy them. For his part, however, Job saw only their continuing strength and enviable security.

Although none of the friends named Job in this cycle, these pointed diatribes formed the basis for Round Three, which turned painfully personal as they accused Job of having engaged in the very same oppressive practices that would make "(the wicked) perish forever, like his own dung" (20:7a).

Carol Newsom downplays the apparently vicious tone of the friends' contributions. In her view, after Job's tumultuous initial outcry their intent was to help him restore his equilibrium (Newsom, *Moral Imaginations*, 94–97). Thus, moving into this second cycle, they pursued narrative threads that were intended to be instructive and therapeutic. The "fate of the wicked" narrative served to address the pressing matter of justice as it should be interpreted in the wider cultural reality. The "hope for the pious" thread encouraged engagement in religious practices as a way of coping with suffering. The friends were not attacking Job in this cycle so much as attempting to alter his narrative understanding of reality (ibid., 105–8).

The Third Cycle: Job Is Guilty!

Because none of the friends successfully scared Job into a confession with more oblique descriptions of "sinners in the hands of an angry God," Eliphaz took it upon himself to accuse Job directly of grievous social sins (ch. 22). His rhetorical technique was brilliant, commencing with two sets of questions. The first set anticipated negative answers (22:2–4), and in this context Eliphaz returned yet again to the matter of fear. "Does he (God) rebuke you for your fear? Will he bring you into judgment?"

He turned his next questions against Job with the clear expectation of positive responses. "Is not your evil great, and is not your sin endless?" (22:5). These questions served as his platform. He declared that Job's moral failures were the cause of the snares and peril surrounding him (22:6–11), manufacturing "facts" about Job's life in order to sustain his own immovable theological position. In Eliphaz's script, Job had exploited those who were already poor, he had withheld basic sustenance from the hungry and thirsty, and he had refused the pleas of widows and orphans. It was likely this false litany that compelled Job to come to his own defense in chapters 29 and 31. These brutal accusations were followed by vague ruminations on what an evil person's response might be. "Oh, God does not see this; what can the Almighty really do anyway?" was the gist of it.

Eliphaz closed this masterpiece with another call to agree with God and to go to God for instruction (22:21–22). If Job would do so, everything would be just splendid. He would be built up; God would be his gold and silver; the Almighty would be his delight and his prayer life would be renewed; and light would shine on all Job's ways. In sum, all would be well. Needless to say, not much of this was particularly fitting, apart from one prescient statement at the end: "(God) will deliver one who is not innocent, and he will be delivered by the cleanness of your hands" (22:30). As it turned out, Eliphaz himself would be the recipient of Job's intercession at the end of the story.

Bildad wisely refrained from any further direct comment on Job's moral standing and simply reminded his audience that, in light of God's sovereign dominion in the heavens, humankind has the status of a maggot. Bildad envisioned God's innumerable armies sustaining light and peace throughout those heavens. Job, on the other hand, noted less comforting aspects of the unseen realms—*sheol* and *'abbadon*, and the necessary destruction of *rahav* and the fleeing serpent (ch. 26). As we have already observed, Bildad's exceedingly abbreviated speech may be a hint that Job simply cut him off just as he was getting started. Perhaps because Job knew what Bildad would say, he mockingly introduced his own version of Bildad with 26:4—"Who helped you utter these words? And whose spirit spoke from your mouth?" Then he went on to mimic Bildad's tone: "The dead are in deep anguish" (26:5a). That's just a possibility.

Zophar even more wisely added nothing at all. At least that is the way the dialogue appears to us. His name is not mentioned. While the sentiments attributed to Job in 27:13–23 could be a Zophar original, it is just as likely that these really were Job's words. In fact, the dialogue disintegrated in its form as well as its substance.

What Do We Do with Friends Like These?

Here we have the efforts of the three friends. If we are honest, we hear ourselves more than we might care to confess. How quickly we assume some type of moral failure underlies the struggles with which our friends and acquaintances wrestle! How quickly we respond in injured pride when our assessment of the case is rejected for what it is—wrong! How much damage and pain we inflict instead of offering consolation!

Or, put another way that might be more to the point: "What egregious missteps can I avoid in this delicate and sometimes gnarly challenge of living with those who suffer?" What negative lessons might we learn from the responses of the friends to what they perceived to be Job's "theologically incorrect" positions? Their understanding of retributive justice was, after all, theologically sound as far as it went. The inherently moral nature of the universe necessitated this teaching—so they thought. How could they be faulted for their ignorance of the dialogue between God and the adversary at the outset? Furthermore, their instruction and counsel for righteous living sound pretty solid.

Just a further reminder: we don't want to miss the fact that Job's ongoing commentary regarding his friends was blistering. He felt deeply the pain that their words inflicted. They added to his torment (19:2) and they pursued him as badly as God did (19:22). They were liars and would have been best off by keeping silent (13:4–5). Job's sharp words would not be called "nice" by our contemporary standards, but they were right on target. Expanding that previous point, the problem inherent in each attempt by the friends to counsel Job was their distortion of the truth in one form or another: "Will you speak wickedly on God's behalf? Will you speak deceitfully for him?" (Job 13:7).

This is an adumbration of God's rebuke to Eliphaz at the end; indeed, they had not spoken truthfully because their words were false given Job's situation. They erred in consistently slipping Job into their moral formulas, subtly at first but egregiously at the end. All of this, in effect, constituted "false testimony" because it ran counter to the public witness to his character (cf. Deut 19:16–19). The friends had to be held accountable for what they did know: Job's long-term reputation and his own testimony. Ignoring those data, they allowed the inexplicable evil to determine wholly the shape of their thinking. They succumbed to the temptation to give out answers without fully hearing—to say nothing of understanding—the *experience* of Job. In the process, they abused their doctrinal knowledge in their crusade to defend God. Formulas were their theological security, and their pride was threatened when their counsel was rejected. In effect, they served as "devil's advocates." In their attempts to get Job to conform to their formulas, they espoused precisely what the *satan* said: Job only served God for what he got out of it.

Having said all that, the friends were most likely not intentionally duplicitous. They spoke very passionately about what they believed. Job's words also burst forth from his experience of the God in whom *he* believed. All were deeply emotional, and often the passion rose from feeling verbally assaulted or offended. When Job rejected the counsel of the friends, their pride was threatened, and their attempts to defend God were increasingly attempts to bolster their own confidence. Sound familiar? Job likewise responded from wounds to his person and pride. Everything he was had been reduced to nothing.

On another level, the friends were blind to the dynamic cosmic dimension of what was happening. Oh yes, they tried, and we must give credit to Bildad, for example, for raising the curtain just a bit on the hosts of heaven. Job, on the other hand, felt and expressed the reality of evil and its presence in the universe (26:5–14). To be sure, the inherently moral nature of the entire universe does necessitate a basic sense of retributive justice. Nevertheless, the friends failed to perceive or acknowledge the vast complexity of the powers and principalities in the heavenly court. Even though Job's awareness was still earthbound, he *knew* that much bigger issues were hanging in the balance.

What is most striking, simple as it sounds, is that the friends talked to Job about God in the most pious terms, admonishing him to pray to God in repentance lest the dismal fate of the wicked in a moral universe overtake him as well. They never addressed God directly. Job, on the other hand, talked frankly about God as he attempted to understand the horror that had overtaken him, but he also appealed again and again to God, evidence of his intimate relationship with God. We know from the prologue that this pattern characterized his life long before the crisis began. Job's practice of offering sacrifices on behalf of his children demonstrated at the outset that he was in the habit of directing his attention to God. This is a lesson that will bear repetition, and we will indeed return to it.

A balancing act: Is there never a place for confrontation and challenge in light of severe moral lapses in the life of the community of faith? Is Job the Old Testament counterpart of "Judge not lest you be judged" (Matt 7:1)? After all, not every situation is a Job situation, and most of us are fairly adept sinners who do need to engage in confession. There is, however, at least one very distinct difference. To all observers, Job's life did indeed back up his claims. That is radically different from behavior and words that clearly need to be challenged. This is yet another reminder to be careful and discerning. With that gentle exhortation, we move ahead to confront God as both Adversary and Advocate.

Consider what it takes to sit in the presence of a deeply suffering person. Explanations, even though we are so often nervously compelled to attempt them, are rarely appropriate, even when our sufferer cries out "Why?" For many, but not all, silent presence is a comfort. Sensitivity to utter weariness that demands our trusting withdrawal for a time is also essential. Attending prayerfully to the promptings of God's Spirit is unfailingly the best path. That avoids dependence on our own limited understanding of always terribly complex situations. For some, it might be helpful to join Henri Nouwen (*The Inner Voice of Love: A Journey through Anguish to Freedom*) as he wrestled through his own dark season and was able to write about it.

CHAPTER 20

God as Job's Adversary, Advocate, and Absent Friend

Introduction

From the prologue, we learned that God was one of Job's greatest fans, echoing the accolades "blameless, upright, God-fearing, and one who avoids evil" from the narrator's introduction (1:1). That might be considered advocacy at its best, except that, of course, God intentionally spoke those words to the *satan*, setting Job on a collision course with that adversary. God's sovereign permission giving Job into the *satan's* hand—twice—placed God squarely on the adversarial side of the ring as well. In other words, God's roles were more than a bit complicated right from the beginning.

It is not particularly comfortable to think of God as divine Advocate *and* Adversary for Job or, even more unsettling, for us. What do those titles mean as the celestial realms intersect with earth? What did Job expect from an Advocate whose domain was somewhere in heaven? Could that Being possibly share identities with the God who was so obviously in an adversarial relationship with Job? Another entirely different way of posing the same set of questions addresses the nature of God in head-to-head combat with evil. Multiple questions flood into our minds. How did the conflict start? Who initiated it? How? And for what end?

I will not claim the wisdom to answer these questions, even though we will do some poking about in various corners. Thoughtful and reflective persons have wrestled with such issues since the garden of Eden. In this chapter, we will take a much more limited approach, unpacking in more detail three passages that we rather summarily skipped over earlier. In preparation for that endeavor, it will be important to explore at greater length the "maximalist" perception of God's sovereignty that Job clearly affirmed. Thus, we first change the lens for the wide-angle view.

Maximalist Sovereignty

Unlike many self-absorbed sufferers, Job consistently articulated a comprehensive sense of God's sovereignty. That is the point of the word "maximalist." To be sure, he addressed God's sovereignty *as it had radically altered his own life*, but his grasp extended far beyond that limited sphere. From the start, he referred to God as Almighty (Shaddai), but not benignly so; instead, the Almighty's arrows were in him and the terrors of God were arrayed against him (6:4). Although Eliphaz urged Job to turn to God, that did not seem possible; Job's God was malevolent. Job did not mince words about the agonies to which God had subjected him, and we will return to those shortly.

Job's vision equally included the immeasurable wisdom and power of God that were evident to him in the natural realm. God removed mountains, shook the earth, shut up the lights of the sun and stars, and trampled the waves of the sea (9:4–10). We linger over these images. The amount of raw power and chronological time needed to remove mountains exceeds our imagination, but this is a minor disruption in God's exquisitely designed creation. Nevertheless, what Job *could* see served as a sufficient link to God's vast domain far beyond Job's own horizon. At this point, however, Job perceived God's design as irretrievably destructive; it was built into nature. In the same way that God destroyed mammoth mountains, wore down rocks, and washed away soil, God was piece by piece destroying human hope: "Nevertheless, the falling mountain crumbles; the mighty rock is hewn from its place. Water rubs away stones; its floods wash away the dust of the earth, and you have caused the hope of humans to perish" (14:18–19).

Job revisited God's wisdom, power, counsel, and understanding, this time in conjunction with the destiny of every human (12:13–21). Nobody can outfox God. Consummate liars and those who are gullible—both are God's. Society's elite classes—let's call them lawyers and supreme court justices, presidents and prime ministers, popes and archbishops—are all exposed as inept (12:16–21). God brings into the light those things that lurk in the darkness. God is in the business of building and taking down nations as well as their leaders, sometimes in humiliating circumstances (12:22–25). God's anger causes the most feared of forces (the "cohorts of *rahav*") to cower (9:13).

In sum, Job knew there was nothing outside God's purview; he remained enthroned on high. The deeper Job's darkness, and the more dreadful his perception of God's sovereignty, the greater was his clamor to engage God. Given what we have just summarized, this took remarkable courage, even more so when Job declared that God was both responsible for the injustice in the world (9:24)—allowing the wicked to prosper (21:7–21)—and inattentive to it (24:1–12).

In light of this overwhelming sense of God's unassailable power, Job initially requested that God would bring his life to an end rather than continue the torment. He recognized his own weakness and potential for denying God (6:10). That, in his mind, would add disaster to disaster. As his journey continued, however, Job insisted that purity comes from going through the fire. "He knows the way that I take, and when he has tried me, I shall come forth as gold" (23:10). This was an extraordinary declaration from one enduring such an unending ordeal.

One final note for now: Job used the titles "God" (*'elohim*) and "Almighty" almost exclusively in the dialogues. "Lord" is absent, with the exception of 12:9. The author(s) of this text conveyed, even with the divine names, God's majesty and transcendence and the current vacuum in Job's world. The divine name Lord is bound up with covenant and relationship. Its Hebrew form is built from the verb "to be" and implies God's eternal self-existence on behalf of his people.

Sovereign God as Adversary and Advocate

Job had no quarrel with the basic truths his friends articulated about God (Job 9:2), although he certainly took issue with their placing him in the crosshairs every time they opened their mouths. Their belief system was his as well. That is why his experience was so shattering for him and why his questions were so anguished. Job spoke correctly (cf. 42:7–8) in that he knew beyond a shadow of a doubt that God *was* responsible for his plight. There was no "minimal sovereignty" in Job's theology book. On the heels of his strongest declarations of God's culpability (9:30–31; 16:7–14), Job expressed his yearning and expectation that *Someone* in the heavens could and would come to his aid. The juxtaposition in each case is compelling. That person would function as a mediator, advocate, and intercessor (9:33–34; 16:19–21) to restore the lost relationship.

Job 9:15–35—The Contests of Strength and Justice

Initially, with good reason, Job sounded uncertain about the possibility of an arbitrator, even though he needed one so desperately. He was undergoing what he described as judicial assault:

> Though (*'im*) I have been righteous (*tsadaqti*), I cannot answer him;
> to my Judge I must appeal for mercy.

If (*'im*) I summoned him and he answered me,
I would not believe that he would hear my voice,
because with a storm he would crush me
and multiply my wounds without cause.
He would not allow me to return my breath,
because he fills me with bitterness.
If it is strength, behold he is mighty.
If it is justice, who will make him recognize me? (9:15–19)

As Job experienced it, this was adversarial injustice in the extreme, and it was coming steadily from the hand of God, whose might and cosmic power Job had just extolled. Job was further confused by his own deep inability to sort through the moral implications of this morass. Who, in the end, was responsible, Job or God?

Though (*'im*) I am righteous (*'etsdaq*), my mouth brings me evil;
I am blameless (*tam*), but he (or "it") made me crooked. (9:20)

Job's provisional conclusion is fraught with moral ambiguity:

[God] destroys both the blameless and the wicked.
If disaster causes sudden death,
he mocks at the despair of the innocent.
The earth is given into the hand of the wicked;
he covers the faces of her judges.
If not he, then who? (9:22b–24)

The expression translated "despair of the innocent" (*massat neqiyyim*) is a bit difficult to pin down. The first word has been understood by some interpreters to come from the Hebrew root *m-s-s*, meaning "to melt away," figuratively understood as "to despair." An alternative rendition takes it as derived from *nasah* ("to test") and would read, "He mocks at the trial of the innocent."

With that indictment, most of us would head for the nearest appellate court, but Job was not quite finished. He circled back to God's meddling with his own attempts to be righteous and blameless:

If I washed myself with the waters of snow;
if I purified my hands with lye (*bor*),
then you would sink me in the pit
and my clothes would loathe me. (9:30–31)

In other words, God was turning justice on its head by making Job filthy. Job recognized the utter futility of fighting against this treatment because he was a man, and God was not. How could they ever meet on an even playing field (9:32)? If only there were someone to intervene—but who? And how? Job's perspective was not hopeful:

> There is not between us an arbitrator;
> he would place his hand on the two of us.
> He would remove from me his rod,
> and his dread would not terrify me.
> I would speak and not be afraid of him,
> for I am not thus with me. (9:33–35)

The first line here might also be rendered "would that there were an arbitrator," which would fit better with the second clause. Neither translation, however, makes it sound as if Job expected a real mediator to remove the painful rod, the dreadful terror. When we get to the last clause, we scratch our heads. What was Job trying to say? Most translations paraphrase this sufficiently that we think we understand it, but this is one of the instances where Job's words ground to a halt. How could anyone possibly articulate what needed to be said or what needed to be done?

Job 16:7–22 — God as Divine Warrior *against* Job

Job's description could not be more stark or horrifying. *God* was unquestionably his adversary (16:9), even though Job hardly dared to name God in such a damning description. This could be another indication of Job's impeccable character; he could not bring himself to juxtapose the name of God Almighty with the forthcoming accusations. Job used words like "hate" and "wrath" to capture the force of God's treatment of him. The imagery combines wild animal and warrior into one raging enemy who seized him by the neck and dashed him. Job felt utterly helpless and torn by the fierce rage of a ferocious beast shaking its prey in its mouth. God set him up as a vulnerable target. Like a city under siege, ranks of warriors poured at him and assailed him. He was shattered, crushed, and cast into the clutches of wicked people (16:7–14). This was the work of an enemy, someone out to destroy him.

Even though some translations include "God" in 16:7 (NIV, ESV, NRSV) and 16:9 (NIV), those are interpretations. A literal rendition of 16:7 is "He has worn me out." The matter is complicated by the second half of 16:7, which says "*you* have made desolate." Only once in this accusation did Job explicitly name God: "*El* delivers me up to evil" (16:11a).

And Job was destroyed. His honor was shattered, and in every describable way he was publicly humiliated. His well-being was completely gone. He described himself in pitiable terms. He covered his scabby skin with sackcloth and buried his strength (*qeren*, "horn") in dust. His face was red with weeping, and over his eyes were shadows of death (16:15–16). Yet from that brokenness, Job envisioned an encounter that could and would and must set everything right. He called on the earth to yield evidence (16:18). This was language used by God's covenant mediators, the prophets. As a matter of course, they summoned heaven and earth to be witnesses when God's covenant was broken (Deut 32:1; Isa 1:2).

As Job called on the earth, he likewise invoked heaven to produce a witness. "Also now, behold, my witness (*'edi*) is in heaven, and my witness (*sahadi*) is on high" (16:19). Just at this critical point, the text turns ambiguous. What does verse 20 say? The primary interpretive options are based on the meaning of one word (*melits*), often translated "intercessor(s)," in the first part of the verse. One possibility is: "My intercessors are my friends (or 'my friends are my intercessors') as my eyes pour out tears to God." This sustains the plural form in Hebrew for the word translated "intercessors" and that matches the plural "friends."

To make this work in the context, we might press the Hebrew syntax a bit further. Perhaps Job was saying "my friends *should* be my intercessors." Or this may have been a plea, something along the lines of "Oh friends, be my intercessors!" Having just referenced a witness and advocate in heaven, now Job called on his friends to be the mediators they should have been all along.

There is, however, another direction we might go. The word interpreted here as "intercessors" has the same root letters in Hebrew as the word for "mock." That would certainly fit Job's perception of his friends' *actual* involvement. It would read, "My friends mock me as my eyes pour out tears." Cruel mockers show up in Job's very next lines: "Surely there are mockers around me" (Job 17:2; the Hebrew word for "mockers" here is a synonym of *melits* in 16:20). In his brokenness, seeing the grave ahead of him, Job perceived them as something akin to scavengers (17:1–2).

Both of these interpretations sound pretty "earthbound." Is there any way that in 16:20 Job might have been referring to a singular heavenly intercessor, especially in light of his affirmation of the heavenly witness and advocate in the preceding verse? That has been the traditional interpretation, both Jewish and Christian. An important contextual consideration is that verse 21a returns to the judicial interface between humans and God: "And he will intercede for a man with God."

> At this point, it will be valuable to explore several additional details of the Hebrew. The first one has to do with the parallel terms translated "my witness" in 16:19. The second one is used in the Bible only here, though a related Aramaic word appears in Gen 31:47 with reference to the heap of stones left as a witness between Jacob and Laban. "Advocate" is one possibility, but the connotations of that may be more positive than what is implied in the word. The ESV has "he who testifies for me." Moving forward to 16:20, Elihu later used the ambiguous word here, *melits*, as a singular noun: "If there were for him an angel, an intercessor (*melits*), one from among a thousand, to declare for a person his uprightness . . ." (33:23). The word also appears in Gen 42:23, where Joseph could understand his brothers but they did not know it because an "interpreter" was between them. Just to complicate the matter, however, a "mocker" in the book of Proverbs is a *lets*; again, the term we are considering is *melits*, and we can see and hear the possible relationship. One more contextual factor might shed additional light on the puzzle. The word translated "intercede" in 16:21a is *yokhaḥ*. If we back up to 9:33, the related participle there (*mokhiaḥ*) refers to the longed-for arbiter. In that context, this is clearly an interceding presence; perhaps so also here as Job seeks someone to intervene *"for"* a man *"with"* God (16:21). This combination of factors may underlie the traditional interpretation of a single heavenly Person who intercedes.

Clearly, the passage in its entirety suggests that Job defied set theological systems, perhaps including his own. His faith was of a magnitude that he wrapped his mind at least partially around the divine Warrior and Enemy also being the perfect divine Advocate and Intercessor. This was one more step in peeling back the layers of Job's faith. His unshakable confidence in God's absolute sovereignty undergirded each succeeding declaration in its context. For the past three chapters, Job's thinking was in the judicial framework. He was about to add another dimension.

> Is this the end of the discussion? No. There are those who presume that Job could never have drawn the identity of his known Enemy, God, together with an Advocate, also God. This is logically irreconcilable and would have taxed his cognitive capacities in the extreme. Instead, from this alternative interpretive framework, Job understood this intercessor as a third party, a powerful celestial figure, perhaps akin to one of the sons of God. We have already seen that the heavens were pulsing with supernatural beings. Job

may have rightly hoped that one of them might step up to the plate on his behalf. As one example of this interpretation, see Norman C. Habel, *The Book of Job*, OTL (Philadelphia: Westminster, 1985), 274–76. This argument, however, fails in the face of Job's understanding of God's sovereignty. Job knew that God overpowers everyone and everything in his path. Even a majestic celestial advocate, if it were anyone other than God, would not be a source of hope for Job. That prospect would simply add to the futility of the case and deepen Job's frustration. Janzen has suggested that seeking to identify the "witness" is misguided. Instead, Job's desperation led him to reach into the utterly unknown (Janzen, *Job*, 125). Balentine focused on the unconventional and unsettling aspects of lament, of which Job 16 is a first-rate example (*Job*, 254–67).

Job 19:6–27—Kinsman-Redeemer

Alongside the visceral physical torment, Job continued to reel from emotional and social shockwaves. All his children had been eliminated in one blow. Losing one beloved family member is unbearable; grief comes in waves of varying degrees of intensity. Job's loss was magnified by ten. In addition, because he was physically repulsive, what should have been his supportive social network melted into the background. Every member of his extensive household treated him like a complete stranger. His servant would not bother to answer when Job called. His wife and brothers found his presence unpleasant in the extreme, and he was mocked by children who should have honored him (19:13–20). In sum, the kinship bond, so important for that culture, was shattered for Job, and Job held God responsible—again (19:21–22). In another clarion call for justice, Job asked that his words would be written, inscribed in a book, and carved into a rock with an iron and lead stylus as a witness (19:23–24).

And here are those words of witness (19:25–27), permanently preserved in a way that likely far exceeded anything Job might have anticipated. The exceedingly literal translation offered here is our first step in probing the depths of this passage.

> And I, I know my redeemer (*go'el*) lives,
> and at the last upon dust he will rise up.
> And after my skin they have struck off thus;
> and/but/yet from my flesh I shall see God,
> whom I shall see for myself; and my eyes have seen and not a
>   stranger.
> My inmost parts ("kidneys") are spent/exhausted in my breast.

This obviously needs some clarification! Of all Job's pleas for a mediating figure, none is better known or more beloved than this. It is, however, also ambiguous. Job *knew* (the Hebrew is emphatic) that his redeemer was living. The title "redeemer" drew on Israelite redemption theology, which had at its core the love of kin that would prompt a relative to buy back and deliver to freedom someone bound in slavery. Even though Job seems to have lived outside that context, his story as we have it was infused with the spirit and worldview of the people of Israel. Their foundational experience was the exodus from Egypt, on which the redemptive themes in the Hebrew are built. In the story of Ruth, for example, we encounter the practice of the kinsman Boaz buying back Naomi's property and acquiring Ruth as a wife at the same time. Isaiah repeatedly used "Redeemer" in conjunction with "the Holy One of Israel" to assure his audience that the God of Abraham, Isaac, and Jacob would restore them (41:14; 43:14; 49:7; 54:5–8).The term in Job is especially fitting in light of the preceding verses, which describe how Job's literal kin had deserted him.

Job declared that his redeemer would rise up, assuming a position of authority with reference to the long-anticipated court scene. The dust may be an allusion to the humiliating place in which Job found himself at that moment. The word for "dust" occurs twenty-six times in the book of Job and underscores his frailty. That in turn points to the broader metanarrative of humankind: "For dust you are and to dust you shall return" (Gen 3:19).

Job 19:25–27 has often been interpreted eschatologically, reading 'aharon as "in the end." Viewed through this lens, Job was anticipating his death, graphically imagined as worms destroying the skin of his corpse, followed by a resurrection of sorts when the Redeemer—here interpreted as God—would rise up to judge, at which point Job would see God. No matter what interpretive lens we train on the passage, about this last point Job was emphatic. He would see God; he would see God for himself; his eyes would behold God. There was no question on this point in Job's mind. (Fast forward to the end of the book; Job *did* see God, and it satisfied him.) In the meantime, depending on how we understand "from my flesh," that vision of God could be either apart from his flesh—a spiritual vision—or from within his flesh, alluding to a bodily resurrection from the dead. The latter reading presumes that Job was thinking of some vision of God after his death.

Nevertheless, it is just as possible that "afterwards" or "at the last" refers to Job's determination to triumph over the devastation of his physical body and, from the perspective of still being alive ("in my flesh"), to see God, again with the same emphatic assurance as we noted above. That ambiguous sentence about his skin could refer to what had seemed like the endless scraping process by which he carved maggots (worms) from his flesh. Perhaps here he was envisioning a time when all those worms would be struck off his flesh.

If this is a possible paradigm, then Job was confident that he would live to see God defend him—even against God himself! That is the paradox with which Job wrestled throughout, and his expressions are founded in his fledgling grasp of God's boundless sovereignty. Thus, this was not hope for his future resurrection in the end times but hope that God would restore and vindicate him in this life.

> When Job spoke of his own direct "seeing" of God, the Hebrew verb is *ḥazah*. Used twice here, it primarily appears in poetic texts and often indicates extraordinary visions of God. See, for example, Isa 1:1; Amos 1:1. When Job returned to his eyes "seeing," the verb used is the more common *ra'ah*.

One more thought from our New Testament perspective: The astounding truth that Job may have grasped regarding God's role as Defender, Redeemer, and Kinsman for his people finds its completion in the finished work of Jesus Christ. In the incarnation, God identified with all of humankind's Jobs and took on the entirety of their sufferings. While those who follow Christ will suffer in this world, he is their Redeemer and Defender before the Father's throne. Job is the earliest expression in the biblical metanarrative of salvation through suffering.

Absent Friend

As Job hurtled along his trajectory, he grasped at the possibilities afforded by a lawsuit of sorts, but the farther he traveled on that route, the more we see his deeper longing simply for the relationship that he had enjoyed *with* God to be restored. The beginnings of that yearning appear almost immediately. There is an emotional and poignant tone to his passing thought that God might seek him after his death *and not find him* (7:21). It sounds like our imaginations when we harbor thoughts about dying and the hoped-for response from people who will care *too late*. We see the same faint hope surface again: oh that God would call him, that God would long for him (14:15).

In Job 19:25–27, the passage we explored in depth above, Job's conviction that he would *see* God drives this even further. God was an absent friend with whom Job increasingly expected to be reunited. This sets the stage for Job's revisiting his past and reflecting on the joyful relationship he and his Friend had shared (ch. 29). We will take that up shortly, but first our trajectory carries us to the far reaches of wisdom. Where may it be found?

CHAPTER 21

Time to Take a Breath: The Far Reaches of Wisdom

Introduction

If we are not reading carefully, it's easy to move from chapter 27 to 28, simply presume that Job continued to speak, and sail right on into chapters 29 and beyond. That's especially true if our reading is guided (as it often is) by headings in whatever translation we are reading. The ESV, for example, shapes our perception with "Job Continues: Where Is Wisdom?" at the beginning of chapter 28. Likewise, the NKJV reads "Job's Discourse on Wisdom." Depending on the edition, the NIV varies between suggesting an interlude, on the one hand, and not including a break between chapters 27 and 28, implying that Job simply continued.

The nature of what we are about to investigate suggests that chapter 28 is an "outsider's" voice. It gives the reading/listening audience breathing space. There had been words in profusion, overwhelming in sheer volume, to say nothing of tone. Thus, time for silent contemplation was essential. This works best if Job himself stopped speaking into the drama.

"Where may wisdom be found?" We might ask: Why inquire about wisdom at this point? Hasn't the disputation been about justice and righteousness? If anything, Job might have been asking, "Where is *God* to be found?" Is this another hint that they had all missed something critical? Is it a preparation for the revelation of God's vast creative wisdom in the final discourses?

Whoever uttered these verses, their contents are rich. The metaphors send us far underground into the darkest mine, back to the heart of the precious metals exchange, and beyond to death and destruction. What a journey! Likewise, the human quest for wisdom ventures into the deepest and loneliest places as well as the teeming hubs of urban life. It seems to come up empty-handed. But wait—that may not be the end of the story.

The Place of This Poem and Its Source

In the previous chapter (27), Job finished his own version of what happens to the evil person. It was full of the same kind of terrors that the friends invoked: floods, whirlwinds, and the dreaded east wind sweeping the sinner away with such ferocity that he could only flee. Then the east wind clapped its hands and hissed, a truly unpleasant personification (27:23). Full stop.

In the biblical text, the east wind is, with only one exception (Exod 14:21), a fierce and destructive force. Jeremiah warned of a scorching wind from the desert as severe judgment (4:11–12). An east wind scattered God's people (Jer 18:17), dried up the fruit of the allegorical vine (Ezek 19:12), and wrecked Tyre in the heart of the sea (Ezek 27:26). Exodus 14:21, however, narrates how the Lord sent a strong east wind to dry up the sea before the departing Israelites; this resulted in their rescue, but the walls of water were the death of the Egyptians.

The very next line (28:1) waxes lyrically philosophical: "There is a place for drawing out silver, a place to refine gold." Continuing: humans search diligently, risking their lives, for these precious metals, along with iron and bronze, because of their extraordinary value. Was this Job speaking? The transition is so abrupt, we can hardly imagine the maggot-covered, beaten man sitting on a pile of dust and ashes suddenly distancing himself so radically from his suffering to talk about the adventure of exploring an underground mining shaft. Yet this chapter does exactly that.

Instead of presuming that Job continued to speak, it might fit better with the overarching poetic development to suggest that the narrator inserted an intentional intermission here. The vigorous battle between Job and the three friends over God's justice had resulted in a stalemate, and it had been a most unsatisfactory experience. Thus, the curtain closed temporarily on the site of the conflict, and the audience was treated to a soliloquy from another voice. This poem compels us to explore why the previous disputations had gone awry. Once this is done, then we pick up the story again. It certainly was not completed; it would now head in a different direction, starting with Job's retrospective (chs. 29–30) and his oath (ch. 31).

Structure and Contents of the Poem

No matter who was responsible for this poem, it is a descriptive masterpiece as it moves the whole drama forward. Wisdom is elusive, and yet its value is so off the charts that humans engage in an endless and intrepid search for it. In the first section of the poem, we come face to face with how lonely and dangerous the quest is. The inestimable value of wisdom is the centerpiece of the second part. The final section affirms that God alone knows where wisdom is to be found; it is bound up with his dynamic creativity.

The Mining Metaphor (vv. 1–11)

In biblical times, mining precious ore took a prodigious amount of labor. It still does, although we have harnessed technology to do the heavy hauling for us. The metals themselves are in darkness, buried deep in the bowels of the earth and difficult to extract. Further, the miner's task was a lonely one, to say nothing of dangerous. He was compelled to burrow into shafts and hang in precarious places. In antiquity, human hands and rudimentary tools were set against massive mountains, and slowly, as the miner kept digging away, he "overturned the root of the mountains" (28:9).

Those who went after iron ore, silver, or gold were driven far underground, forgotten by people above them going about their daily tasks. Even the most keen-eyed creatures, birds of prey, would have missed the enterprise; it was completely hidden from sight. Mighty creatures whose rule of the wild places was incontestable did not walk in those paths. Nevertheless, the smallest degree of success was enough to compel the miner forward into further darkness. We cast our memory back into American history, recalling that mere flecks of gold sent thousands out to stake claims and spend countless hours panning for gold.

Mining is a telling metaphor in terms of the search for wisdom. Even though some aspects of the human quest for wisdom bring light (vv. 3 and 11), the ultimate goal continues to be elusively in the shadows, always somewhere farther ahead. Like mining, the search for wisdom is arduous, takes a very long time, and is a lonely endeavor. At the same time, both wisdom and the prospect of precious metals draw us like magnets.

There are additional dimensions to this metaphor that make it particularly fitting in the context of Job. Lonely suffering and endless seeking are at the heart of the Job narrative. Our lived experience repeatedly demonstrates that wisdom seems best grasped, even if temporarily, when we are at the painful end of ourselves or beside ourselves with grief. Perhaps we come closer to elusive wisdom when, like Job, we turn to God with questions and accusations that scare the daylights out of would-be comforters. To repeat: the way of suffering is, like the search for precious ores and true wisdom, a lonely and difficult path. It thrusts us into the darkness that terrifies; a recurring theme in Job is darkness and the deep shadow of death. At the same time that suffering saps our strength, it compels us to press further. "Mining" for precious ore, for wisdom, for peace of mind and heart, for understanding, for relief from anguish—all drive us well beyond our inherent strength.

The metaphor may send us one last direction, although the connection is more tenuous. The components of ore and metal are static. Once they are at the surface, they can be refined and shaped, but not dramatically altered. So it was too with the traditional wisdom of the friends. By way of contrast, the miner keeps exploring, venturing farther into the deep recesses and readjusting tools and perspective. That was characteristic of Job in his quest.

The Inestimable Value of Wisdom (vv. 12–22)

The author paused to recalibrate: "But wisdom, where shall it be found, and what is the place of understanding?" (28:12). These questions recur in verse 20 as well. Each refrain is followed by flat-out responses that are not encouraging if we want answers and not mystery. Wisdom is not in the land of the living, and no living creature can see it. The deep and the sea, both fearsome places, say "nope, not with us." *'Abaddon* (destruction) and death are beyond the deepest digging that humans could ever do, and they have heard only an echo. Each of these terrible places is personified, and they all come up lacking. At least death has something to report, perhaps because dying begins to draw us out of ourselves and closer to wisdom. It makes sense. Nonetheless, each of those brief quests as to "where" we might find wisdom is not the main issue here. The metaphorical connection between the first part of the poem and the second is the value of the treasure that is brought to the surface by the intrepid and undeterred miner. It is far beyond every precious metal that is known and far beyond the sum total of mined ores and gems.

> Five different words for "gold" appear in the space of five verses in Job 28: *segor* (v. 15); *ketem 'ophir* (v. 16); *zahav* (v. 17); *paz* (v. 17); *ketem tahor* (v. 19). These words are heaped up, like an overabundance of wealth. Together they suggest the processes of refining and purifying so that this is the *best* gold. Interlaced with the additional exquisite gems, the beauty and value of the whole collection is breathtaking.

How can the imagery of Job 28 be made real for garden-variety twenty-first-century readers, who seldom see an abundance of pure gold, silver, rubies, topaz, and sapphires up close? We think of the court of Solomon, in which gold, silver, precious gems, and spices were visibly abundant

(1 Kgs 10; 2 Chr 9). That may have been the political and economic back-drop for the description in Job 28, but most of us do not deal in gold and precious gems. Even if we did, our small claim would be a tiny fraction of the whole potential. Consider what treasures lie in retail stores around the world, await refining in industrial complexes, or still rest underground. The numbers are staggering. If the mind-numbing figures about national debts roll past our ears without making much impression, certainly these sums will as well. Wisdom is more valuable than billions and billions of dollars of forgiven debt. Wisdom exceeds what all the monarchs of the world hold in their Swiss bank accounts. Wisdom far surpasses the value of the crown jewels. Would we forego the opportunity to have any or all of that if we could be assured that we would be wise? If we cannot compute these ideas of value, it remains a very theoretical question and, of all things, the need for wisdom must not be theoretical!

Let's try it from the other side. What would it mean to be truly wise—all the time? We would no longer make stupid missteps. Decisions would be ones that truly resolved critical problems, and were able to do so without favoring one side or another. We would not endanger the well-being of individuals, family members, whole groups, or entire nations.

As is evident, I have been flailing about without articulating either side of the equation satisfactorily. The odd conundrum of this section of the poem and of our lives' quests is this: what we want and crave and need the most is always, forever unattainable in our human efforts. It is both valuable and hidden. Yet we know we must search for it. This will be an unfulfillable, lifelong frustration because human brilliance and ingenuity only get us so far. This sounds suspiciously like Qohelet. On the other hand, depending on what perspective we bring to the task, this could also be a joyful quest. That may be God's challenge to Job at the end of the story.

> Set yourself to the task of "valuing wisdom." Write down the most astonishing sums of valuable items that you can wrap your imagination around. Then, write down what characterizes the kind of wisdom you wish you intrinsically had. Pause to consider how these columns correspond to each other in your own "value metrics." Which would you honestly seek more fervently?

God Knows the Way to and the Place of Wisdom (vv. 23–28)

At this point the poet creates for us a resting place, and it is a necessary one, given the emotional roller coaster of the preceding stanzas. Our mortal enemies, death and destruction, have been proven helpless in this regard, but *God* knows. That may be too pat an answer for some, but at least it is a counterpoint to the human limitations we have just encountered. And it allows us another lens on the issue, one that will bring some light into the dark spaces and then help refocus that light.

"Wisdom" is not specified in these successive verses; the text simply refers to "it" throughout. More vital in this description are the verbs. God *understood* and *knew* wisdom's way and place (28:23). These two verbs are perfect tenses in Hebrew; the simplest rendition is what we think of as past tense. While Hebrew verb tenses can be particularly fluid in poetry, we might at least say that God from the very beginning knew and understood, and continues to do so, because of wisdom's part in the very processes of creation. The continuing dimension is reflected in following future (imperfect) verb forms. God *looks* and *sees* in the far reaches of earth and heaven the ongoing and dynamic creativity still being unveiled (28:24). There is a profoundly mysterious connection—we get it faintly—between wisdom's place and God's mighty creative activities.

We hear faint whispers of the coming whirlwind of chapter 38 in God's acts of measuring wind and water, setting a decree for rain, and establishing the ways for thunder and lightning. All these are part of wisdom. Just one small observation: we are repeatedly astonished as we watch lightning streak across the sky in always unpredictable patterns. God knows each one. These God-ordained weather-related snapshots are again drawn into the wisdom web, and they are the prism through which we see multiple, beautiful, and sometimes terrifying facets of wisdom. Here is a parenthetical subtext: all of this is well beyond our capacity to wrap it up into a neat theory.

Wisdom too gets tested by its Author. God "saw it," "declared it," "established it," and also "investigated it" (28:27). "Then he (God) said to the man (*'adam*), 'Behold, the fear of Adonai (Lord, Master), this is wisdom, and turning from evil is understanding' " (28:28). Whereas human efforts can never attain to wisdom, making correct moral choices is the light toward that path. What an incredible paradigm shift!

In the End: "The Fear of the Lord Is the Beginning of Wisdom"

The echo from Job 1:1 is unmistakable, and we are not to miss it. Job feared the Lord and turned away from evil. God declared that the pattern of obedience that characterized all of Job's life represented actively engaged wisdom. The only change in this context is the substitution of Adonai for the divine covenant name YHWH (LORD). This ties the narrator's far-reaching philosophical/theological adventure right back into the narrative. Job's is the next voice we will hear, and he will continue to maintain his integrity, based entirely on his stubborn fear of God and refusal to compromise his truthfulness.

A second observation is really a question: Presuming that God made this declaration, to whom and when was he speaking? "To the man (or person)" suggests a human audience. Was this intended to represent a primordial address to Adam? Was it intended as a distillation of wisdom for general human consumption ('adam representing humankind)?

In this declaration lie hope and joy. Wisdom is not entirely off-limits and is not always elusive. As the book of Proverbs repeatedly indicates, there is a lot that we can *do* that will weave wisdom into the fabric of our lives. God has hidden a great deal from us this side of heaven, but he has also revealed the path we ought to take step by step in obedience. "Fear of the LORD" is not paralyzing anxiety or dread. On the contrary, it is life-sustaining.

Proper fear of the Lord is also germane as we face the vexing problems of suffering and death. Rather than swirling away in the vortex of unanswered questions, we can revel in the fact that God remains Master Designer of the universe, and the Master's instructions are sufficiently clear for our lives. Obedience is the beginning of wisdom. Does God want us to have wisdom? Absolutely, as it serves to guide and protect us. How are we to know how far to press the limits in our quest for wisdom? How do we know when we have exceeded those limits? Here is one possible response: creative interaction with God's world is never out of bounds, even as we acknowledge it will never get us beyond God's world into supernatural spheres. Those are his domain, and we trust him to be Master there as well.

CHAPTER 22

Job's Life in Retrospect

Introduction

"And Job added to his discourse (*mashal*)" (29:1). This same rhetoric introduced Job's words in chapter 27. Up to that point, Job had just "answered" each of the friends' admonitions. In both chapters 27 and 29, Job headed in new directions. In 27, Job had ventured wholesale into the paradigm of the friends, perhaps particularly of Zophar, with regard to the fate of evil persons. Picking up the challenge again (ch. 29), he began to build the foundation for the radical move that would close his words. Neither direction was a previously trodden path for Job. Perhaps that is why the narrator framed Job's words in each case as a *mashal*. The word refers to a likeness; in this case, it established a connection between the new venture and the earlier, more familiar path.

> *Mashal* is often translated "parable." Job also used a form of this word to describe his own condition: "I liken myself to dust and ashes" (30:19). In the larger discourses of chapters 27 and 29, Job was constrained to think in terms of comparisons and contrasts with what he already knew, because he had not been on either of these playing fields before. For one thing, to argue through Zophar's lenses (ch. 27) might have seemed very awkward indeed. On the other hand, cobbling together a self-defense and subsequent set of oaths against himself was something far removed from anything he had experienced in the city gate.

Chapters 29–31 represent a dramatic turning point for Job. To understand him, we need to remind ourselves of previous developments. Chapter 29 sounds as if Job was boasting about himself, but that is a superficial reading of his words. In fact, he revisited his own better days to counter the false accusations that Eliphaz had cruelly lobbed at him (ch. 22). Job's declarations and the deeply pained descriptions of chapter

30 form the basis for the oaths against himself (ch. 31) that served as his final, last-ditch means to summon God.

Above all, Job mourned his lost relationships, both with God and with people. The theme of friendship has been high profile all along, through the failure of Job's friends and the apparent absence of God's friendship. The transition from Job's lament over his absent relationship with God to the series of oaths that would compel God to reappear is breathtaking.

Yearning for His Lost Relationships (ch. 29)

More than anything else, Job was broken over the inexplicable dissolution of his friendship with God. He longed for God's presence—not just for the blessings (although they were abundant) but for God's friendship. This was a precious relationship, and Job desired above all else to have it restored. The images of light (29:3) and rich oil (29:6) were woven through his remembered well-being. So were spreading and luxuriant trees (29:19). Every benefit that he had bestowed on others was because God had initially blessed him, and he knew it. Put in the terms of the heavenly encounter between the *satan* and God, Job was *not* being good for what he got out of it. His perspective was one of stewardship.

Job's description of his life prior to the catastrophe indicates that he indeed was a source of hope and blessing for both the nobility and the indigent in his city. He was respected by everyone, young and old, at the city gate, where he enjoyed public honor. The city gate was the ancient counterpart to city hall or the state house. Job held a high position, perhaps even serving as a ruler of the city.

Utter deference is the best way to describe the effect that Job had on those who were in his presence. Young men withdrew in respect; the aged rose, a sign that they too held him in the highest esteem. As an example, think of the United States Congress rising as the president enters to deliver the annual State of the Union address. It is the honor due the office. A general silence reigned in his presence; mundane chatter would have been entirely out of place. Even nobles were so overwhelmed by his presence that they became tongue-tied. Others waited for his advice and took it to heart, listening in silence.

All of this was because, contrary to Eliphaz's accusation, Job's social justice credentials were impeccable. This was not boasting; it was truthful self-defense in the face of falsehood. It was a known fact that Job responded to appeals for help from all sorts of people. Israel's Torah required God's people to sustain "widows, aliens, and orphans" as the paradigmatic marginalized people groups. Even though he was likely outside the covenant community, Job did so as well. He clothed himself with righteousness and justice (29:14). There is an echo of God's clothing himself with salvation, righteousness, and vengeance in order to do justice (Isa 59:15–18).

What an image this is! Whether we acknowledge it or not, we often consciously select our literal clothing to define us for the watching audience. We know the terms for certain costumes: "casual professional" or "Sunday best." Here Job's "clothing" spoke volumes about his concern for his fellow human beings, both in terms of his own integrity and his efforts to renew broken lives. Job was an advocate for justice as a matter of course. These were consistent and evident features of his life. In the face of them, Eliphaz's accusations were patently false.

The continuing list could be read at an awards ceremony: Job interrupted his own agendas to help the blind as they groped for the way, to assist those who could not walk, to comfort the fatherless, to take up causes for the broken, and to go after thugs and perpetrators of violence. He was tireless in his efforts to maintain security for those under his care. There seems to have been a number of people who did rest in the shade of his protection. He mentioned being a chief and living like a king among his troops.

Whatever these figures represented in Job's own culture, he was a source of encouragement, wisdom, and justice for many. He engaged in all of these activities joyfully as a response to the goodness God bestowed upon him. God's blessing was not something he longed for as an end in itself; it enabled him to be good to others. In this framework, the tone of his self-description is not troubling. It is simply Job's honest assessment and reflection on the conditions that he missed dearly. Of all the changes in Job's life, his inability to help others no doubt grieved him terribly. This chapter reflects a momentary reverie before he was hauled back to reality by his shame and pain.

Job's Lament (ch. 30)

That's the way it had been; all classes of his social world had honored him. But now! Now, he was a laughingstock. Shriveled and nameless creatures poked fun at him and taunted him. Street urchins spat when they saw him coming. The social cruelty of this scene taxes our imagination. Few of us live with this kind of degradation. We know clever insults and put-downs; but a directed stream of saliva is repulsive in the extreme. It transcends the power of verbal abuse.

It seems the mockers drew courage to treat Job with physical cruelty because they saw that God had degraded him (30:11). "On my right hand the rabble rise; they push away my feet; they set against me their ways of destruction" (30:12). They were intentionally tripping him up to watch him stumble and fall. All of the previous honor, accolades, and gratitude for his goodness to them were out the door, gone. Instead, these bands of mockers came after him to destroy him. "Terrors are turned against me; my honor is pursued as the wind and like a cloud my salvation passes away" (30:15).

It is no wonder that Job's description of those who assailed him was so stinging (30:2–8). They were from the lowest dregs of society, from families whose honor was nonexistent. They grew up on the fringes of civilization. We might find a contemporary parallel to these images of gnawing dry ground, eating saltwort, and ingesting broom bush roots in huddled masses living in the garbage heaps of large cities, scavenging for any food they can find. We hear of shantytowns and read of slums; the pitiable homes of Job's mockers were dry riverbeds and caves in the rocks, sheltered only by bushes. It all exceeds our worst imaginations. They were nameless (30:8)—no identity and no honor, outcasts in every way. It may be that Job's refusal to put them with his sheepdogs (30:1) was because they were so beaten that they lacked any strength for work. His apparent disdain might shock us except that he immediately added that he was lower than they. All of their shame was his in excess.

Job returned to his own despair over his unending pain (30:16–19). This pain tore him apart and gnawed at him. The clothing that touched him added to his extreme discomfort, binding him around the neck. He was hurled into the muck and had become dust and ashes again (30:19). The combination "dust and ashes" appears only here, in Job 42:6, and in Gen 18:27. In the other two passages, it represents abject humility as well as standing up to (as it were) God! The same is true here.

In no uncertain terms, Job accused God. "I cry out to you, but you do not answer me; I have stood up, but you merely consider me. You are turned to a cruel stranger for me; with the might of your hand, you hold a grudge against me" (30:20–21). Not only was God silent; God was cruel and intending to harm Job. What follows is an abbreviated paraphrase of 30:24–31: "God, put this together for me because I cannot. I helped those who cried out. I wept for those who grieved. But you have not done any of this for me. Instead, there are just days and days of darkness, days of crying out for help in public—utter humiliation—but I need help. I am no longer ashamed to shriek like a wild animal as my whole body collapses in terrible pain."

Job put himself in the company of wild animals, owls, and jackals who shriek in the wilderness. He could not be more outside—in every way. It was a place of horror for Job, and this was his final accusation against God. As we read ahead, however, wild creatures will roam freely throughout God's discourses; perhaps Job's words here are an adumbration of that radically altered perspective.

Job's Oaths of Innocence (ch. 31)

From the depths of his agony, Job did the only thing left. It was a radical move. Knowing that he was innocent, he went on the offensive. Up to this point, he had been defending his honor and integrity against the torrents of innuendos and attacks from Eliphaz, Bildad, and Zophar. His responses to them were substantial; his "defense" zeroed in on their ineptitude, on God's recognized sovereign powers and right, on the affliction that God had dealt out with a very unkind hand, and on his demand for a judicial hearing in God's presence. The last was apparently not forthcoming, even though Job repeatedly begged for an advocate of some sort. Thus, Job brought himself to trial. If he had committed any of the moral offenses, he asked that he be punished in kind. This was much more serious than simply asking for an audience. This would compel God as supreme Judge of Job's world to respond with measure-for-measure justice.

Job started with a remarkable declaration: "I have made a covenant with my eyes; how then could I possibly look upon a virgin?" That statement encapsulated Job's integrity. No human would know what was going through his mind, but he knew God would see his ways and number his steps (31:1–4). Jesus echoed that same challenge in the Sermon on the Mount: "But I say to you that everyone who looks at a woman with lustful intent has already committed adultery with her in his heart" (Matt 5:28 ESV). The divine Judge would know.

Following that introduction, Job launched into his claims to innocence by enumerating possible sins that he may have committed. He had just taken God to task for *not* responding in kind to his good deeds—the measure-for-measure justice so central to the Israelite understanding of God (30:24–26). Now, in a judicial tour de force, he demanded that God dole out measure-for-measure *punitive* justice if Job had engaged in sin. Although he did not *name* God, he certainly invoked God's presence; if God was God, he had to respond. For each possible sin, Job specifically called down upon himself the ill consequences that a transgressor would deserve.

This set of oaths was not haphazard. Job started off with those failings that would generally be hidden from the public eye or that could be sufficiently retooled to not look like sin. He started with deceit, always so insidious and damaging because, by its very nature, it can look good. He asked that he would not enjoy the fruit of any of his labor if it had been mingled with falsehood. Following on the heels of deceit was adultery, always initially concealed but with horrifying effects, especially if and when it becomes public knowledge. It was iniquity, a fire that consumes as far as 'abaddon, and utterly destructive (31:11–12).

Moving more to the public sphere, Job enjoined punishment upon himself if he had refused in any way to care for his servants, the poor, the needy, the widow, the orphan, or any kind of destitute person. He asked that the source of his own power to work, his arms, would be broken, placing him in the same helpless condition as the poor or the destitute. He uttered further oaths in regard to trusting in his own wealth, engaging in idolatry, being gleeful when his enemies came into difficult times, concealing his own sin out of fear of public shame, or abusing the land that was his. What a recital this was! It was audacious in the extreme, but Job was determined that his character would not be maligned. He was blameless and upright, he feared God, and he shunned evil. Taking these oaths would prove that.

Job's Closing Words

Just before his final oath, Job called the accuser to write out the accusation against him, declaring that he would wear it like a crown on his head and then boldly approach the Almighty (31:35–37). There are echoes here of things we have already heard: earlier, he longed for his own words to be permanently inscribed, as he affirmed the living presence of the kinsman-redeemer whom he expected to see (19:23–24). Even more compelling, when Job had been administering justice for the poor and needy at the city gate, he was clothed with righteousness and justice (29:14). Now, as a suppliant, he was clothed with an indictment, but he would wear it confidently!

And then, "the words of Job are ended" (31:40).

Robert Gordis has counted fourteen declarations in Job's final oaths. This is twice the symbolic seven, perhaps another way that Job emphatically affirmed his unassailable integrity. The Hebrew words for "oath" and "seven" are related. (We see it also in the name Beersheva, "well of seven" and "well of oath"; Gen 21:22–31). The distinct spheres Gordis recognized are:

1. lust (31:1–2)
2. deceit in business (vv. 5–6)
3. coveting property (vv. 7–8)
4. adultery (vv. 9–12)
5. unjust treatment of servants (vv. 13–15)
6. hard-hearted treatment of the poor, widows, and orphans (vv. 16–18)
7. lack of pity for the needy (vv. 19–20)
8. perverting justice regarding orphans (vv. 21–23)
9. love of and dependence on wealth (vv. 24–25)
10. idolatry—worshipping sun and moon (vv. 26–28)
11. rejoicing at devastation of foes (vv. 29–30)
12. not practicing hospitality (vv. 31–32)
13. concealing sins for fear of public scorn (vv. 33–34)
14. using the law to take the land of others (vv. 38–40)

(adapted from Robert Gordis, *The Book of Job: Commentary, New Translation, and Special Studies* [New York: Jewish Theological Seminary, 1978], 542).

CHAPTER 23

Elihu as Arbiter and Adumbration

Introduction

What are we to make of Elihu? By his own admission, he was younger than all the rest and, in respect to them, a combination of deferential and boldly critical. He was the one who said, "I was afraid of declaring my knowledge to you" (32:6c) and "I waited for your words; I heard your reasoning; while you were searching for words, I gave to you my attention" (32:11–12a). At the same time, he comes across as rather self-assured: "I lift up my knowledge from afar; to my Maker I will give righteousness, for surely my words are not false; one complete in knowledge is with you" (36:3–4). One wonders whether he intended his audience to think the "one complete in knowledge" was God or himself.

Elihu seemed concerned not to offend. Nevertheless, every time he opened his mouth, he was sufficiently angry to be offensive! We are told three times of his anger with Job and the friends (32:2–5); he had a difficult time containing himself (32:18–20). His impetuous nature confounded itself on occasion as he alternately told Job to "be silent," to "speak up," and again to "be silent and I will teach you wisdom" (33:31–33). In sum, no matter how we assess the literary role of this interlude and Elihu's role in the narrative, these next five chapters are quite the ride.

Elihu the Latecomer

A significant number of commentators suggest that chapters 32–37 are a later addition to the text. There are credible reasons for this conclusion. For one thing, we have neither any warning that Elihu was lurking on the sidelines nor any follow-up to his vigorous assertions. God did not bother to include Elihu in his rebuke to the other three friends. In addition, Elihu has his "own" prose introduction followed by four separate poetic sections, so the whole unit could stand alone. There are also some scholars who do not consider Elihu to have added anything at all beyond what the friends had already said.

Furthermore, the language in these chapters is different from the rest of the book. There is not uniform agreement on just how the differences should be characterized or what to do about them, but the poetry is distinct from that of the surrounding speeches. That is saying something, since the Hebrew of all of Job is notoriously difficult. Nonetheless, there are more foreign words in this section, possibly reflecting a more international flavor. Some of these foreign words seem to be Aramaic, the language of commerce and diplomacy spoken across the ancient Near East. (English is the best contemporary parallel, as it is used internationally for these same purposes.) Perhaps the younger Elihu represents a more cosmopolitan perspective in the narrative.

Nevertheless, Aramaic appears elsewhere in the book as well, and all the friends had come from afar. Instead of these unusual words reflecting a foreign origin for Elihu alone, they may be a literary device designed to convey the sense that he was particularly unusual. From a wider stylistic perspective, Elihu's pronouncements seem more prosaic than those of the friends; they lack the striking imagery and compelling figures of speech that were laced through the words of Job's counselors. This could simply be another reflection that he was younger and had not gathered a repertoire of poetic metaphors.

Seow's cogent assessment (*Job 1–21, 31–37*) of the integrity of these chapters is invaluable. Here is just a sampling to whet our appetites. The presumed Aramaic influence evident in Elihu's speeches is almost equally present in the discourses of Bildad. Nevertheless, certain vocabulary differences do seem to set Elihu's speeches apart from the prior discourses between Job and his friends. When Elihu referred to himself, the first-person singular pronoun is different; he used *'ani* instead of *'anokhi*, the pronoun regularly employed by Job. Elihu had multiple occasions to refer to "knowledge." In his vocabulary, that was *dea'*, instead of the more typical term *da'at*. It may be that Elihu substituted *dea'* for *da'at* to signal his sense of divine inspiration (36:4); this was not just garden-variety knowledge, and he wanted his audience to know that. Elihu also used *'el* to refer to God, instead of *'elohim*. To be sure, Bildad did so as well, so that is not a reason for presuming these chapters are a later addition.

The challenge for readers is what conclusions to draw from the differences. Elihu's language may indeed represent his youth and cosmopolitan background, but that does not necessitate his speeches being a separate text. Conveying a foreign flavor fits well with the nature of this narrative and all its characters; they were not provincial, rural types. Further, we remember that the narrator included chapter 28, with its far-reaching quest for wisdom; the new tone and approach of Elihu's addresses follow well.

Even presuming we could make a case that Elihu's chapters were a later addition, we still have to ask why they were added if they were that disparate. If Elihu's connection to the surrounding discourses is indeed elusive, it would be so no matter when these chapters became part of the poetic drama. Let's try a different lens. Elihu's discourses serve effectively as a well-placed transition from the gravity of Job's oaths to the grandeur of God's appearance. If we view them in this framework, then Elihu did not interrupt an otherwise seamless poetic drama; rather, his outbursts were an integral part of its development. Elihu responded to Job and the friends on the judicial level, but also summoned them to a place from which to see and hear the approaching storm. That whirlwind was the medium for God's revelation about his own wisdom.

Who Was This Character and What Did He Contribute?

His full name was Elihu ("He is my God"), son of Barakh-el ("God has blessed"). His keen spiritual sensitivity seems evident; he attributed to God Almighty his very life and breath, as well as his ability to understand (32:8; 33:4). His opening remarks were an extensive justification for why he was speaking at all (32:6–33:7). If we contend that Elihu's speeches did add significantly to the narrative development and were not simply a repetitive string of others' ideas, it will be important to establish what roles he filled.

Adjudicator

Elihu expressed his frustration with the collapse of the disputation. Like a lawyer, he summarized what he had heard, both from the defendant, Job, and from the ineffective prosecution, the friends. In the process, he also responded to key points from the preceding dialogues. There are echoes of Eliphaz (33:12–18) and of Job (33:23–24; 34:14–15, 22). Elihu synthesized, piecing together affirmations from all parties, and engaged in a certain amount of "creativity" as he restated the arguments and shaped his presentation of the evidence. In the course of his summary statements, he seems to have put words in Job's mouth.

He attributed to Job a declaration of sinlessness (33:8–9), using the terms "pure," "without sin," "clean," and "free from guilt." It is not entirely clear that Job had been so definitive about himself. It was God who had said that Job was blameless and upright and that he shunned evil and feared God (1:8). Job repeated the term "blameless" in response to the accusations of his friends (cf. 9:20–21) that he had sinned grievously. He stated that he had led a righteous life (23:11–12) because he feared the Lord (31:23), a clear reflection of God's assessment at the outset. Nevertheless, lodged within Job's agonizing were ongoing doubts about his own innocence (7:20–21; 9:29; 10:14–15; 13:23; 14:16–17). At the close of his final self-vindication, his apprehension surfaced again: "If I covered my transgressions as 'adam did, hiding in my bosom my sin . . ." (31:33).

Job held God accountable for what had happened to him, and he was vexed that he had been denied justice. In that respect, the second part of the words that Elihu attributed to Job are closer to the truth: "Behold, he finds occasions to be hostile against me, he reckons me as his enemy; he puts my feet in the stocks and watches all my paths" (33:10–11). Job repeatedly placed the responsibility for all his ills at God's feet.

Elihu further "quoted" Job as saying, "I am righteous but God denies me justice. Concerning my justice, I am considered a liar; I am . . . without transgression" (34:5–6). When Job declared, "I am righteous" (9:15, 20), this statement was preceded by "if." That is a significant difference. Elihu attributed to Job the attitude that there is nothing to gain by refraining from sin (34:9; 35:3). According to Elihu, Job said God's "anger never punishes, and he does not take the least notice of wickedness" (35:15). Elihu was determined to declare God entirely just (34:10–12) and to defend God (36:2) while twisting Job's words. In sum, Elihu did sort through and augment the growing legal tangle, but his additions were not helpful in light of Job's integrity.

Cajoler

Elihu was also bent on getting Job to reconsider, and he explored new territory in the process. Early in his first speech, he shifted gears temporarily away from Job's presumed declarations of innocence. Instead, acknowledging the great gulf between God and Job, he posed the question, "When humans absolutely need to hear from God, how does God speak?" In Elihu's presentation, God uses multiple media.

Elihu drew on the same numinous terrors to which Eliphaz had appealed as grounds for the credibility of *his* revelation (4:12–19) that no human could be considered righteous before God. According to Elihu, however, God used these fearsome circumstances for the purpose of warning people away from sin. "In a dream, a vision of the night, when deep sleep falls on men, while they slumber on their beds, then he uncovers the ear of men and terrifies them with disciplines" (33:15–16). Those warnings included pain and affliction (33:19–21). Elihu acknowledged the severity of suffering, but never named it as *Job's* suffering. His "sufferer" was on the verge of death as his soul drew near the pit and his life came face to face with the dead (33:22). Sounds grim.

In that very context, however, Elihu introduced the person for whom Job had been longing. Job had begged for an arbitrator (9:33–34), a witness, an advocate, an intercessor (16:18–21), and a kinsman-redeemer (19:25) to prove his righteousness and provide vindication. Elihu's mediator walked out of that strictly courtroom context. Initially called a messenger (*mal'akh*), this mediator (*melits*) would declare what was right and then request the life of the sufferer because a ransom had been found (33:23–24). In other words, the mediator's role worked in both directions.

As a result of restoration, the sufferer prayed, rejoiced, and confessed. With this, Elihu turned the friends' approach around significantly. They had been pressing Job to confess in order to be renewed. Here, the provision of the ransom just at the seemingly hopeless point of death should have elicited a confession of wonder at the redemptive grace and favor that were unmerited (33:26–28). This was a major advance beyond the judicial paradigm, and it sounded persuasive.

Elihu started out well but subsequently fell into the same pattern that dogged the friends' counsel. In his excessive attempts to defend God's justice (34:10–12), he accused Job of hobnobbing with sinners (34:8) and rebelling against God (34:37). In an extraordinarily cruel attack, he wished that Job would be tested to the utmost (34:36), as if that were not already the case!

Mercifully, from this point on Elihu's focus was primarily on the nature of God's justice and power rather than on Job. He echoed the themes of the friends to the effect that God knows all the ways of the wicked and punishes them (34:21–26). In that context he addressed the problem of God's silence and seeming inattentiveness (34:29; 35:12–13). In his view, God does not respond to the pleas of the wicked. Implicit in this was Elihu's assessment that Job was wicked.

In response to the hypothetical question that Elihu put in Job's mouth as to the value of refraining from sin (35:3), he explored the implications of God's transcendence (35:5–8). Could God possibly be affected by human sin? Initially, the answer seemed to be no. Nevertheless, Elihu had more to say. We're not surprised. He declared that God is intimately involved with both the wicked and the righteous (36:6–7). There is a disciplinary value in affliction (cf. 33:19), and God uses it to inform people that they have "sinned arrogantly" (36:9). After this tentative foray into the potentially interesting territory of God's silence and transcendence, Elihu retreated to the friends' platform, concluding that God corrects, commands repentance, rewards obedience with contentment, and punishes the godless (36:8–12). His initially general tone turned personal as he got Job in the crosshairs one last time (36:16–21).

Forerunner

Twice Elihu used the expression "one perfect in knowledge is with you." The initial instance sounds as if he was referring to himself, and it smacks of arrogance (36:4). The same description crops up again, however, shortly thereafter (37:16). By this time, Elihu had begun to address the wondrous works of God (37:14), especially as they are manifest in the realms of storm and whirlwind. Here is how he began:

> Behold, God is great, and we know him not;
> the number of his years is unsearchable.
> For he draws up the drops of water;
> they distill his mist in rain,
> which the skies pour down and drop on mankind abundantly.
>   (36:26–28 ESV)

From that gentle beginning, Elihu's response ranged through rumbling thunder, flashes of lightning, snow, the mighty downpour, and the whirlwind (36:29–37:13). Then he turned to question Job. Did Job know how God did any of this? Was Job able to accomplish these mighty works? All of this was pointing directly to what God would say and do when he finally appeared. If we couch this in some kind of historical context, Job, the friends, and Elihu might have been sitting together watching and hearing, with fascination and deep fear, the blinding lightning and deafening roar as the tempest approached.

Elihu's final role was his most dramatic. He was singing a magnificent hymn of praise to the mighty power of God, particularly as it was displayed in the coming storm. In doing so, he also offered a corrective to Job's preceding declarations. God does indeed respond to humans, and we need to be warned because that response is never tame.

From a literary perspective, Elihu's speeches brought some sense of closure to the human arguments, even though his thought trajectory suffered from the same kinds of lapses as did those of the friends. What is significant, however, is that his final oration provided the perfect segue to the appearance of God. Because it had proven futile to cajole Job, Elihu returned to the sovereign power and transcendence of God. From God's initial acts of drawing together drops of water, forming clouds, and providing showers (36:27–28), Elihu reveled in the majestic displays of thunder and lightning that are at God's command: "He unleashes his lightning beneath the whole heaven and sends it to the ends of the earth. After that comes the sound of his roar; he thunders with his majestic voice" (37:3–4 NIV).

Get Ready

"Listen to this, Job; stand and consider the wonders of God. Do you know . . . ?" (37:14–18). Elihu's series of questions was a tiny foretaste of what Job was about to experience from the Divine Inquisitor. In the meantime, Elihu affirmed God's radiance (37:21–22), his exaltation, and his perfect righteousness in dealing with humankind (37:23). He closed with the basic recipe of wisdom—the fear of the Lord (37:24).

CHAPTER 24

Responses from the Wild Wind: A Cosmic Tour

Introduction

Elihu prepared the way for God's arrival on the stage with his vivid description of the impending storm, followed by a doxology:

> From the north, golden, he is coming. Upon God is terrible majesty.
> The Almighty—we have not found him; he is exalted in strength.
> In his justice and great righteousness, he does not oppress.
> Therefore, humans fear him,
> for he does not have regard for those who think themselves wise.
>   (37:22–24)

"Then the LORD (YHWH) answered Job out of the storm" (38:1). God's covenant name reappears at this point. In the preceding poetic dialogue and monologues, with the exception of 12:9, the divine person was "God" or "the Almighty," transcendent and powerful—and, as far as Job was concerned, absent. Here, however, the Lord shattered all the silence barriers; the very name indicates God's active engagement in the relationship.

Characteristically, the Lord of the covenant revealed himself in the stormy power of clouds, thunder, and lightning (Exod 19–20; Judg 5:4–5; 2 Kgs 2:1), demonstrating his transcendence above and control over all of these phenomena, which, with their destructive might, so terrify humans. The Hebrew word for storm (se'arah) also figures in Ezek 1:4 in a context that vibrates with power: "I looked and behold, a wind storm (ruah se'arah) was coming from the north, a great cloud with fire flashing and streaking about it, and from the middle of the fire was a source of brilliant light." The Lord's stormy approach to Job was wild, uncontrollably wild; so was the universe that God described. There was no gentle voice here. We have to ask ourselves, after all Job had been through, why *this* approach? It hardly seems a comforting or heartening response to a broken person.

From the forceful intensity of the storm, the Lord taunted Job: "Who is this who darkens counsel, with words without knowledge?" (38:2). Unless it was intended as a dismissive one-liner to Elihu, this jab seemed a low blow to Job, who had been pouring out his heart, his very soul, in tears and anger to God. How could the honest description of his anguish and the oaths as to his innocence be "words without knowledge"? Was every aspect of his experience of no value? Were his attempts to clarify simply muddying the waters? How could God think so little of Job's request to see God? What "counsel" and "knowledge" had Job completely missed?

Moving to center stage, the Lord surged on with a barrage of words, squelching Job and affirming the Lord's own intimate knowledge of, delight in, and absolute jurisdiction over his creation. The divine Judge did not answer Job's plea for justice directly—ever. Instead, the theophany, the poetry, and the rhetorical questions prodded Job into an entirely different and sublime realm.

There are two distinct responses from the Lord, each beginning with "Bind up your loins like a man. I will question you and you shall cause me to know" (38:3; 40:7). In other words, God commanded Job to prepare for the battle that this verbal onslaught would be! Girding up the loins was preparatory to close physical combat, notably wrestling. Don't miss the fact that the Lord invited Job into this. Through the first of these encounters, he opened up vast new panoramas for Job's consideration and exploration. The second round moved in for much closer scrutiny of wildness beyond the edges of Job's reality.

Scene One: "What Do You Know and What Can You Do?"

The Lord's rhetorical questions took Job on a tour of the entire created order, from the far reaches of the universe to exquisite terrestrial creatures. They verbally sailed past the singing morning stars and the sons of God, the gates of the shadow of death, cruel ostriches, and soaring eagles. "Where?" "Who?" "On what?" "Do you know?" "Can you command, lead, send forth, hunt?" Torrents of questions pounded Job, who could not have had the foggiest notion how to answer any of them. This was God's design, not his. It was a deductive process; because Job could not respond to these foundational questions, how did he have the audacity to dabble in the moral fabric of God's universe? That would mean entering unseen spheres to encounter order, chaos, and untamed beauty, all equally compelling and intricately intertwined. Did Job have the where-withal to sort through right and wrong in that tangle of threads? Job's knowledge indeed was fledgling, and his legal ventures were a fleeting dark shadow against the radiant Presence at the very center of all realities.

Our initial inclination is to read the incessant questions as continued slaps in Job's face, cruel at best. It may be, however, that God's questions were not meant to demean and silence Job, but to invite him to adopt a radically altered perspective. If so, the questions emphasized possibilities and hope rather than limitations (Balentine, *Job*, 644–66).

Echoing Gen 1:1, this divine Presence emerged first as the consum-mate Architect. Accompanied by a celestial chorus, God measured the foundations of the earth, set its footings, and established its cornerstone (38:4–7). In the context of separating the waters above and below, God's role shifted to Midwife. The powerful sea, viewed as a chaotic and fear-some part of the creative process in surrounding cultural myths, is por-trayed as an infant being birthed from the womb. God was there to wrap it up for protection, and set limits lest its boisterous presence overreach boundaries (38:8–11). Because God brought it into being, he did not need to subdue it. The apparent source of chaos was already entirely under God's control. The theme of giving birth continues as the focus moves to the creatures under the Lord's care and in God's dominion (ch. 39).

We might envision creation as God's cosmic temple. As King, God was lay-ing the cornerstone, and the chorus provided the liturgy. We have encoun-tered "sons of God" already (Gen 6:1–4; Job 1:6; 2:1). Here they join their voices with "stars of the morning." Job had asked those brilliant stars of the dawn to be darkened (3:9), but in God's temple they shouted in exultation. This mighty chorus was a diverse lot! Not only were the "sons of God" in Gen 6:2 headed the wrong direction as they "took daughters of men"; we also meet a "star of the morning" in Isa 14:12 who was likewise headed the wrong direction: "How you have fallen from heaven, O bright star, son of the dawn." While Nebuchadnezzar is the primary referent in Isaiah (14:4), the chapter also points beyond the immediate earthbound context to *sheol* below and the heavens above. Nevertheless, this cosmic temple was rever-berating with shouts of praise from hosts of celestial creatures.

In the interval, however, the tour ranged through inaccessible places: light and darkness, the depths of the sea and the heights of heaven, the paths of storms, and the desolate wastelands in times of drought. Job had cursed the day of his birth; God celebrated morning, dawn, and the dwelling place of light. Perhaps in response to Job's preoccupation with death, the Lord chided Job: "Have the gates of death been shown to you? Have you seen the gates of the shadow of death?" (38:17). God as Commander shaped water in all its forms: snow, hail, rain, dew, ice, and frost (38:22–30). He set in place the constellations, maintaining order in spheres far beyond Job and yet observable to him.

Whereas Job had been focused on obtaining justice and righteousness, these moral concerns were a lesser component in God's response. The Lord mentioned evil a total of two times, and the poetry is so exquisite that we hardly pause on the "evil" aspect: "(Have you) caused the dawn to know its place, to grasp the wings of the earth that evil ones would be shaken from it?" (38:12b–13), and "Their light is withheld from evil ones, and the exalted arm is broken" (38:15).

Returning from the extraterrestrial spheres, God next staged a parade of wild creatures, starting with predatory lions (38:39–40) and ending with birds of prey that ominously hover wherever the dead lie (39:26–30). In between, God gave Job a bit of a breather from the interrogation, and reveled in the oddities of the flapping ostrich and the powerful warhorse. The questions and descriptions vibrate with life and disdain for domesticated ease and comfort. Mountain goats and deer give birth in the open. Wild donkeys and oxen scorn the harness that binds them to labor. The bloodthirsty eagle soars aloft. There is a scent of death intertwined with the hawk and the eagle; they thrive on the cusp of death. This echoes Job's awareness that his life was on that edge as well. Even so, here God emphasized vigorous life whereas Job had been caught in the downward suction of death prayers.

God inserted "wisdom" into this remarkable picture, but it happened so subtly that we may miss it, especially since it involves ambiguous words and cross-cultural connections. "Who placed wisdom in the *tuhot*, or who gave understanding to the *sekhvi*?" (38:36). What are we to do with this? Most modern translations (ESV, NIV, NRSV, NASB) include as the primary translation something along the lines of "inward parts" for the first and "mind" for the second. That works. See Ps 51:6 [8]—"Surely you desire truth in the *tuhot*; you have caused me to know wisdom in sealed places." This is the only other place in the Bible in which the word *tuhot* appears; and *sekhvi* only appears in Job 38:36. The Lord's question stands. God alone gives wisdom to humans. Nevertheless, these two rare words may possibly be translated "ibis" and "rooster." This could be an even more subtle allusion to God's superb assignment of wisdom. In Egyptian tradition, both birds supposedly possessed extraordinary wisdom (Balentine, *Job*, 657; Gordis, *The Book of Job*, 452–53; Dhorme, *Commentary on the Book of Job*, 593). Wisdom given to birds, not humans! "Birdbrain" takes on another level of meaning.

This exhibit of wild creatures served as a prelude to the forthcoming appearance of the formidable Leviathan. The message was clear. God viewed each of these creatures with joy and pride; they were his. Not one of them is presented as an enemy of God. Strikingly, God said nothing whatsoever about humans in this recital! Instead, the Master of the universe commenced with the utterly unknown in the beginning of time and then moved on to "simpler" things right around Job. Even about those creatures Job had to confess ignorance. His existence had been "sheltered" from the wild aspects of God's world. Perhaps, however, he was to infer that because God knew and nurtured all the others, God also cared for him. In addition, perhaps he was to be mindful that too much of his attention had been on himself.

Scene Two: The Wild Gets Wilder

The "intermission" between the first and second speeches is brief. God paused after the line about birds of prey and essentially asked "So? What do you have to say now?" (40:2). Job had time only to catch his breath and acknowledge that he had nothing to say (40:3–5). Or so it seemed. We might ask what it meant that he "laid his hand on his mouth." Earlier, he had remarked that society's elites had done the same thing in his presence (29:9). That was out of respect and perhaps some sense of being intimidated. We could presume the same here about Job, but could there be more to it? Was this to suppress something that he was about to blurt out but knew should not be said? Was his refusal to say anything laced with some degree of defiance?

God demanded an answer (40:2); Job said unequivocally, "No!" There is a parallel here that at least merits mention. Job had spoken extensively and demanded a response from God, and God was silent. Now God spoke extensively and demanded a response from Job, and Job was pretty much silent. It was as if Job had the chutzpah to say, "Take a bit of your own medicine!" His "response" acknowledged that he was of little account, but he did not yet renounce his challenge. Thus, God continued.

"Be God!"

Something about Job's words compelled God to issue the same challenge a second time. "Brace yourself; get ready. I will ask the questions and you will answer" (40:7). God charged Job with impugning God's justice in order to maintain his own rightness (40:8). Then God challenged Job to "be God" if he could. "Assume God's voice and majestic splendor; pour out anger against the proud and the wicked; bring them all down to dust—and below" (an abbreviated paraphrase of 40:9–14). At first glance, this is a cutting rebuke. God knew Job could not do these things, and this was one more way to reduce him to utter submission.

On the other hand, it could also be an invitation to Job to step up to the plate and take on the high calling of being God's "regent" (Balentine, *Job*, 682). In that case, God was subtly restoring Job to his place of lost honor—in fact, raising him far above where he had been before. Job was now privy to the faint traces of God's design of the cosmos and, just as Adam before him, Job was instated as God's image-bearing representative in the earthly realm. This task would not be easy. The summons was a prelude to lengthy portrayals of Behemoth's strength and the untamable might of Leviathan, two most proud and fearsome creatures. They represented the epitome of the pride that Job was challenged to confront. "Look at every proud one, and humble him, and trample the evil ones under them. Hide them together in the dust; cover their faces in the hidden darkness" (40:12–13). What would Job know of Behemoth and Leviathan? What could Job do with them?

Behemoth and Leviathan

At this point, a host of questions boils to the surface, and they are not from God. They come from us, the readers of this text. Here's a sampling: What was the point of God's lengthy reference to Behemoth and Leviathan? What were these creatures? Were they simply huge and daunting animals? Were they of such mythic proportions that there is no connection with what we might call physical reality? Or were they on the boundaries between the wild and the mythical? What biblical and extrabiblical connections might help us make sense of these remarkable sketches?

The Mythic Pair

Several observations are in order at the outset. As presented, both of these creatures were sufficiently powerful to cow Job and anyone else who might be tempted to meddle with them. Nevertheless, God evidently delighted in their brute strength, and he praised them at length—especially Leviathan, whose description reaches fantastic proportions.

There is considerable debate over the purpose(s) of God in waxing eloquent about what initially appear to be a hippopotamus and a crocodile. Both of these creatures might have been known to Job in his ancient Near Eastern geographical setting, at least in the area of the Jordan River (cf. 40:23) and the nearby Nile in Egypt. Further, both were formidable and potentially dangerous. Thus, they were good figures to challenge Job with his own human frailty.

Beyond those comparisons, however, lie additional possibilities. *Behemoth* is the plural form of *behemah*, a generic word for living creatures other than humans (cf. Gen 1:24). The singular form of the word occurs frequently and refers to the more domesticated varieties. Think cows and related benign creatures. While the plural form appears a number of times in Scripture with reference to herds of those domesticated animals, in this context (40:15–24) it may signify the ultimate in sizable beasts, "first among the ways of God" (40:19). "First" could point simply to the size advantage, which, to be sure, was there. On the other hand, with this statement, perhaps God subtly put Job in his place. Maybe Job and all other humans along with him were not the sole focus and pinnacle of God's creative activities.

Behemoth and Leviathan may merge physical and mythic characteristics, and may exist on the edge ("liminal"), somewhere between natural, observable reality and supernatural realities. If so, they would represent the undefinable realms of chaos on both land (Behemoth) and sea (Leviathan).

Images of the hippopotamus and the crocodile were intertwined in Egyptian depictions of the goddess Ammut, a destructive deity who doled out retribution in the afterlife. See Richard H. Wilkinson, *The Complete Gods and Goddesses of Ancient Egypt* (London: Thames & Hudson, 2003), 218–20. The biblical description of Behemoth is particularly intriguing. Hints of sexual virility may be woven into 40:16–17; the "tail" could be a euphemism. Herodotus describes the hippopotamus and crocodile as denizens of Egypt (*Histories* 2.68–71).

In truth, Behemoth actually sounds a bit lazy in this context, lounging in the shade of the lotus plants and not being particularly bothered. That, however, is deceptive. This creature could afford to be peaceable, given its size and strength, and caution was in order if someone intended to trap him (40:24).

Leviathan, on the other hand, was unquestionably fierce, apparently uncontrollable, and something with which God also contended. Leviathan makes appearances in several other biblical passages and is linked with additional names of fearsome creatures, (*tannin* ["sea monster"] in Job 7:12 and *rahav* in 9:13 and 26:12). These all merit a brief detour. Then we will propose several possible interpretations of God's relationship to Leviathan, and explore how this figure works in conjunction with the Job story.

An Excursus: Tracking Leviathan

The start of our "detour" actually takes us backward in the text. We initially met Leviathan when Job begged that "those who curse days (or the sea) curse that day, those who are ready to rouse Leviathan" (3:8). Something of the dread and terror of Leviathan was already evident in Job's temporary venture into that dark realm. The traditions he knew and cited included cosmic battle: "With his strength he agitated the sea; by his understanding he shattered *rahav*. By his breath the skies were fair; his hand pierced the fleeing serpent" (26:12–13).

Outside the book of Job, Leviathan was an enemy of the Lord, and a fierce and terrible one at that: "In that day, the LORD will visit with his fierce, great, and powerful sword Leviathan the fleeing serpent, Leviathan the coiling serpent; he will kill the monster (*tannin*) of the sea" (Isa 27:1). Like Litan, who shows up in the Canaanite myth of Baal and Anat, this monster serpent had multiple heads:

> You split open the sea by your power;
> you shattered the heads of the monsters (*tanninim* [plural]) on the
>   waters.
> You crushed the heads of Leviathan,
> and gave him as food to the people of the desert. (Ps 74:13–14)

Job's reference to *rahav* (Job 9:13; 26:12) opened up additional connections. "Was it not you who cut *rahav* to pieces, who pierced that monster (*tannin*)?" (Isa 51:9b). "You crushed *rahav* like one of the slain" (Ps 89:10b [11b]). Done deal—Leviathan represented evil in its most terrifying manifestations, and God dealt it violent blows in order to crush it out of existence.

Close to Israelite culture, the Canaanite combat myth of Baal and Anat sheds light on the biblical Leviathan. The twisting and coiling serpent (Lotan or Litan, very similar to Leviathan) was done in, presumably by the storm god Baal. Its description bears quoting:

> Though you smote Litan the fleeing serpent,
> finished off the twisting serpent,
> the encircler with seven heads,
> you burned him up,
> and thus you brightened the heavens.
> (KTU 1.5.i.1–8; trans. William D. Barker, "'And Thus You Brightened the
> Heavens . . .': A New Translation of KTU 1.5.i 1–8 and Its Significance for
> Ugaritic and Biblical Studies," *Ugarit-Forschungen* 38 [2006]: 1–52)

"Brightening the heavens" here seems to parallel the "skies becoming fair" in Job 26:13. The seven heads also remind us of the multiheaded dragons slain in the battle between Tiamat and Marduk, most familiar from *Enuma Elish*, the Mesopotamian creation epic. For an accessible version of that narrative, see Matthews and Benjamin, *Old Testament Parallels*, 11–20. You may find a fuller version of the Leviathan connections in Elaine A. Phillips, "Serpent Intertexts: Tantalizing Twists in the Tales," *Bulletin for Biblical Research* 10 (2000): 233–45.

But not so fast. The psalmist sang:

How numerous are your works, O Lord!
All of them with wisdom you have made;
the earth is full of your creatures.
This is the sea, great and wide,
which teems with creatures without number,
living things, the small with the great.
There the ships go to and fro;
Leviathan, this you formed to frolic in it. (Ps 104:24–26)

"Frolic"? Leviathan, created by God and forcefully subdued by God, also had a playful and wildly free side given to it by none other than God, who was certainly not out to slay this dragon. Instead, God admired Leviathan—from his tough skin to the "doors of his face" (41:14 [6]), lined with teeth; from the rows of shields on his back to flames and sparks darting from his mouth, and the smoke bellowing from his nostrils. In this context, the flames and smoke are not fantasy images for dragons. These are the same elements that swirled about God when he chose to manifest his presence. Theophany is the word. In ways that are beyond our imagining, God identifies with the chaotic and terrible as well as the orderly parts of his cosmic temple (Chase, *Job*, 268–74).

Be that as it may, every human attempt to establish a relationship with Leviathan—speaking softly, making a covenant, putting him on a leash as a pet—would fail miserably. Leviathan thrashed about, leaving destruction in his wake. If Job were to choose combat, woe betide him! Swords, arrows, and clubs would be useless. As if to set Job's rash plea in 3:8 in proper perspective, God said, "No one is so cruel that he would rouse him" (41:10a [2a]). In sum, "Job, don't even think of meddling with those who styled themselves as capable of rousing Leviathan!"

God's description closed with the following accolade for this terrifying monster: "There is not on dust one like him—made without dread. He will see all height; he is king over all proud creatures" (41:33–34 [25–26]). There are important evocations here. Remember Job's declaration that his Redeemer would rise up "on dust" (19:25)? Even though "on dust" no doubt means "on the earth," the mention of "dust" is a reminder of the fragile mortality of humans: "To dust you shall return" (Gen 3:19). Yet, when the Redeemer figure rose up in the court context, Job perceived that as vindication.

The Hebrew word translated "one like him" (*moshlo*) sounds like the word "to rule" (*mashal*). Perhaps we are to interpret the first clause of this passage on more than one level. "There is no one on dust ruling him—or like him" might convey the proper sense. God continued in the very next verse to call this creature "king." It fits and perhaps is also a gentle jibe at Job, who had called himself king (29:25) in the midst of his prior social context. Not only was Leviathan king; he was king over *all* the prideful ones. God had invited Job to humble all the proud and the wicked (40:11–14). We presumed God limited that challenge to humans Job might engage. Not necessarily. Here was exhibit A of those Job could assuredly *not* bring down.

Now, so what? The question for students of Job for millennia has been: What do we do with Leviathan? Was this description intended to represent in a very indirect way the *satan* of chapters 1 and 2, thereby claiming God's victory over that adversary without honoring him by title? That presumes the *satan* was an embodiment of the consummate evil adversary. If this was so, then at least part of God's message to Job was that God has triumphed over evil. Further, if the cultural connections that we have briefly noted were all part of Job's frame of reference, God's second speech hinted that much more was going on in the cosmic sphere. While God did not tell Job outright about the forces in those realms, he may have been alluding to a massive cosmic conflict and may have been indicating that he is Lord of those forces as well. Not only that, if the two speeches of God spanned from before creation to the end of the ages, then God claimed his sovereignty through the reaches of time. This would be an extraordinary announcement of the end of evil, personalized in later sources as Satan. What a stinging defeat for the adversarial figure who so brashly challenged God in the first chapters! It would also be humiliating; neither the *satan* (nor Satan) was accorded any specific mention at the end.

Not everyone agrees. At this point, we need to revisit the first two chapters with another lens in place. A number of scholars have suggested that perhaps the *satan* was more of a snarky prosecuting attorney in the heavenly court, challenging the Judge and Master of the universe as to the wisdom of his overarching design. In other words, it was not Job who was on trial, but God. The adversary was not Job's adversary but God's, and the *satan* presumed he had God pinned in a very difficult place. If goodness was merely a matter of "I'll do it for what I get out of it," the verdict would be "flawed design"—cheap, if you will. To demonstrate otherwise, a truly good person would have to undergo horrific suffering. If that person continued to love God for the sake of loving God, then God's universe was indeed a masterpiece, founded on gratuitous love. Once this trial of God got rolling, the *satan*'s role ended.

If we disconnect the *satan* of chapters 1 and 2 from Leviathan, there are additional provocative possibilities. Perhaps Leviathan was not necessarily a representation of the supernatural, powerful evil that is the ruination of humankind. Perhaps instead it was the epitome of that which is wild and chaotic. To be sure, this does not make Leviathan benign; it would still be terrifying and potentially destructive, but not necessarily devastating. The word exhilarating might come to mind. In fact, could Leviathan be not God's enemy but a reminder that God's sovereignty also embraces wildness and chaos? The interpretation of 41:10–11 [2–3] may be critical in addressing these questions.

> No one is so cruel (or fierce— *'akhzar*) that he will rouse him;
> and who is he who will stand before me?
> Who has preceded me that I should repay?
> Everything under all of heaven is mine.

The fiercest of humans ought not tangle with Leviathan; that is clear. What comes next is somewhat more ambiguous. Is it referring to Job's clamor to stand before God? Is it the would-be rouser of Leviathan? Or is it Leviathan himself? Whatever the case, implicit in God's declaration is that *no one* will stand before God; no one has preceded him; he owes nothing to anyone because everything that exists is God's. End of story. Wild creatures, fearsome events, inexplicable and unbearable pain—it's all God's to address. There is no indication that God had any intention of subduing Leviathan. Instead, the Almighty clearly enjoys this terrifying creature.

In sum, while there are numerous variations on the themes, they boil down to two basic scenarios. On the first stage, two majestic and powerful cosmic entities do battle with one another, and God slays the dragon, the serpent from of old, Satan (Rev 12:9). The reassurance in that picture is palpable, even though it often seems to be long in coming. In the second, God alone is majestic and sovereign, bringing and keeping in his domain forces that are wild and chaotic and that are called evil by humans. He does not eradicate them but does set boundaries for them. In this way, God nurtures the freedom of all parts of creation. This too is reassuring although much more challenging. It calls for deeper trust. In light of that, perhaps one subtext that we trace through this drama is that God was giving Job time to get beyond the fear that so permeated Job's earlier life.

Commentary: Was God's Verbal Response Truly a Response?

Our first response to this question is a resounding "no." How could it be? Job had asked for an "audience" with God, for an explanation, and for justice. His sense of justice was primarily limited to the judicial scene that he invoked numerous times with his legal language. Earlier treatments of the book of Job have frequently addressed how effective it is as a theodicy—providing a solution to the problem of evil in the face of both God's goodness and God's omnipotence. However, the "solution" these treatments described was vague at best because God did not seem to answer at all.

While the theodicy question was compelling for thinkers steeped in modernity, this entire approach may seem insufficient in a more postmodern framework. Instead, the mystery of wisdom allows readers to revel along with God in the explosive richness of the creation, acknowledging the unfathomable wisdom of the One who made it and sustains it. God waxed lyrical over his own vast, sovereign freedom. God addressed justice (40:8) but framed the discussion in the wider arena of his rule over creation. Put another way, justice was a subset of God's wisdom.

Contrary to scholarly allegations that God's responses have nothing to do with Job's deep distress, let's try this. Job was experiencing excruciating suffering that was closely related to the natural world. The wind storm, fire, and crushing disease were all products of creation's untamed nature. Both God and the *satan* had been involved in the beginning, but it is telling that God's response declares that *God* reigns supreme over all of it. No adversary. Thus, for God to lay clear claim to all aspects of nature was tremendously important at this point. In addition, God invited Job into a place where he could for the first time consider the vast panorama of God's creative wisdom and find his (small) place amidst the array of creatures upon whom God clearly showered attention. While his circumstances were slower to change, the new and enlarged perspective engendered both humility and awe. I use "awe" in the best sense of the word—terrified joy and hope.

Here is a suggestion for further reading in regard to the beauty of chaos and wildness: Terrence E. Fretheim, *Creation Untamed: The Bible, God, and Natural Disasters* (Grand Rapids: Baker, 2010).

Permeating God's verbal response is the resounding declaration that God designed this world and that he thus knows and ties together all of life's processes; nothing on earth is random, even though it may play at the edges of chaos. Even more, the universe does not revolve around humankind as we attempt to explain and control it. We see and hear echoes of God's transcendence and majesty, but we cannot explain him. These chapters are hymns of praise to the Master of the universe who is at once both frighteningly powerful and eminently good and faithful. This revelation from God to Job was entirely sufficient and reassuring.

One final thought merits at least passing mention. This remarkable display could also be intended for the friends, who had presumed to have the whole of the moral universe neatly wrapped up. They would have to start all over again.

In sum, it was enough for Job that the God whose very *word* had flung all of the created order into being was *speaking* to *him*. It was individual attention of the most humbling but at the same time the most exalting kind. God more than restored Job's honor by inviting Job into this vigorous exchange. Finally, from a longer perspective, it would be that same *Word Incarnate* who would suffer (also apparently unjustly but accomplishing ultimate justice) on behalf of all of humankind.

CHAPTER 25

The Epilogue: Job and God Respond

Introduction

How are we to interpret Job 42? One thing is for certain; every aspect of it comes as a complete surprise. First, Job's final words to God are mind-bogglingly ambiguous, leaving us to wonder just where Job ended up. Furthermore, God's words catch us off guard. Why rebuke the friends, even to the extent of their needing an intercessor? Why characterize their exhortations as so deficient alongside Job's outbursts? Finally, the two-fold restoration of Job's property and family seems to subvert the entire point of the dialogues and to support the contention the adversary made at the very outset—to wit, Job was faithful to God because of what God did for him. We have our work cut out for us as we tie together the implications of these responses, both Job's and God's.

Job's Final Words: Repentance, Resignation, Rebellion?

What could Job possibly say once God stopped talking about Leviathan? Good question—and not only what could he say, but what did he really say? To be blunt, after Job's opening affirmation of God's absolute power and purposes for creation (42:2), it is not clear what he said, or how he said it. His "confession" is notably fraught with challenges of translation and interpretation. What sounds on the surface like contrition about his overreaching demands for vindication and possibly sinful accusations could also be Job's turning away from his humiliated posture and claiming a renewed sense of equilibrium. From another angle, he may even have declared his disdain for God. That's how perplexing this is. We will give it our best interpretive shot, acknowledging that there are most assuredly other ways of understanding just about every line. This is another place where you definitely want to have several Bible translations open as we work through this chapter.

> Even Job's statement in verse 2 is challenging. We have already encountered the very occasional distinction in the Hebrew text when what is "written" in the consonants is slightly modified when the text is read. This is always marked in the margins of the Hebrew Bible. Here, the written form of the Hebrew text has Job saying, "You know that you can do all things." In other words, Job knows that *God* knows. The "read" form, however, preserves the traditional understanding and says, "I know that you can do all things."

In verse 3, Job appeared to quote God's prior words (38:2 — "who is this who darkens counsel with words without knowledge?"). Of course, we recall that even at that point, it was not certain just who was the target of those words — Job, Elihu, or the friends. Here, if we insert an interpretive "You asked" prior to Job's restating of God's question, it appears that Job confirmed his own deficient knowledge and understanding. That is what God had said, and Job affirmed it. If so, this would be the perfect grounds for his later retraction (in verse 6) of his previous, hastily spoken words.

There are, however, two subtle differences to note in Job's reiteration of the query. He said, "Who is this *who hides* counsel without knowledge?" As Job modified and abbreviated God's question, he may have actually been lobbing it back at God. In other words, "How can you, God, expect someone to have knowledge when you have been hiding it?" In addition, Job mentioned nothing here about words, because until God's torrent of words at the end, God had said nothing to enlighten Job or anyone else. As a result, Job had been left to speak about things beyond his understanding, things far exceeding his human knowledge, things of which he was only now becoming aware because of the unique cosmic tour.

So now what? It seems that Job continued to use God's initial challenge to come back with his own. God had said, "Gird up your loins for a wrestling match; I will question you and you will cause me to know" (38:3). Now Job continued, "Please hear and I (the pronoun is emphasized) will speak; I will question you and you will cause me to know" (42:4). Sarcastic retort? Or perhaps the lines manifest a momentarily bolder Job, different from the man who previously clapped his hand over his mouth (40:4). To be sure, many readers see this as Job simply quoting God's demand, especially since Job does not pose any further questions. To make this work, they insert another interpretive "You said" at the beginning of 42:4. Following that declaration, verses 5 and 6 then acknowledge Job's submission before the Master of the universe.

Nevertheless, two clues in Hebrew ("please" and the emphatic "I") ought to make us pause, even if only briefly. Job was speaking back to God, this time *with* a modicum of knowledge because he had been privileged both to hear *and* to see, and that was sufficient. The Q & A session would not be necessary after all. Other interpreters do not necessarily see Job so quickly quelled. We may not have his questions back to God, but he was still boiling at this point.

However we read verses 2–5, we have to contend with verse 6! Here it is, complete with exceedingly amplified translation possibilities. The words in brackets are options for what might be the unwritten direct object of the first verb, which itself has a range of possible meanings.

Therefore, I reject [life, you, dust and ashes] / despise [myself, my words, life, you, dust and ashes] / retract [my words],

and/yet I am comforted / changed my mind / relented / repented

in/on/concerning dust and ashes.

> For a comprehensive treatment of every aspect of this challenging verse, along with a careful assessment of the wider contexts and the scholarly literature, see Bartholomew J. Votta, "The Nature of Job's Response (42:6) to YHWH's Self-Disclosure" (MTh diss., Biblical Theological Seminary, 2005). See further Dhorme, *Commentary on the Book of Job*, 646. John Briggs Curtis ("On Job's Response to Yahweh," *Journal of Biblical Literature* 98 [1979]: 497–511) suggested that Job ended in outright rejection of God.

There are six separate words in the Hebrew of this verse, and only one of them has an assured meaning in this context. That is the compound word translated "therefore." The two verbs are particularly challenging, but we also must inquire as to whether "dust and ashes" is metaphorical and if so, how does it function? At another level, are any of these puzzles elucidated by earlier references in Job or the wider context of the Hebrew Bible? Depending on how we untangle these knots, Job's final words have been variously interpreted as an about-face from his adamant demands for vindication, a changed perception of the place of humans in God's vast creation, comfort even in his persistent distress, repentance from what he now perceived to be sinful words in his accusation of God, ongoing rejection of the position to which he had been reduced, or ongoing disdain for and rebellion against God. Perhaps there are other directions to explore as well, but this will be enough for us to occupy ourselves.

Let's get started. It is not clear what or whom Job despised or rejected. The verb is never used reflexively elsewhere, so it is unlikely that he "despised himself," as the NIV and others render it. Did he despise God, to whom he had just referred? Or was he retracting the case, complete with the set of oaths that he made? Did he reject his wasted state? To make a muddle even more perplexing, the first verb might also be translated as "melting" or "wasting away" instead of some version of "despise" or "reject." If so, this might be Job's commentary on his ongoing physical dissolution to the point of fading away. An alternative interpretation of that translation might be that the overwhelming divine presence had reduced him to almost nothing.

The first verb is puzzling enough, but the second one really affects how we interpret Job's self-understanding. Did he repent/change his mind/relent, or was he comforted? Whatever Job said here needs to fit with what the Lord said about Job's words immediately after this. It seems that God did not think anything Job said or did warranted repentance—as if those words were sinful.

The problem is that the Hebrew verb form (*niham*) has two distinct spheres of meaning. The first includes "repent," "change one's mind," and "relent." All of these presume that some factors have effected change in the subject's perception of the given issue. The second possible meaning has to do with being comforted or consoled.

For Hebrew readers, the *piel* and *niphal* forms of this word look the same for the first-person singular perfect. When the *piel* appears, it primarily means "to comfort." This is how the Septuagint translates most *piel* forms of the word that occur elsewhere. The *niphal* usually means "to repent" or "to change one's mind," and almost uniformly God is the subject of this verb form in other occurrences in Scripture.

Half of the occurrences of *niham* (no matter what the specific grammatical form) have the Lord as the subject. And in more than two-thirds of the cases in which the verb is interpreted as "to change one's mind" or "to relent," the Lord is the subject. These facts ought to make us wary of interpreting what Job does as repenting of a sinful act. That is hardly something we would ascribe to the Lord; thus we may not want to jump to the conclusion that Job repented after having uttered sinful words. For that reason, I would offer a tentative reading to the effect that Job was consoled in spite of his unchanged circumstances.

Add to that the expression "dust and ashes." The two words appear together only in Gen 18:27, Job 30:19, and this passage. Both other uses suggest a position of humility in addressing God. It may be that as a result of Job's new reality framework, his posture before the Lord changed. He retracted the most radical claims in his lawsuit and changed his perspective. Or perhaps he was repenting of arrogance in accusing the Lord of the universe of injustice. On the other hand, "dust and ashes" could equally suggest that Job was still adamantly opposed to what dust and ashes symbolized; he rejected everything that had transpired, and likewise the humiliation to which he had descended. But on yet another hand, presuming we are allowed more than two hands, he might have been asserting that he found comfort even though he was still sitting on an ash heap. Having seen God, he knew that the matter that had most troubled him, his broken relationship with God, was now restored. Nothing else mattered.

God's Final Words

Of equal interest in stitching together the entire fabric of the book is what God said in the epilogue. In light of what each of the participants had contributed in the course of the soliloquies and dialogues, God's rebuke in 42:7–8 is possibly the crux of the interpretation of Job, and it comes as a bolt out of the blue.

Twice the Lord told Eliphaz that he was angry with the friends "because you have not spoken unto (*'el*) me in the right manner (or 'truth' — *nekhonah*) as my servant Job has" (42:7–8). While modern translations (NIV, NASB, ESV, KJV, NJPS, NRSV) render this dual testimony about Job's friends and Job as a matter of speaking the truth *about* God, the Hebrew is simply *'el*, which, in its most general usage, indicates motion or direction toward, either physical or mental. To be sure, a preposition as extensively used as this one has a wide range of nuanced meanings, and "with regard to" can be one of them. It might not necessarily be the best rendition here, however, and that case is strengthened by consulting the earliest translations of this text. Both the (Greek) Septuagint and the (Aramaic) Targum on Job have the equivalent of "to" or "unto" as the meaning. In other words, Job repeatedly addressed God, while the friends never made any appeal whatsoever on behalf of Job to the God whom they were at pains to defend.

For a survey of the usage of *dibber* plus *'el* in the Hebrew Bible along with the Septuagint and Targum readings, see Elaine A. Phillips, "Speaking Truthfully: Job's Friends and Job," *Bulletin for Biblical Research* 18 (2007): 31–43. God's two declarations in Job 42:7–8 are "framed" by the same grammatical structure meaning "speak to." Job 42:7a reads, "After the LORD spoke these words to Job . . . ," and Job 42:9b indicates that the friends "did as the LORD had spoken to them."

It is also necessary to address the implications of speaking "the truth" or "rightly." What Job had said *to* God was *nekhonah*, possibly in his choice of "Addressee," in how he said it, and/or in its content. That content would include the accusations, challenges, and curses. We must resolve the perceived tension between this affirmation of Job and God's accusation that Job darkened counsel with ignorant words (Job 38:2). The issue is how the *substance* of Job's speech could be both ignorant and correct. Here is an initial response. Job's barrage of anger and pain was the truth about his circumstances, and it was rightly spoken to God. We might hold out for more detail later.

The verbal root of *nekhonah* means "to be set, established, or fixed." In Ps 5:9 [10], *nekhonah* clearly refers to "that which is right." Here it might also have the implication that the friends had not spoken *to* God what is right. It is equally possible, however, to read this as an adverb, meaning "to have spoken correctly." In sum, it may be that God declared unequivocally (two times) that speaking correctly meant speaking *to* him and, in the process, properly representing both Job's situation and God himself. Job did so; the friends did not, suggesting that, in addition to their limited view of the situation, they completely lacked the relationship with God that infused Job's every utterance. See also Stanley E. Porter, "The Message of the Book of Job: Job 42:7b as Key to Interpretation?" *Evangelical Quarterly* 63 (1991): 291–304. Porter suggests that God's declaration that Job spoke what was *nekhonah* unequivocally affirmed all the elements of the classical theodicy argument. In other words, it is appropriate to question the claim that God is both omnipotent and perfectly loving when we live in a world where evil abounds. The problem of why undeserved suffering exists is never resolved, but Job raised all the right questions.

This declaration (42:7–8) is also interesting in light of God's apparent rebuke of Job in 40:8–14. There, God seemed to challenge Job's audacity in putting *God* on trial and summoned Job to an impossible task: "exercise the same power as God, and thus be God's equal." This challenge came after rehearsing at length evidence of God's wisdom and majesty as sovereign Master of the universe (chs. 38–39). Job was unquestionably put in his place, and the reader initially squirms on behalf of Job. Nevertheless, the echoes of Ps 8:5–6 in this passage are not to be ignored. This was an invitation to engage as God's image-bearer more fully in exploration and governance of the wildness and sublime nature of God's created order. Job's sole focus on the issue of God's justice was demonstrated to be only one small lens; there was much more at stake.

One last conundrum for now. It appears that God himself would take responsibility for potentially doing something in the realm of folly if Job's prayer and sacrifice did not intervene (42:8). Most modern translations shift the "folly" to the friends because it is certainly more theologically comfortable. (The ASV, NASB, RSV, HCSB, and NIV are representative.) The NIV reads ". . . not deal with you according to *your* folly . . . ," as God addressed Eliphaz. The literal translation, however, is "in order not to do with you folly (disgrace)."

This "folly" would have been the punishment of well-meaning defenders of God's justice. To think of the friends' words as verging on blasphemy takes us aback. Weren't they just trying to help and restore Job to a proper spiritual state? Yet their lives were in jeopardy because of the way they had spoken. It is as if *they* had cursed God and would die unless Job mediated for them. The sin enmeshed in their words necessitated sacrifice for their very lives. And it was a major command:

> Take for yourselves seven bulls and seven rams and go to my servant Job, and offer a burnt offering for yourselves, and Job my servant will pray for you. *Only* then will I accept him (his prayer), and avoid doing harm (a paraphrase of the "folly" line) to you, because you have not spoken unto me in the right manner as my servant Job has. (42:8)

The clause associating "doing something disgraceful" with God (42:8) is both syntactically awkward and potentially troubling. The idiom, 'asah nevelah, appears frequently with the sense of doing a morally reprehensible thing (Gen 34:7; Deut 22:21; Josh 7:15; Judg 20:6, 10; 2 Sam 13:12; Jer 29:23). Gordis (*The Book of Job*, 494) understood the term as indicating "an evil action of major proportions." The prospect of God as the subject of this activity is unnerving. Thus, translations and interpretations are inclined to preserve God's integrity by shifting the force of *nevelah* to the friends. The NJPS is an exception; it reads, ". . . and not treat you vilely, since you have not spoken the truth about Me." One further note on a key Hebrew phrase. While *ki-'im* generally introduces an exception to a preceding negative clause, here it seems best to translate it as "only." In other words, it was *only* because Job would pray for Eliphaz and company that God would restrain his anger to which he referred in the preceding verse.

The prospect of God engaging in anything even approaching what we would call "folly" is sobering in the extreme. Nevertheless, we must remind ourselves that Job had been terribly wronged, not least by their words. Because God's justice ultimately does ensure appropriate and measured punishment for sin, the damage done by their words was serious and necessitated an equivalent punishment for them, extraordinary and disgraceful as it might have seemed.

These words of God must be addressed both on the level of content and in regard to relationship. Job was audacious and honest, and his deepest concern was his life with God—not his wealth or health. Honest confrontation of ambiguity, fear, and injustice occurs only in a personal relationship. Toward that end, Job spoke *to* God. What's more, Job had sought an advocate, one who would speak on his behalf, also to God. Intercession had been a pattern in his own life, but no human intercessor was found for him, even though he repeatedly expressed his longing for one. That is where the friends failed so miserably, and that is what prompted God's rebuke and declaration that, in the great irony of the closure, Job, so greatly in need of their intercession, would pray for them lest they be destroyed.

God's Final Action: The Restoration of Job's Family, Possessions, and Status

In addition to speaking, God *acted*. That, too, is unexpected unless we already know the story. Does the metanarrative of the whole book lose its power once God restored Job's status, physical possessions, and family? From one perspective, this single maneuver seems to undercut everything that transpired in the agonizing exchanges between Job and his friends, as well as "between" Job and his silent God. What the friends repeatedly said turned out to be true; Job retracted his words, and God restored his fortunes. Case closed, and no need for God's remarkable self-revelation from the whirlwind.

A related conclusion: the adversary himself was also correct. The created order had a design flaw so that God's image-bearers would never love and serve God simply "because." There always would be an expectation of reward—or a fear of punishment if Job might be caught falling short. And Job's fear was a factor.

Looked at through another lens, however, God's choice to restore Job's possessions was a remarkable "confession" on the part of God. In the Torah, a thief was required to make restitution for stolen property—two-, four-, or fivefold, depending on what was stolen and whether or not it was recoverable (Exod 22:1–4). God restored to Job the stolen property, as his possessions were doubled. This was tantamount to admitting that God had stolen from Job for the sake of the trial. That takes our breath away!

To press this further, the restoration of Job's property would have been interpreted by what might have been a large watching audience as a sign that Job's "trial" was over. While Job was entirely vindicated by God's appearing to him, this would have served as public confirmation both to the human audience and to those celestial observers among the "sons of God" who would not have been unmindful of the follow-up to the adversary's challenge to God. Job's character remained unsullied.

> Ephesians 3:10–11 might be a source of hope in connection with the painful realities of inexplicable suffering. We (the church) have a part in making known to the rulers and authorities in the "heavenlies" the manifold wisdom of God.

What is of continuing interest is the possibility that it was God and God's policies for running the universe that were on trial, not Job. If that indeed is the larger part of this narrative, then God's choice to restore Job was an act of justice and wisdom. Job maintained his full-orbed relationship with God, with all of its sputters and railings, and after a long silence, God reentered Job's sphere. God's choice to intervene on Job's behalf in fact confirmed what God had said concerning his sovereign power in chapters 38–41. Both Job's "rightness" and God's comprehensive wisdom were confirmed by divine action.

To be sure, we are still left with questions. To what extent was Job irreparably altered by his suffering, and could we possibly consider his ordeal good in any sense? (The answer here may be yes.) What about the loss of his children? While God paid back double in terms of Job's possessions, his children did not return to him from the grave. Job himself had observed that. He was left with the memories of the first set while he enjoyed and was grateful for the second. Nevertheless, when we look back through our New Testament lenses, we affirm the hope toward which Job pointed with his expressed confidence in his Redeemer.

In addition, his deep pain, followed by his tour of God's astonishing creation, undoubtedly made him see beauty in an entirely new way. We might see hints of that in the details about the names of his daughters.

They were, in order, Turtledove, Cassia (the spice), and Horn of Eye Paint. Not exactly in the top ten for contemporary name choices, but resonating with a sense of gentle, precious, and beautiful things. Perhaps he also saw different levels of justice; we must not miss the fact that he doled out inheritance to his daughters as well as his sons.

Were God's Responses Sufficient?

The answer to this question depends on who sets up the criteria for "sufficient," and who is the judge of the case. For a critic seeking resolution to the bedeviling problem of theodicy, the answer is most likely "no." The fact of the matter is, there is no emotionally satisfying explanation in the face of suffering. Excruciating hardship of any stripe demands something that goes well beyond words, no matter how wise they might sound. It certainly requires more than well-reasoned pontification. The latter is all too close to the friends' attempts at explanation and "comfort." Job found them wanting, and God did as well.

It comes back to the matter of relationship and what that truly entails. Job's painful laments morphed into a longing to see God, to have his knowledge of God's character fully affirmed, and to experience at the deepest levels the restoration of his previous friendship with God. God's self-revelation was what Job needed. What satisfied Job was that he knew God even better, though the road to that destination was tortuous at best. In the end, the relationship was knit back together, and based on a much greater self-understanding on Job's part.

As the result of his exposure to the vast, vast reaches of the universe and what he could not understand or control, he learned better how to live in a world that was beyond his control. He had always presumed the glorious sovereignty of God and God's control. It was important to draw that into his own experience.

Fretheim reminds us that natural disasters and illness are a significant contribution to Job's suffering and that these are intrinsic to creation itself. The question then is "Why?" Fretheim writes, "God's commitment to human freedom . . . means that God's relationship to this world is such that God no longer acts with complete freedom. God is committed to the structures of creation, to letting the creatures be what they were created to be" (Fretheim, *Creation Untamed*, 87). This is God's willed design, and it interfaces with perceived justice in exceedingly complex ways. Explore Fretheim's entire chapter on Job ("Natural Disaster, the Will of the Creator, and the Suffering of Job," 65–92).

God's endorsement of Job's words silences those who say that we ought not articulate the difficult truths about the apparently gratuitous evil infesting our fallen world. That had been implicitly the position of the friends, who were unnerved by the force of Job's protest. What Job said represented reality, although it was an incomplete picture, as is that of any human observer. Job's expressed anguish and his refusal to back down were what prompted the unparalleled revelation of God in the whirlwind. What God said at that point was only that Job spoke in ignorance (38:2).

While it seems so simple, the consequences were profound. In God's perfect design, even the colossal failure of the friends meant that Job would articulate his fledgling belief in the greatest Advocate, the Kinsman-Redeemer whom he would see with his own eyes, and who would fully restore the shattered relationship between God and him (Job 19:25–27). In the rich interweaving of adumbrations throughout this text, here is the culmination. That perfect Advocate, the sinless Word of God, would and does speak as Intercessor on behalf of his friends.

For Further Reading

Andersen, Francis I. *Job: An Introduction and Commentary*. Tyndale Old Testament Commentaries. London: InterVarsity Press, 1976.

Balentine, Samuel E. *Job*. Smyth & Helwys Bible Commentary. Macon, GA: Smyth & Helwys, 2006.

Brown, William P. *Character in Crisis: A Fresh Approach to the Wisdom Literature of the Old Testament*. Grand Rapids: Eerdmans, 1996.

———. *Wisdom's Wonder: Character, Creation, and Crisis in the Bible's Wisdom Literature*. Grand Rapids: Eerdmans, 2014.

Chase, Steven. *Job*. Belief: A Theological Commentary on the Bible. Louisville: Westminster John Knox, 2013.

Clines, David J. A. *Job 1–20*. Word Biblical Commentary 17. Dallas: Word, 1989.

Curtis, John Briggs. "On Job's Response to Yahweh." *Journal of Biblical Literature* 98 (1979): 497–511.

Dhorme, Edouard. *A Commentary on the Book of Job*. Translated by Harold Knight. Camden: Nelson, 1967.

Driver, Samuel Rolles, and George Buchanan Gray. *A Critical and Exegetical Commentary of the Book of Job*. International Critical Commentary. New York: Scribner's Sons, 1921.

Freedman, David Noel. "Is It Possible to Understand the Book of Job?" *Bible Review* 4 (1988): 26–33.

Fyall, Robert S. *Now My Eyes Have Seen You: Images of Creation and Evil in the Book of Job.* New Studies in Biblical Theology 12. Downers Grove, IL: InterVarsity Press, 2002.

Gordis, Robert. *The Book of Job: Commentary, New Translation, and Special Studies.* New York: Jewish Theological Seminary, 1978.

Habel, Norman C. *The Book of Job.* Old Testament Library. Philadelphia: Westminster, 1985.

Hartley, John E. *The Book of Job.* New International Commentary on the Old Testament. Grand Rapids: Eerdmans, 1988.

Janzen, J. Gerald. *Job.* Interpretation. Atlanta: John Knox, 1985.

Nam, Duck-woo. *Talking About God: Job 42:7–9 and the Nature of God in the Book of Job.* Studies in Biblical Literature 49. New York: Lang, 2003.

Newell, B. Lynne. "Job: Repentant or Rebellious?" *Westminster Theological Journal* 46 (1984): 298–316.

Newsom, Carol A. *The Book of Job: A Contest of Moral Imaginations.* Oxford: Oxford University Press, 2003.

Phillips, Elaine A. "Serpent Intertexts: Tantalizing Twists in the Tales." *Bulletin for Biblical Research* 10 (2000): 233–45.

———. "Speaking Truthfully: Job's Friends and Job." *Bulletin for Biblical Research* 18 (2007): 31–43.

Polzin, Robert. "The Framework of the Book of Job." *Interpretation* 28 (1974): 182–200.

Pope, Marvin H. *Job: A New Translation with Introduction and Commentary.* Anchor Bible 15. New York: Doubleday, 1965.

Porter, Stanley E. "The Message of the Book of Job: Job 42:7b as Key to Interpretation?" *Evangelical Quarterly* 63 (1991): 291–304.

Pyeon, Yohan. *You Have Not Spoken What Is Right About Me: Intertextuality and the Book of Job.* Studies in Biblical Literature 45. New York: Lang, 2003.

Rowley, H. H. *The Book of Job.* New Century Bible Commentary. London: Marshall, Morgan & Scott, 1976.

Sasson, Victor. "The Literary and Theological Function of Job's Wife in the Book of Job." *Biblica* 79 (1998): 86–90.

Seow, Choon-Leong. *Job 1–21: Interpretation and Commentary.* Illuminations. Grand Rapids: Eerdmans, 2013.

Votta, Bartholomew J. "The Nature of Job's Response (42:6) to YHWH's Self-Disclosure." MTh diss., Biblical Theological Seminary, 2005.

PART FIVE

Wisdom and Love: Song of Songs

Our journey through the biblical wisdom texts has taken us along trails that seem to intersect only sporadically. Proverbs is a field trip through all kinds of practical wisdom. Ecclesiastes and Job follow routes into the depths of uncertainty, pain, suffering, and death. Sometimes road markers are hard to come by. At this next turn, we might ask why Song of Songs is even on the itinerary. For what reasons might we visit these love poems in our quest for an understanding of biblical wisdom?

Responding to this question will compel us to merge the well-traveled thoroughfares of genre and interpretation. We will examine the indicators that help us read this text with greater understanding. A guide is essential as we venture along this particular track. This journey compels the traveler to linger in vineyards and gardens, gaze at hillsides with flocks of sheep and goats, and savor flowers, fruit, and scents in abundance. The scenery we pass is rich and varied. What on earth are we to make of it?

If there are significant connections to be made between this text and Proverbs, Ecclesiastes, and Job, they are not immediately evident. Nevertheless, because wisdom wrestles with the truly challenging aspects of being human, it will inevitably encounter the mysteries of love. Of all the perplexing parts of life, dealing with the power of love is right up there at the top. Uncertainty abounds in love just as it does in suffering and death. It is love that often causes unspeakable agony as well as ecstatic delights. On a mundane level, we might revisit the nagging spouses of Proverbs and inquire what went wrong. In sum, this part of the journey will be as compelling as the others.

CHAPTER 26

This Is "The Best Song"

What Does the Title Imply?

In Hebrew, the title of the book is "Song of Songs." To be sure, we often call it the "Song of Solomon," and we will address the reasons for that shortly. In the meantime, "song of songs" is a way in Hebrew of expressing the superlative—in other words, "the best song." (We saw the same thing with the key expression in Ecclesiastes, *havel havalim*, "utter transience.") Perhaps you are prompted to ask at this point, "What makes *this* the best song?" or "The best song about what?" These are good questions; the answers have to do with how we choose to read and interpret this book. For the sake of clarity for now, we will simply refer to this text as "the Song."

Contemplate one further detail. In traditional Judaism, this text is read at Passover, the annual festival celebrating Israel's redemption from bondage in Egypt and God's leading them to Mount Sinai, where he made the covenant with them. That sequence of events had everything to do with God's covenant love relationship. This is a profound connection.

The Significant Characters: The Young Woman and Her Lover—and Solomon

The first line of the book reads "the song of songs, which is Solomon's." If this song belonged to Solomon, does that mean he authored it, commissioned it, or was its prime subject, viewed from afar? If the last, does the poem look with favor upon him or not? Just for the record, the Hebrew here could also mean that the song was "for" Solomon or "about" Solomon. However we read this, his presence is woven into the text, and we will explore its significance in relation to the other two characters.

The major speaker throughout the poem is a young woman; the number of lines she utters is almost double that of the lover. As she described her lovely and dark complexion, she likened herself to the "tents of Kedar" and the "curtains of Solomon" (1:5). This might make us think of Bedouin tents, some very large and elaborate, made of dark goats' hair. These tents, still in use across swaths of Middle Eastern deserts, are contemporary reflections of ancient Near Eastern dwellings for leaders, who were often portrayed as shepherd-kings.

Just prior to this, the young woman declared that the king brought her into his chambers (1:4). Is this a delicate allusion to Solomon? She mentions the king on his couch later in the chapter (1:12), but that picture is fleeting, and it seems jarring immediately after her quest for her shepherd lover who was engaged in caring for his flock (1:7). In fact, that royal bed may be the foil against which she declared that the couch she would share with her beloved shepherd was green, overshadowed by real cedars and pine. In other words, *they* were outdoors, and their most tender and intimate moments were framed by outdoor and sheltered imagery.

This same juxtaposition continues. Someone brought the young woman to the "house of wine" for festivities (2:4), an image that may not fit well with the young shepherd who, verses later, was leaping over mountains and hills, shyly gazing through a window, and inviting her to savor the beauty of the flowers, fig trees, and vineyards (2:8–13). How do we interpret these two male figures? Perhaps each reference to the king (Solomon) is an intended contrast with the person the young woman truly loved. At the end of the book, Solomon is said to have had an enviable vineyard that yielded an extraordinary amount of fruit, but the woman saw that as less attractive than "my vineyard, mine" (8:11–12).

In a scene that certainly looked like a royal wedding, Solomon rode in splendor on a silver, gold, and purple "bed." His entourage was complete with precious incense and spices, men of valor to guard him, and the crown with which his mother crowned him on his wedding day (3:6–11). The reader cannot help wondering wryly which wedding, as Solomon had a multiplicity of wives (1 Kgs 11:3). An array of court women—queens, concubines, and virgins—seems to be a foil for the loveliness of *this* young woman, whose beauty eventually drew even their praise (6:8–9). In contrast to all of these court trappings, the lovers escaped to the fields and villages as their trysting places (7:11–12). In sum, we are left wondering just who was the object of the young woman's passion.

Portraying Solomon as a shepherd-king is not quite the picture we have in the historical books, which mention his palatial dwelling in Jerusalem (1 Kgs 7:1–12). If he was the single male lover of the poems, why describe him in a wholesale pastoral context? Was the powerful figure of the king instead a threat to the idyllic love between two rustic young folks, whose lives were shaped by the natural beauty surrounding them? Did his regal presence and expressed desire tempt the young woman away from her true beloved for a time? Here is one additional question for now. If the text is primarily describing the love of a tender young woman for her shepherd, how would they know of the abundance of precious spices that tantalize our sensory imaginations? These were certainly far too precious for them to experience.

Perhaps the figure of Solomon is embedded in the poem(s) as a commentary on the royal marriages of Solomon, far too numerous to be exemplary. It may be that Solomon's reputation as a king with a sizable harem served primarily as a symbol for marital love without specifically involving him in the story—if there was one. We also must ask if the references to the king as lover have allegorical/symbolic overtones. This last question redirects us into an intriguing path through the history of interpretation.

No matter how we read Song of Songs 3, our observations on the symbolism bound up with royal marriages must include some reflection on Psalm 45. It is a royal wedding song, indicated by both the psalm title and the contents. The king is a handsome and majestic warrior in the causes of truth and righteousness. He is also the human figure pointing to God on his throne (45:6–7). The author of Hebrews draws on this theological connection; the Son is the one who occupies that throne forever and ever (Heb 1:8–9). The poetry moves elegantly to the chamber of the lovely princess, arrayed in multicolored and golden robes. When she is led to the king, they enter the palace, and the psalm delicately ends with the promise of generations of progeny. Needless to say, the echoes of God's people as the bride are unmistakable.

A Brief Survey of Interpretation History and Interpretive Possibilities

While it may seem unlikely to some twenty-first-century readers, Song of Songs was an immensely popular book for centuries because it was read as an allegory describing, according to Judaism of late antiquity, God's love for Israel. In Christian circles, the paradigm shifted to Christ and the church, but the symbolism was maintained. The church father Origen (third century CE) added an individual dimension to the picture as well, saying that the theological relevance of the text lay in both the Bridegroom and Bride imagery as well as the soul's love for God. Maimonides, a twelfth-century Jewish philosopher, likewise suggested that the Song expressed the individual soul's longing for God. Reformation scholars tended to stay within the symbolic "fold," if not opting for wholesale allegory.

> After Maimonides' lengthy discourses on the problem of suffering and evil, the purposes of the law, and the nature of wisdom, he reflected on the relationship between the Creator and humans. "When we have acquired a true knowledge of God, and rejoice in that knowledge in such a manner, that whilst speaking with others, or attending to our bodily wants, our mind is all that time with God; when we are with our heart constantly near God, even whilst our body is in the society of men; when we are in that state which the Song on the relation between God and man poetically describes in the following words: 'I sleep, but my heart waketh: it is the voice of my beloved that knocketh' (Song v. 2) . . ." (*Guide for the Perplexed* 3.51, trans. M. Friedlander, 2nd ed. [London: Routledge & Sons: 1910], 387).

These readings are compelling from a theological standpoint. They transform a book that is clearly sensual on the surface into a statement about God's covenant love. Although that is not the direction most contemporary interpreters head, we don't want to lose the deep theological connections that emerge with these allegorical readings. We will return to this point.

In the meantime, modern scholarship has drawn on cultural connections with the wider ancient Near East. Love poems, some rather more explicit than Song of Songs, were in circulation. They were short, secular, and had no particular narrative development to them. Egyptian love poems, the closest parallels, were erotic, depicting sexual delight and exploration.

> Papyrus Harris 500 contains the text of nineteen love poems that were found in the section of the temple at Karnak added by Ramesses II (1290–1224 BCE). Here are the third and fourth songs, attributed to the young man and his lover respectively.
>
>> My lover is a marsh,
>>   My lover is lush with growth. . . .
>> Her mouth is a lotus bud,
>>   Her breasts are mandrake blossoms.

Her arms are vines,
>Her eyes are shaded like berries.
>Her head is a trap built from branches . . . and I am the goose.
>Her hair is the bait in the trap . . . to ensnare me.

>My cup is still not full from making love with you. . . .
>>My little jackal, you intoxicate me.
>I will not stop drinking your love,
>>Even if they beat me with sticks into the marsh,
>Even if they beat me north into Syria,
>>Even if they flog me with palm branches south into Nubia,
>Even if they scourge me with switches into the hills,
>>Even if they force me with clubs into the plains,
>I will not take their advice,
>>I will not abandon the one I desire.
>(Matthews and Benjamin, *Old Testament Parallels*, 323)

Perhaps the "best Song" of the Hebrew Bible reflects slices of love life from Israelite society. If so, however, there is still a nagging question: Was this Song intended to be a singular poetic narrative that portrays the agonizing and delicate dance toward sexual consummation within marriage? There are hints that might suggest this, but it is not a foregone conclusion by any means. Strong opinions exist on all sides of this argument. Some tease out a development from courtship to betrothal to marriage in the first four chapters. Others claim that the clearly expressed sexuality encountered right at the outset makes that interpretation impossible. The poem's contents *do* change as we move through it, and we will probe this more deeply.

Adjusting the cultural lens somewhat, perhaps this series of poems functioned as ritual drama. If so, interpreters need not be concerned to identify a plot development or figure out how the characters interact with one another to bring meaning to their literary lives. Instead, the context in which these poems flourished was that of worship. Yes, you read that correctly, even if it sounds peculiar. In this interpretive framework, it is presumed that poems of this sort were used to enact, on the human level, divine love relationship(s) in order to prompt the gods to bestow abundant fruitfulness on the worshipping devotees. In other words, Israel was awash in and deeply influenced by the pagan rites of surrounding cultures; the poems of the Song are thought to be a reflection of that. While that depiction of the culture was sadly true, it may be less likely that canonical Scripture would unquestioningly absorb these attitudes without commentary. In addition, ritual drama focused primarily on the presumed sexuality of the gods and goddesses. These poems celebrate human sexuality. As with our allegorical reading, however, we do not want to discard this track entirely. Hang on to these ideas as well.

No matter which direction we turn for interpretive help, we are faced with the fact that this text is unusual. It includes no religious vocabulary, no explicit naming of God, and about 10 percent of the words in the text are not used elsewhere. The woman's voice is the dominant one. If nothing else, that gives us pause on a solely allegorical reading of the text, in which we would expect the figure of the Bridegroom and Husband (as God) to be preeminent. Here, however, the "narrative" comes through the woman's eyes and in her language. She is also more fully and lovingly described. In the next chapter, we will address the unfamiliar imagery and how it works to convey the extreme sensual experience that sexual love brings. The bottom line for us is this: we have work to do in order to properly interpret this "best Song."

A Message That Deserves to Be Included in the Canon

In the meantime, Solomon's presence in the book puts it in good company with Proverbs and Ecclesiastes, both of which are also linked in some way with that venerable person. Even though we cannot determine date or authorship, we do not want to ignore the Solomon connection. It might be one of the reasons that the text is included in the canon of the Hebrew Bible, even though it raised the eyebrows of some early Jewish interpreters. Reasons for that are not difficult to unearth; we will explore the many (and tasteful) allusions to sexual intimacy in the next chapter.

For now: Why is this in the Bible? After all, have you heard very many sermons on the Song of Songs? What are we missing if we treat it with embarrassed reserve or give it a thick and modest allegorical garment? To be sure, the allegorical interpretations, both Jewish and Christian, have dominated the reading of this text because it *does* rest in the canon of sacred Scripture, and that is a weighty concern. If it were not in the canon, the book would simply be treated as a collection of love poems.

I am indebted to George Schwab for the suggestion I am about to summarize. It is powerful because it emerges from an exploration of the ancient geographical and cultural contexts in which Israel always struggled to maintain its faithful relationship with God. Israel, by the way, most often lost that spiritual battle.

George M. Schwab, "Song of Songs," in *The Expositor's Bible Commentary*, ed. Tremper Longman III and David E. Garland (Grand Rapids: Zondervan, 2008), 6:375–76.

Here's how it works. God planted his people, Israel, in a semiarid climate where drought and famine were always threatening. The surrounding cultures almost exclusively worshiped Baal or whatever the local counterpart might have been. It's easy to see why. According to Canaanite religion, Baal was the god of thunder, storm, rain, and agricultural fertility. It behooved the people, it was presumed, to appeal to this powerful deity if they wanted to survive, let alone prosper. How was that most effectively done? At this point, you are seeing the connections with the ritual drama interpretation we noted above.

Part of Baal worship was public ritual sex, representing intercourse between Baal and his consort, Anat. It was not simply a benign reenactment. Fertility cult activity in the temple context presumably stimulated divine sexual activity in the heavenly realms. That was expected in turn to result in fertility in crops, livestock, and humans. It was an entirely different worldview from that of biblical Israel because it manipulated sex in conjunction with religion and the economy. In other words, God's people were tempted—severely—to turn to culturally accepted means of ensuring their economic stability. Hold that thought.

God knew this would be so. In the Torah, God defined the consequences for this kind of infidelity (Lev 26:3–5, 14–20; Deut 11:13–17). If the people were disobedient, the heavens would be shut, there would be no rain, and the land would dry up. We read a compelling example of this in the Elijah narrative (1 Kgs 17–18). Through the prophets, God warned Israel over and over again against idolatry; it was adultery. Hosea's call to live out the role of the brokenhearted husband dealing with a straying wife leaps to mind. Hosea had to *experience* her adultery to get the point across to a dull-hearted people who were violating the covenant marriage bond with God by their idolatry. In sum, it was a major problem in that culture.

Here in the "best Song," God presented a powerful attack on idolatrous abuse of sexuality. It is compelling because it is so unexpected, especially for us. Instead of the Baal myth, with its public copulation that was intended to bring to fruition all manner of fertility, these poems celebrate the private and tender enjoyment of sex as everyday people delighted in it. The biblical view of sexuality and that of Baal worshippers could not be more different. In other words, the "best Song" was a subtle polemic against the exploitation of sex. Lest we think that worldview is relegated to the ancients, let's just ponder for a moment our contemporary advertising and entertainment worlds. Sex is publicly exploited for economic purposes—over and over again. We are still very much in need of the challenge to rethink how we view sex. The "best Song" is an unusual and therefore excellent starting point.

That, however, is not all. The central imagery of the garden (to which we will return in the next chapter) draws our theological reflections back to creation and the beauty of the relationship that Adam and Eve enjoyed in the garden. Sexual expression was governed by God's design, and it provides an image of his deep love for his people. It was the superlative gift from God right from the beginning. Even better, we need not dismiss the allegorical reading. God's love for his people and Christ's love for his church are deeply embedded in the interpretation of this culturally significant text. We are called to be a distinctive Bride.

CHAPTER 27

A Garden of Spices: How Do You Describe *Your* Beloved?

Introduction

Think of walking into a small spice shop. It is filled with delicate aromas. The scents that waft past your nostrils carry you away, perhaps back to childhood in your grandmother's kitchen, perhaps to exotic locations you have visited, perhaps to the memory of someone you adored. This sensory journey occurs somewhere inside, in a place too deep for words. When you attempt to describe it to someone else, you falter. And yet you are compelled to try because these nostalgic moments are precious, and you want to capture them just as they have captured you.

The richly textured poetry in the Song is likewise evocative. We shut our eyes, inhale deeply, and imagine cinnamon, incense, and the scent of roses. We savor the memory of fine wine, perfume, and blossom honey. Through our imaginations run idyllic scenes of small villages, fields, orchards, vineyards, and gardens. When these images and sensations are locked together in our hearts with a lover, our response is visceral; it actually hurts to feel so overwhelmed with love. This Song is intended to be sensuous. Each place is important, each sight unforgettable. The two young lovers allow their eyes to linger and feast on each other's beauty, first in a delicate manner, and then with passionate abandonment at the sight of beguiling nakedness.

This Song is written for the incurable romantic, and romantics do not speed-read. When we read a love story, chances are we linger at the most heart-throbbing moments. In the case of this Song, however, the heart-throb comes only after an interpretive exercise, something that threatens to diminish the power of the subject and the poetry. Nevertheless, we must try.

Much of the imagery is foreign to us. Instead of feeling our heart beat faster as the lovers describe each other, we find ourselves scratching our heads to figure out why *that* particular body part comes across in such a bizarre way, or what might be the double meaning of the words at hand. In this chapter, we are going to unpack some of these figures and explore how they have been knit together so that passion returns to the actual reading of the love song. To make this "exercise" a bit more palatable, we will start at the end of the Song; the imagery in that context transcends cultural barriers a bit more easily!

The Power of Love

Set me like a seal over your heart;
like a seal on your arm.
For strong as death is love;
hard as *sheol* is jealousy.
Her sparks are sparks of fire—a mighty blaze.
Many waters are not able to quench love,
and rivers will not overwhelm it.
If a man gives all the possessions of his house for love,
it would completely shame him. (8:6–7)

Try an exercise here. Think of all the possible associations that you have for the word "seal." Pause before you read ahead. Perhaps you want to jot your thoughts down. Here are my suggestions; you may have others. First, I would be remiss if I failed to include the sleek water creature, even though any connection with this passage would be a stretch! More to the point, we seal letters so nothing inside is either lost or viewed by unwelcome eyes. Sometimes the seal involves not only some adhesive but also a personalized impression. In that way, we identify ourselves with that letter. In the ancient Near East, seals indicated property. As we read the Gospels (later than this text, to be sure), we are reminded of a seal placed on the tomb of Jesus to prevent his body from being stolen. Just this one word—seal—has so many potential implications. If the lover responds to his beloved's request and sets *her* as a seal over his heart, there will be security and permanence to their love; they will identify with each other and possess each other. These are precious indeed.

To permanence, we add power. There are admittedly unsettling parallels between love and death, jealousy and *sheol*. Remember that *sheol* is a poetic way of referring to the shadowy realm of the grave. It is no surprise that the poem establishes a connection between love and jealousy as well. Not one of these lets go—ever. The grave and death do not release their captives; neither do love and jealousy. True love has a deeply jealous component; no one, no one should break into that loving bond, and if someone does, that transgressor is in danger. Parenthetically, that is why God is called a jealous God. He is rightfully angered and utterly grieved when his wayward children break their covenant vows with him and go after idols. We might have a better understanding of this if we contemplate the prospect of our beloved spouse (or future spouse) being stolen from us by someone else.

Love is passionate, growing in intensity from showers of sparks to fire, and then bursting into a mighty flame. Sparks are brilliant and unexpected in their timing and direction. They turn into a steady blaze. Some would translate "a mighty flame" in 8:6 as "a flame of the LORD," seeing in the word a shortened form of the divine name—which, in turn, implies the utmost superlative. That consuming fire cannot be doused, no matter the size and force of the water reservoir. Think of terrible wildfires that rage across vast areas of forest. Human efforts to contain them are feeble in contrast to the devastating flames. Likewise, attempting to restrain the impulses of love often results in heroic failure. This is the stuff of grand opera and classic movies.

Finally, material goods are worthless in the face of love. Wealth, inheritance, status, or name—we turn away from all of them when overwhelmed by love. They are nothing in the face of our aching desire. This entire description gives us pause. Not only is love a source of ecstasy; there is also a place for caution and even fear. Love is dangerous! And yet it is irresistible—so we plunge forward.

The plunge at this point is an interpretive one as we desire to relish the ecstasy in these poems as fully as possible. First, it is important to note that the lover and his beloved rhapsodize over each other. In other words, they don't just describe the person they are in love with using hackneyed terms, like "awesome" or "cool." They gush; they sing; they are over the top; they choose the most remarkable images to force us to picture for ourselves the exquisite beauty with which they are overwhelmed. There are no common comparisons that work sufficiently for *this* person's beauty. Physical attractiveness is couched in terms of elaborate bird and animal imagery, floral patterns, jewelry, spices, choice foods (honey, wine, and milk), celestial bodies (sun, moon, and stars), and even geographical references! Because sexuality and sex are knit together with procreation, the Song includes manifold allusions to the fruitfulness of nature. Apples and raisins (2:5), acknowledged aphrodisiacs in the ancient Near East, intimate the sensuous joy of their love—under the gentle shade of the apple tree (8:5).

Precious Treasures

The senses of taste and smell are stimulated by wine, honey, nectar, milk, and precious spices. All are likened to the intimate sweetness of lovemaking. However we understand the role of Solomon, when his entourage arrived across the wilderness, it was awash with myrrh and frankincense (3:6). These were greatly valued in the ancient Near East, and it is no surprise that they would accompany the king. Nevertheless, they were not limited to the royal circles. The lover anticipated his sexual union with his beloved as going away to the "mountain of myrrh and the hill of frankincense" (4:6), a place of both intoxication and untold value. Those enchanting scents are joined by henna, nard, saffron, calamus, and cinnamon, all mingling to captivate and transport the lovers—and to confound the modern reader who may not have a clue as to the properties of these aromatic spices, apart from cinnamon.

> To help those of us who have little contact with the world of exotic scents and flavors, here is a quick guide. Henna has fragrant flowers and is a reddish-orange cosmetic; nard is likewise an aromatic plant used for ointment; saffron is bright orange and is used to color and flavor foods; calamus is an Asian plant known for its aroma.

As the young woman described her lover to the daughters of Jerusalem, we know immediately how immeasurably she valued him. Gold, jewels, ivory, sapphires, and alabaster—that was her lover through her eyes, and those were treasures of kings. He was like a cedar of Lebanon, a strong, stately, and glorious tree used to build temples and palaces (1 Kgs 5:6–10). But he was not simply hardened metal or powerful wood; his eyes were like doves, his cheeks like beds of spices, and his lips were lilies. She saw in him a captivating mixture of strength and gentleness.

In his turn, the lover returned multiple times to her allure. His description is discreet at first, extolling the beauty of her hair, teeth, lips, cheeks, and neck, but stopping delicately with her breasts (4:1–6). Even that much is breathtaking, but once he entered into "his garden," his description is much more daring. He knew her body intimately, and he actively desired more of her, climbing and grasping her breasts (7:1–9 [2–10]).

In each description, the imagery is rich. He likened her eyes to doves; her teeth were ewe lambs coming up from the washing; her breasts were like fawns. These are gentle creatures, soft and inviting. He found her eyes especially compelling, even behind her veil (4:1, 9; 6:5). We know what the lover meant; at the same time that direct and lingering eye contact unsettles us, we long for more! Doves, lambs, and fawns are vulnerable. As a contrast, the sight of a flock of sturdy goats streaming down the hills of Gilead, constantly moving back and forth, served as a perfect figure for her dark, freely flowing hair. Her cheeks were like the halves of pomegranates, a traditional symbol of fruitfulness because of the hundreds of succulent seeds they contained.

These features were visible to all, but the lover also reveled in his own "private viewing" (7:1–3 [2–4]). He cherished the masterfully crafted jewels of her thighs; her navel captured mixed wine; her belly was a mound of wheat surrounded by lilies. Touch and taste joined together to present a sumptuous repast of sexual enjoyment. In addition to these inviting qualities, however, she was also a formidable protection for him. This woman was strong, her neck like a tower with shields of warriors hanging on it (4:4).

The Garden and the King's Garden

Orchards, vineyards, and gardens were the trysting places for these lovers, secluded from intruders and redolent with fruit of all kinds. They were an appropriate scenic backdrop, to be sure, but we need to augment our understanding even further. Our first task is to rescue the term "garden" from our own context, in which it usually means an individual flower plot or a public expanse for the enjoyment of the masses. In antiquity, by way of contrast, gardens were often the property of kings— walled, private, and locked so that outsiders could not access them.

In the Song, two words signify the garden. One is the "garden-variety" Hebrew word *gan* (4:12, 15, 16; 5:1; 6:2, 11; 8:13). We will return to its significance momentarily. At one point (4:13), however, the text also includes the word *pardes,* a Persian term that provides the connection with royal gardens noted above. It is translated as "orchard" (NRSV, ESV), but even the look of it reminds us of the "paradise" that was the garden of Eden prior to the fall. Hold on to that possible connection. The choice aromatic spices (4:13–14) in this *pardes* indicate that this was an exquisite and exceedingly special location.

The locked garden (*gan*) of 4:12–5:1 represents the woman herself, further described as a "closed fountain" (4:12). She was a virgin; that was treasured and protected. It was only when she invited her lover to enter her garden that their love was sexually consummated. The pleasures there were intoxicating, and the lover enjoyed them to the full; now it was not only her garden but "his" as well (4:16). It is not an accident that this description is at the center of the Song. It follows a crescendo of his growing anticipation, excitement, and his invitation to her to "come away" with him as his "bride" (4:8–10).

> While our familiar Western literature generally builds toward a climactic moment at the end, a standard ancient Near Eastern pattern brought the most critical part of the narrative to the center. This is called chiastic structure, after the Greek letter *chi* (X). Each narrative development that leads up to the centerpiece is then echoed. It might be best illustrated by the following: A, B, C, D (the center), C′, B′, A′. We see it in a number of the stories in the Hebrew Bible. Perhaps the most compelling one is the book of Esther, which has at its center the fact that the king could not sleep (6:1). Even though the name of God is not mentioned in the entire book, that single event turned the entire narrative around from pending disaster for the Jews to survival. It speaks volumes to God's "fingerprints" in the book.

In addition to the sexual intimacy so delicately described here, we also find rich theological connections. Circling back to Gen 2:8, God planted a garden (*gan*) in Eden. In it, Adam and Eve, who shared "bone" and "flesh," became "one flesh." The perfection and beauty of that garden were set off-limits as a result of their disobedience, becoming a "locked garden." As the lovers of this Song continued to seek and long for fulfillment, there is a faint echo of our longing for the restoration or renewal of the perfection of that garden that is truly the King's garden.

> It is striking that the word translated "desire" in Gen 3:16 appears only two additional times in the Hebrew Bible. One of them is in Song 7:10 [11]—"I am my beloved's and his desire is for me." (The other is in Gen 4:7, where the connotation is significantly more negative; in fact, it is parallel to the tragic tone of Gen 3:16.)

Even Geography

It would push far beyond our imaginative limits to attach such names as Mount Everest, London, the Riviera, or Sri Lanka to our effusive praises of the persons we love. Yet geographical references are interwoven with the ardent descriptions in this Song. They were local and recognized names in that cultural context, and no doubt they sparked particular associations. We can only begin to follow those possible threads, but let's try. The young woman extolled her lover as a cluster of henna blossoms from the vineyards of En-Gedi (1:13). We have already explored "henna";

now it helps to know that En-Gedi is a lush spring above the shore of the Dead Sea, or more properly, the "sea of salt." The spring at En-Gedi was a dramatic contrast to its immediate, barren surroundings, and it was known as a haven (David retreated to En-Gedi in 1 Sam 23:29–24:1).

The beauty of the beloved was likened to Tirzah and Jerusalem (6:4). Both are nestled deep in the hill country, protected from those outsiders whose greedy ambitions occasionally tempted them to enter the land. Further, when dawn comes gently in those hills, the mists rise around the trees, and the coolness of the nighttime lingers. These are evocative figures.

Familiar places are infused with additional meaning. The fertile Sharon plain was the referent for the famous "rose of Sharon, lily of the valleys" (2:1). The beloved's tresses, flowing and dark, were like goats streaming down the slopes of Gilead (4:1; 6:5), a fruitful region across the Jordan River from Israel where flocks of sheep and goats brought the hillsides to life. Elegance is conveyed by the allusion to her head crowning her like Carmel (7:5 [6]), the promontory jutting out into the Mediterranean Sea, visible from afar.

Lebanon appears most frequently. It was a place of majesty, but one from which the lover intended to draw his beloved away (4:8). At the same time, he was captivated by the fragrance of Lebanon (4:11) and its flowing streams (4:15). In turn, his stature was like a cedar of Lebanon (5:15) in her adoring eyes. While the name Lebanon was associated with fruitfulness (4:8, 15), it was also an allusion to power, along with Damascus and Carmel, even power over the king himself (7:5 [6]). Perhaps that sheds some faint light on the puzzling picture of the beloved's nose being likened to a tower of Lebanon that looks toward Damascus (7:4 [5]).

"I Charge You . . . by the Gazelles"

What does this expression mean? Everyone always asks! It is the introduction to an oath, odd as it may seem. In its full form, it occurs twice. The "daughters of Jerusalem" were made to swear "by the gazelles and the does of the field" not to awaken love before its time (2:7; 3:5). Just prior to each of these charges, the two lovers were intensely and passionately aroused. Question: Was this shaped as a warning for them—and all lovers like them—to put the brakes on? Or was it a warning to anyone nearby not to disturb this most intimate lovemaking?

There are two additional variations on the theme. The daughters of Jerusalem were charged again after the lover entered his garden, but this time the message was different (5:8). The creatures around which the oath was constructed were left out, and the plaintive message is simple;

the young woman is heartsick over her lover, who has left—temporarily, it turns out. In the book's reprise, the daughters of Jerusalem were put under oath one last time not to awaken love (8:4), this time also with no reference to gazelles and deer!

Why would the "narrator" or poet refer to these particular creatures in conjunction with an oath about the perils of hastening sexual fulfillment? Sworn oaths were serious. For example, one of the hot theological discussions in Jesus' day had to do with whether it was appropriate to swear by the temple, the gold on the temple, the altar, the gold on the altar, or heaven (Matt 23:16–22). Those were weighty references. By contrast, what substance could a few wild creatures bring to this business of oaths?

Two initial suggestions, neither of which really has to do with oaths, have been put forward, and we ought at least to mention them. Perhaps these shy animals that flee quickly represent something about the elusive nature of love. Or perhaps they are especially sexually potent. If you do not find these suggestions particularly compelling, you are joining the ranks of a number of other readers. Here is one more, which does enter the realm of oaths and also enters the realm of Hebrew language. It turns out that there are subtle connections between the Hebrew words for these animals and words that may hint to the presence of God. Yes, you read that correctly. Let's see if we can unpack it without getting too buried in details.

The first thing we need to recall is that, unlike in English, in Hebrew, nouns are either masculine or feminine. In any sentence, the gender of nouns, verbs, and adjectives all match. In the delightful imagery of this song, our young lover is likened to a gazelle (*tsevi*) or a young stag (*'opher ha'ayyalim*) as he bounds over hills toward his beloved's home, where she is protected by a wall and is behind a latticed window (2:8–9; see also v. 17). The Hebrew verb forms for "leaping" and "jumping" that describe the approach of this fleet-footed creature are masculine—fitting for the context. In the oath, however, both noun forms are feminine plural. We might be inclined to bypass this detail except that the feminine plural of *tsevi* is *tseva'ot*, and *that* word appears in the expression "Lord God of Hosts" where "Hosts" is *tseva'ot*. Intriguing, isn't it? Likewise, in the oath (2:7; 3:5), the *'ayyalim* (masculine) of 2:9, 17 has shifted to *'ayelot* (feminine) and is followed by the Hebrew word for "of the field" (*hassadeh*). *'Ayelot hassadeh* sounds a bit like El Shaddai, the Hebrew for God Almighty. Possibly, just possibly, these are veiled allusions to the divine Presence woven right into the stunning sensuality of the book. As such, they remind us that the ecstasy, danger, and sweep of emotions are not outside God's design.

For a fuller explanation of how the elements of this oath work, see Schwab, "Song," 386–87.

Putting It Together: Brief Notes on Structure

Many commentaries on the Song present an outline of the book, suggesting that it might be more than simply a collection of discrete poems. In other words, we can possibly trace a unifying thread through the eight chapters; the poetry "goes somewhere." While there are variations on the basic divisions, the following overarching contents and development are evident.

Attraction, Exploration, Anticipation (1:1–2:7)

Each of the young lovers recognized the compelling draw of sensual attraction, but the young woman was especially uncertain. There are questions and somewhat disjointed exchanges, along with a variety of images that are not developed at this point. Beauty is important, but detailed physical descriptions are not. The lovers anticipated being in bed together (note the "couch"), but this section ends with the warning not to awaken love before its time (2:7).

Mutual Seeking (2:8–3:5)

As the young lover eagerly arrived, he was like a shy creature, leaping, hovering, timidly looking through the lattice, and then inviting her away. The young woman longed for him so much at night that she headed out to seek him, boldly inquiring of the watchmen. Her desire is evident in the way she referred to him; "the one whom my soul loves" was on her lips four times. In between these "his and hers" longings is the declaration "my beloved is mine and I am his" (2:16). Nevertheless, the caution was still in place: don't awaken love before its time (3:5).

Interruption of the Idyll (3:6–11)

Solomon arrived with his splendid entourage. Majestic though it was, complete with expectations of his wedding day, it seemed to be on the perceptual fringes for the two lovers, who were utterly enchanted with each other. At most, Solomon's interest may have been a temptation to the young woman.

Captured and Consummated (4:1–5:10)

As their emotions heightened, the lover's description was more detailed but still discreet. He invited her away from possible threats to this intimate moment. He was "hearted" (4:9—a particularly engaging verb form from the noun for "heart"), and what he anticipated was utter sweetness. The garden encounter was just around the corner, and is found at the center of the book. Here we have no admonition about not awakening love; the lover entered his garden.

Mutual Seeking—Again (5:2–8)

This time seeking was mingled with uncertainty and missed opportunity. They longed for ecstasy again, but their attempts were thwarted by timing and by the abuse of outsiders; the watchmen were not sympathetic or at all helpful. The daughters of Jerusalem were enlisted to find her lover and tell him that she longed for him. The perfect relationship was threatened by realities outside their own sphere—but not irreparably so.

Mutual Admiration (5:9–7:13 [14])

Back together, they rhapsodized over each other's exquisitely beautiful bodies; they knew them intimately. They were in the garden, the vineyard, and the orchards, and were freely loving: "I am my lover's and he is mine" (6:3).

Nostalgic Reprise (8:1–14)

These verses revisit the sweetness of their love (8:3; see 2:6). In this later context, the abbreviated oath to the daughters of Jerusalem simply served as a reminder. The one who came from the wilderness was not Solomon in all his glory. It was the woman, leaning on her lover. Perhaps they were older here, bound together in different ways and increasingly aware of the lasting power of love (8:6–7). Various vignettes appear in succession: protection for a little sister, the woman's own strength, remembering Solomon's abundance but affirming that her choice was the right one, fleeting memories of the gardens, the swift and agile gazelle, and the abiding allure of spices.

Closure

This Song is a feast for the imagination, and all the more as we linger to relish the images. Above all, it is a lovely and unsullied view of sexuality, one that stands in stark contrast to the tragic exploitation of sex found in so many contexts. The centrality of the garden reminds us that as Adam rejoiced over Eve, he was engaging in profound worship of the God in whose image they were made. This is indeed the best Song, sung powerfully in marriage, celebrating one-flesh sexual union, and pointing upward and ahead to the eschatological oneness of God with his people, Christ with his church.

For Further Reading

Carr, G. Lloyd. *The Song of Solomon*. Tyndale Old Testament Commentaries 17. Leicester: Inter-Varsity Press, 1984.

Davidson, Richard. "Theology of Sexuality in the Song of Songs: Return to Eden." *Andrews University Seminary Studies* 27 (1989): 1–19.

Fox, Michael. *The Song of Songs and the Ancient Egyptian Love Songs*. Madison: University of Wisconsin Press, 1985.

Garrett, Duane. *Song of Songs*. Word Biblical Commentary 23B. Nashville: Nelson, 2004.

Gault, Brian P. "An Admonition against 'Rousing Love': The Meaning of the Enigmatic Refrain in Song of Songs." *Bulletin for Biblical Research* 20 (2010): 161–84.

Hess, Richard S. *Song of Songs*. Baker Commentary on the Old Testament Wisdom and Psalms. Grand Rapids: Baker, 2005.

Longman, Tremper, III. *Song of Songs*. New International Commentary on the Old Testament. Grand Rapids: Eerdmans, 2001.

Provan, Iain. *Ecclesiastes, Song of Songs*. NIV Application Commentary. Grand Rapids: Zondervan, 2001.

Schwab, George. "Song of Songs." Pages 367–431 in vol. 6 of *The Expositor's Bible Commentary*. Edited by Tremper Longman III and David E. Garland. Grand Rapids: Zondervan, 2008.

———. "Song of Songs 1: Book of." Pages 737–50 in *Dictionary of the Old Testament: Wisdom, Poetry and Writings*. Edited by Tremper Longman III and Peter Enns. Downers Grove, IL: InterVarsity Press, 2008.

Weems, Renita. *The Song of Songs*. New Interpreter's Bible. Nashville: Abingdon, 1997.

EPILOGUE

What Next?

The Problem

It seems presumptuous to write a conclusion. Among other things, it suggests an end to the study, whereas we have really only begun, or at least that is my sense. The greater question ought to address how I bow out of this conversation and leave it to my faithful readers to continue. Part of me would like to take your metaphorical hand in mine and say, "Now, let's start over again and see what we learn this time." That, however, might not be welcomed!

Let's turn this into a different question: What might we take away from this endeavor? There could be value in all of us actively engaging this challenge, rather than my barging in with premature or ill-formed thoughts. They would only serve to submerge your excellent observations and reflections. Further, any exercise I might devise could easily be artificial. (I've already tried; it's artificial.) Instead, I have chosen to offer some rather simple observations, along with further questions. That is a wisdom recipe of sorts, isn't it?

Most of us have experienced at least one terrifying event in our lives, and we remember it vividly. In the aftermath, we vow that our lives will never be the same, that this has indeed been life altering, that we will discipline ourselves to become virtuous in every way. In other words, we will become wise stewards of the astonishing gifts that enrich every day of our lives. Yet—and now I speak for myself—more often than not, I simply continue to go about my daily business with little modification of my bad habits, my self-centered perspectives, and my colossal neglect of God's astonishing goodness and protection. To be sure, I now issue "reminders to self" on occasion to be eminently thankful for the daily gift of life as each day passes safely by. But the profound impact of the dramatic events in our lives tends to fade. This troubles me! Where is wisdom residing for me day by day? How do I pursue its riches? It seems I need to return—again—to a more basic message.

"Trust and Obey—For There's No Other Way"

"Fear of the LORD" is front and center in the wisdom books. It seems to be an inseparable companion to wisdom no matter where we look. It's a good thing—and a safe place to be. In the face of everything from slight apprehension to abject terror, from tiny twinges of desire to overwhelming temptation, we flee to God. Where else is there to go?

Nevertheless, slightly nagging questions remain. How do we nurture our longing for God's presence no matter what the circumstances? And how do we train ourselves to run toward God instead of in the opposite direction? How do we live out a healthy and courageous fear of the Lord? And how do we retain a posture of humility? Are you noticing traces of Proverbs and Job in these questions?

My tentative response is going to sound deceptively simple and impossibly difficult at the same time: trust and obey. It's an old hymn title— and one that captures the essence of Christian living. The *only* way I know even to begin to make that combination a part of my moment-by-moment existence is to be utterly infused with God's promises—so infused that I accept each event, whether mundane or a crisis, as part of my Master's design. That is really easy for me to write, but oh so difficult to do. And perhaps for you as well.

In the meantime, we *can* work on the "infusion" part. We can dust off the parts of our brains that are made to memorize, and put them to work. If it helps, let me suggest that you find someone who will join you in the process.

Here is one last suggestion for now: learn to sing biblical and theological truths. Music not only helps our memories; it also reaches more deeply into the core of our being. When we need that gem of truth, it will surface in the form of a sung text, accompanied by a deepening, growing, and enlarged sense of God's reality that far transcends any immediate circumstances. Don't forget that the morning stars sing together (Job 38:7). What a privilege to join them!

I'm barely started on this journey. I would invite you to join me as we move forward. In closing, I offer one of my favorite hymn texts. It is by Paul Gerhardt (1656) and translated by John Wesley (1739):

Give to the winds thy fears; Hope and be undismayed;
God hears thy sighs and counts thy tears, God shall lift up
    thy head.

Through waves, and clouds, and storm, He gently clears thy way;
Wait thou His time; so shall this night Soon end in joyous day.

Leave to His sovereign sway To choose and to command;
So shalt thou, wondering, own His way, How wise, how strong
    His hand!

Far, far above thy thought His counsel shall appear,
When fully He the work hath wrought That caused thy need-
    less fear.[1]

Notes

Chapter 2

1. Gordon D. Fee and Douglas K. Stuart, *How to Read the Bible for All Its Worth: A Guide to Understanding the Bible*, 1st ed. (Grand Rapids: Zondervan, 1982), 187.

Chapter 5

1. Miriam Lichtheim, *Ancient Egyptian Literature*, vol. 1, *The Old and Middle Kingdoms* (Berkeley: University of California Press, 1973), 62–63.
2. Ibid., 68.
3. Translated by Miriam Lichtheim in *The Context of Scripture*, ed. William W. Hallo and K. Lawson Younger Jr. (Leiden: Brill, 1997), 1:62.
4. Ibid., 1:111.
5. Ibid., 1:119.
6. Translated by H. L. Ginsberg in *ANET*, 428.
7. Ibid., 429.

Chapter 6

1. The Hebrew verb form is feminine because both "commandment" and "instruction" are feminine nouns.

Chapter 8

1. Abraham Joshua Heschel, *A Passion for Truth* (New York: Farrar, Straus & Giroux, 1973), 158.

Chapter 12

1. Michael V. Fox, "The Meaning of *Hebel* for Qohelet," *Journal of Biblical Literature* 105 (1986): 414–27; *A Time to Tear Down and a Time to Build Up: A*

Rereading of Ecclesiastes (Grand Rapids: Eerdmans, 1999), 8–11, 30–42. Fox explores extensively the connections with Camus.

2. Robert V. McCabe, "The Message of Ecclesiastes," *Detroit Baptist Seminary Journal* 1 (1996): 94. McCabe presents an excellent summary of the possibilities in regard to the translation of *hevel*, so we will not linger on all of them here.

3. Fox, *A Time to Tear Down*, 49.

Chapter 18

1. This is the only place this Hebrew root (*s-l-d*) appears in the Hebrew Bible, and it is difficult to determine a specific meaning.

Epilogue

1. Quoted from *The Hymnal*, published by the General Assembly of the Presbyterian Church in the United States of America (Philadelphia: Presbyterian Board of Christian Education, 1933).

Index of Scripture References